Praise for *Permanent Partners*

"*Permanent Partners* is a truly wonderful book, long overdue but well worth waiting for. Berzon writes with such insight and sensitivity that gay and lesbian couples will discover themselves on every page . . . This book celebrates diversity and difference, and that stands in stark contrast to the discrimination and despair that has been the lot of gay and lesbian people for so long."
—Bonnie Strickland, Ph.D., past president,
American Psychological Association

"A masterpiece! This book ought to be around for a century. *Permanent Partners* is the book that gay people have needed from the beginning . . . Everyone knew this book was coming some day, and now it is here."
—George Weinberg, Ph.D.,
author of *Society and the Healthy Homosexual*

DR. BETTY BERZON is a psychotherapist specializing in work with lesbians and gay men since 1970. She edited the classic *Positively Gay: New Approaches to Gay and Lesbian Life,* first published in 1979, third edition in 2001. She is the author of *Permanent Partners: Building Gay and Lesbian Relationships That Last,* 1988, updated edition in 2004. Her other books, *The Intimacy Dance: A Guide to Long-Term Success in Gay and Lesbian Relationships* and *Setting Them Straight: You Can Do Something About Bigotry and Homophobia in Your Life,* were published in 1996, and her memoir, *Surviving Madness: A Therapist's Own Story,* was published in 2002, and won the 2003 Lambda Literary Prize for autobiography. She also writes a weekly relationship advice column, *Love Letters,* on PlanetOut.com.

A longtime activist in the gay and lesbian community, Dr. Berzon was national president of the Gay Academic Union for three years, served on the boards of National Gay Rights Advocates and the Los Angeles Gay and Lesbian Center, and is the founding board chair of Gay and Lesbian Adolescent Social Services (GLASS). She has been a member of the American Psychological Association since 1964, and has been listed in *Who's Who of American Women* and *Who's Who in America.* She lives in Los Angeles with her partner of thirty-one years, Teresa DeCrescenzo. Learn more about Dr. Berzon and her books at **http://members.aol.com/bberzon**.

P9-DEI-189

"Betty Berzon is a saint of nurturing. This is a needed book, honestly and expertly exploring the terrain, parameters, and dimensions of gay and lesbian relationships."
    —Malcolm Boyd, author of *Take Off the Masks* and *Gay Priest*

"This is an innovative, practical, highly readable psychological resource for gay and lesbian couples. A must-read for therapists and all couples."
    —Andrew Mattison, Ph.D., and David McWhirter, M.D.,
    coauthors of *The Male Couple*

DR. BETTY BERZON

PERMANENT PARTNERS

Building Gay & Lesbian Relationships That Last

A PLUME BOOK

PLUME
Published by the Penguin Group
Penguin Group (USA) Inc., 375 Hudson Street, New York, New York 10014, U.S.A.
Penguin Group (Canada), 10 Alcorn Avenue,
Toronto, Ontario, Canada M4V 3B2 (a division of Pearson Penguin Canada Inc.)
Penguin Books Ltd, 80 Strand, London WC2R 0RL, England
Penguin Ireland, 25 St Stephen's Green, Dublin 2, Ireland (a division of Penguin Books Ltd)
Penguin Group (Australia), 250 Camberwell Road, Camberwell,
Victoria 3124, Australia (a division of Pearson Australia Group Pty Ltd)
Penguin Books India Pvt Ltd, 11 Community Centre, Panchsheel Park,
New Delhi –110 017, India
Penguin Books (NZ), Cnr Airborne and Rosedale Roads,
Albany, Auckland, New Zealand (a division of Pearson New Zealand Ltd)
Penguin Books (South Africa) (Pty) Ltd, 24 Sturdee Avenue, Rosebank,
Johannesburg 2196, South Africa

Penguin Books Ltd, Registered Offices: 80 Strand, London WC2R 0RL, England

Published by Plume, a member of Penguin Group (USA) Inc. Previously published in a Dutton
edition and published simultaneously in Canada by Fitzhenry and Whiteside Limited.

First Plume Printing, January 1990
First Plume Printing (revised edition), October 2004
10 9 8 7 6 5 4 3 2 1

Copyright © Betty Berzon, Ph.D., 1988, 2004
All rights reserved

Grateful acknowledgment is given for permission to quote from the following works:

American Couples, by Phillip Blumstein and Pepper Schwartz. Copyright © 1983 by Phillip Blumstein
   and Pepper Schwartz. Reprinted by permission of William Morrow & Company.
Handbook for Commitment Ceremonies. Reprinted by permission of Rev. Rex A. Coots of the Unitarian
   Universalist Church, Canton, New York.
Jealousy, by Gordon Clanton and Lynn G. Smith. Copyright © 1986 by Gordon Clanton and Lynn
   G. Smith. Reprinted by permission of University Press of America.
A Legal Guide for Lesbians and Gay Couples, by Hayden Curry and Denis Clifford. Copyright © by
   Hayden Curry and Denis Clifford. Reprinted by permission of Nolo Press.
Positively Gay, edited by Betty Berzon. Copyright © 1984 by Betty Berzon. Reprinted by permission
   of Mediamix Associates.
Sexual Awareness: Enhancing Sexual Pleasure, by Barry McCarthy and Emily McCarthy. Copyright ©
   1984 by Barry and Emily McCarthy. Reprinted by permission of Carroll & Graf.
Excerpts from the Introduction and Chapters 2 and 4 of the treatise *Sexual Orientation and the Law,*
   by National Lawyers Guild Anti-Sexism Committee of San Francisco Bay Area Chapter, Roberta
   Achtenberg, Editor. Copyright © 1985, 1987. Reprinted by permission of Clark Boardman
   Company, Ltd., 435 Hudson Street, New York, New York 10014.
Wills Give You Power: A Guide for Gay Men and Women. Reprinted by permission of National Gay
   Rights Advocates, Public Interest Law Firm, San Francisco, California.

Ⓟ REGISTERED TRADEMARK—MARCA REGISTRADA

CIP data is available.
ISBN 0-452-28621-2

Printed in the United States of America
Original hardcover design by Earl Tidwell

Without limiting the rights under copyright reserved above, no part of this publication may be
reproduced, stored in or introduced into a retrieval system, or transmitted, in any form, or by
any means (electronic, mechanical, photocopying, recording, or otherwise), without the prior
written permission of both the copyright owner and the above publisher of this book.

PUBLISHER'S NOTE
The scanning, uploading, and distribution of this book via the Internet or via any other means
without the permission of the publisher is illegal and punishable by law. Please purchase only
authorized editions, and do not participate in or encourage electronic piracy of copyrighted
materials. Your support of the author's rights is appreciated.

BOOKS ARE AVAILABLE AT QUANTITY DISCOUNTS WHEN USED TO PROMOTE PRODUCTS OR SERVICES. FOR
INFORMATION PLEASE WRITE TO PREMIUM MARKETING DIVISION, PENGUIN GROUP (USA) INC., 375 HUDSON
STREET, NEW YORK, NEW YORK 10014.

To Teresa DeCrescenzo,
Ti amo moltissimo

"I think it is important for us to remember that we began, and are empowered and have lived and survived on the value, the energy of our passion . . . that we have been pushed around, slandered, driven away from our families . . . but we have survived on our passion. . . . It is what has made you alive, what has made your life even happen . . . so that you didn't almost live. . . . Oh, how really difficult it has been . . . to maintain this love against all the pressure, all that pressure in the other person, in ourselves, in the great world around us. . . . This has been our energy, our force, our strength, our power. They have made it hell and we made it beautiful. Never forget the nights of your love in the days of your working for its freedom, its expansion to fill the world with the roses of those moments out of time . . . an army of lovers not only can't fail but they could convert revolution into music, into the power of eros. And, in fact, really what was it we wanted to bring to this place anyway, if it wasn't love."

KATE MILLETT
Speech to the Gay Academic Union
Los Angeles, California 1978

CONTENTS

ACKNOWLEDGMENTS

I would like to thank Victor Sun, the late Dr. Griff Humphreys, and Craig Ketchum for their efforts in the preparation of the manuscript for the first edition of this book.

Jane Hoose helped keep me grammatically correct. She and Bronwyn Anthony offered valuable observations as the text was being developed.

Drs. Laura Brown and Rex Reece assisted me with their expertise in the chapter on sexual issues, as did attorneys Leonard Graff of National Gay Rights Advocates and Roberta Achtenberg of the Lesbian Rights Project in the chapter on legal issues. Brent Nance was kind enough to review the material on insurance matters.

I very much appreciate Roberta Achtenberg and Judge Mary Morgan allowing me to include mention of their family in the section on having children.

In my search for an appropriate publisher for this book I was particularly helped along the way by Dr. Drew Mattison, Jim Bennett of Lambda Rising Bookstore, John Preston, and Armistead Maupin. That trail led me to Jed Mattes of International Creative Management who (happily for me) became my agent.

I am grateful to my editors, Carole DeSanti at Dutton and Gary Luke at New American Library for their valuable help in the final polishing of the manuscript for the first edition.

I owe a debt of gratitude to my partner, Teresa DeCrescenzo, for so graciously putting up with several years of preoccupation with the writing of this book. Her love and support eased a sometimes arduous passage.

Finally, I want to thank the many gay and lesbian couples who have shared their lives with me over the last three decades. If this book does provide substantive guidance to gay men and lesbians in building strong and satisfying relationships it is because, in learning what I needed to know to write it, I had the best possible teachers, my clients.

Special thanks to Carole DeSanti for supporting this new edition at its inception, to Lexy Bloom and Molly Bruce Barton for making it happen so efficiently and expeditiously, to Dusty Jones for making the technical end so easy, and to Teresa DeCrescenzo, whose help in getting this edition out parallels the help she gives me in every other part of my life.

INTRODUCTION
TO THE 2004 EDITION

WHAT HAPPENED?

It is Thursday morning, February 12, 2004. A small group of people slips quietly into San Francisco City Hall. At the center of the group are two women, Phyllis Lyon, seventy-nine, and Del Martin, eight-three. Accompanying them are newspaper reporters, an Academy Award–winning filmmaker, members of Mayor Gavin Newsome's staff, and a retinue of civil rights attorneys. The group proceeds to the office of the city assessor/recorder, Mabel S. Teng. The purpose of the visit is, so far, a well-kept secret.

Del Martin and Phyllis Lyon have been lovers and partners for fifty-one years. They are about to be married. City Assessor Teng has been deputized to perform the ceremony. A marriage license is applied for and issued. At precisely 11:06 the wedding vows begin.

A tsunami of social change has been set in motion.

By February 19, one week later, the number of same-sex marriages sanctioned in San Francisco alone reached nearly 3,000. The majority leader of the U.S. Senate calls it a "wildfire" as the movement for same-sex marriage spreads to New Mexico, Oregon, and New York. Television brings the scenes into America's living rooms—gay men and women of all ages, races, and backgrounds standing in line, in the rain, all night, waiting to be married to their same-sex partners. Many of those lined up are there with their children, intact families, bound together by love and kinship and a shared determination to be acknowledged and affirmed.

The dramatic impact of what is happening becomes hard to ignore. The relationships that are at the center of the lives of most gay and lesbian people are suddenly on display. These partnerships, rarely seen by the public, are the context in which we quietly live our lives. These are the families that give our community stability, continuity, and strength.

And now America sees us and learns that our couples are being denied the sanctity of marriage—even though we love, bond, and commit to one another in exactly the same way as the statistical majority. What is different is that we do this with a partner of the same gender. In every other respect, our relationships are no less real, no less imperative, no less complete.

I can hardly believe that in 1988, in the first edition of this book, I suggested that a way to gain legal status for our partnerships was to *adopt* our partners, or to *hire* them under contract. Such a suggestion now seems so old-fashioned, so primitive as to be ludicrous. No more games.

The gay marriage "wildfire" is now spreading across the country, as courageous city and county officials in new places challenge equal protection constitutional issues, following the lead of the Massachusetts high court earlier in 2004.

One thing is certain. The genie is out of the bottle, and it is not going back. Our families can no longer be ignored. Invisibility is no longer an option. Our issues are on the agenda of powerful individuals and groups who care about freedom and fairness. With the help of our allies, we must continue to demand our rights, in the streets for those who are so inclined, with our friends and families and in our workplaces for those attuned to a gentler advocacy.

We must also work to make our spousal relationships the very best they can be, as free as possible of the tensions that are inevitable when two people are building a life together.

What lies ahead? What is in our future as we move through

the battles for equality, the marriage licenses that will be issued, the ceremonies and celebrations? How will our new marital status affect the relationships that we are already in or that are ahead for us?

I have answers from over thirty years of counseling gay and lesbian couples. What works? What doesn't work? Where are the pitfalls? What are the best ways around trouble? What are the paths back to compatibility when crises demand reorganization? What are the common, everyday aspects of relationship to keep an eye on as we move through a shared life with this complicated person we love and are committed to, and don't always understand?

Here are just a few of the challenges that most of us will encounter.

Communication: We must make our needs known to our partner, keeping the voice of the relationship strong and always available to express dissatisfactions as well as love and affection. Guessing games don't work in intimate relationships. There's too much at stake.

Conflict: When there are two human beings with differing needs, values, and beliefs at odds; when missions of the moment are not in sync, there is going to be conflict. The ways in which that conflict is dealt with mean everything to the overall health of the relationship. There is always important information to be learned from conflict when it is dealt with honestly, and not avoided.

Building Family: Two gay or lesbian people in a relationship are a family, probably with an intentional family of friends attached. Most often there is a family of origin, including in-laws to contend with, either joyously or diplomatically. These days there is a very good chance that there will be children and the many decisions that go along with that wonderful but demanding enterprise.

Dealing with Change: There is always going to be change—time, age, evolving status, new challenges. How we deal with change can make a significant difference in the quality of a couple's life. Sometimes people fight change because it feels safer when things stay the same and life is predictable. But change is inevitable, despite our fears and doubts, and expecting change (good or bad), allowing it, integrating it rather than fighting it, can assure growth in a relationship and strengthening of the partners' bond.

These are just a few of the cautions and rewards that are a part of every intimate partnership. Our job is to work to make our spousal relationships as sweet, affirming, energized, and enduring as possible.

This book is dedicated to helping you achieve that goal.

Read on.

REFERENCES AND RESOURCES IN THIS BOOK

No longer a sidebar to history, same-sex partnerships and gay marriage are topics about which reams have now been written. Since the original edition of this book, attention to this topic has spread around the world as the relationships of same-sex couples have come out of the closet in country after country. Reaction to the demand for change has varied from domestic partnership accommodation for gay couples in some places to legal marriage in others.

What the future holds for same-sex couples in the United States is still evolving, but as Jonathan Rauch states in his book, *Gay Marriage*: "The river of history has rounded a bend." Things are changing so quickly that even what I have just written here about the subject will soon become dated. That is how fast the train is moving on this track. I will, therefore, present throughout this book only a sampling of references and resources with the understanding that in years to come, the picture will change and change again.

THE STRUGGLE FOR SAME-SEX MARRIAGE
IN THE UNITED STATES

Hopefully, you will want to know about the history of same-sex marriage in the United States. These books cover the landmark events, the issues, and the politics:

Baird, Robert M., and Rosenbaum, Stuart E., eds. *Same-Sex Marriage: The Moral and Legal Debate.* Amherst, N.Y.: Prometheus Books, 1997.

Boswell, John. *Same-Sex Unions in Premodern Europe.* New York: Vintage Books, 1994.

Cabaj, Robert P., and David W. Purcell. *On the Road to Same-Sex Marriage.* San Francisco: Jossey-Bass Publishers, 1997.

Eskridge, William N., Jr. *Equality Practice: Civil Unions and the Future of Gay Rights.* New York: Routledge, 2002.

———. *The Case for Same-Sex Marriage: From Sexual Liberty to Civilized Commitment.* New York: Free Press, 1996.

Gerstmann, Evan. *Same-Sex Marriage and the Constitution.* Cambridge, U.K.: Cambridge University Press, 2004.

Kotulski, Davina. *Why You Should Give a Damn About Gay Marriage.* Los Angeles: Advocate Books, 2004.

Moats, David. *Civil Wars: A Battle for Gay Marriage.* New York: Harcourt, Inc., 2004.

Rauch, Jonathan. *Gay Marriage: Why It Is Good for Gays, Good for Straights, and Good for America.* New York: Times Books, 2004.

Strasser, Mark. *Legally Wed: Same-Sex Marriage and the Constitution.* Ithaca, N.Y.: Cornell University Press, 1997.

Sullivan, Andrew, ed. *Same-Sex Marriage: Pro and Con. A Reader.* New York: Vintage Books, 1997. Revised edition, 2004.

Wolfson, Evan. *Why Marriage Matters: America, Equality, and Gay People's Right to Marry.* New York: Simon & Schuster, 2004.

INTRODUCTION: ABOUT US

It is more important now than it ever was that we make our gay and lesbian relationships work.

Wherever we have deluded ourselves in our pursuit of love everlasting, we must now sort out truth from illusion, shadow from substance, to find the real core of intimacy in our partnerships. Where we were lacking in information, guidance, inspiration, and motivation supplied by others, we must now supply our own.

No more excuses. No more distractions. No more illusions.

We have to get down to the work of constructing a new gay and lesbian partnership style.

We must choose our allies in love with care. We must bind our pairings together into a solid foundation of family, chosen family, gay and lesbian family.

This book is dedicated to that task. I have sought here to provide information about the dynamics of intimate partnerships. I have tried to give guidance and inspiration from my own life and from the lives of gay and lesbian people I know and work with.

The motivation already exists to be in, and to build, enduring relationships. I know because I hear about it everywhere I go: "If only I could find a lover." "If only we could work it out." "If only we can keep it together."

We've had a lot of excuses, haven't we? "It's hard to be gay." "It's hard to find someone who's compatible." "It's hard because there's no support for our relationships." "It's hard because they don't understand us."

A lot of excuses.

We've certainly had our share of distractions. There were the '70s discos and the clubs of the '80s. The music was like a heavy current carrying us away from our troubles, into a sea of bodies moving in a mass of denial that there was anything left to believe in but this deafening beat. It was as if we were all trapped there for a while, like running through a dream slowly, not getting anywhere. The drugs didn't help. We just thought they did.

Then there was the politics. Now that was some exciting stuff. We strategized, and we confronted. We lobbied, and we rallied. We gave our speeches, and we sang our songs. We marched and demonstrated. We raised money in astonishing amounts. We built whole new institutions. We created a community where there had never been one. We made the world sit up and take notice of us. We turned the tide of history for gay and lesbian people. We were goddamned heroes!

Who had time for relationships? And, anyway, how could any relationship compete with all that heady stuff?

A lot of distractions.

And, we've certainly had our illusions: "Love conquers all." "Everything will be all right as long as we're in love." "It works as long as it's fun."

A lot of illusions.

And now it's time for reality. Oh, the clubs are still there, and there is plenty of political work still to be done, but let's face it, folks, it's time to get some balance in our collective lives. It's time for relationships that work, that endure, that satisfy. It's time to get serious about partnerships that are permanent.

Permanent partnerships for gay and lesbian couples? Not exactly something you heard a lot about from Mom and Dad. How could you? Even if they *were* disposed to extol the virtues of long-lasting, same-sex relationships, how could they know that you were going to turn out this way? How could they know what was in store for you?

They didn't grow up gay. They didn't struggle with the feeling of being different, the sadness, the resentment, the perplexity. They didn't live with the long search for meanings, the fantasies, the joy of finally discovering how good it felt to be touched in a way that had seemed so wrong. They didn't know the ecstasy of allowing the feelings to come through, the release of tension, the relief of knowing you were not the only one. They didn't have to face the dilemma of a newly forming identity, the decisions about whom to tell, the choices about what to do with the rest of your gay or lesbian life. They didn't have to figure out how to integrate it all and feel good about it. And, for heaven's sake, they didn't have *them* to deal with.

So, you had to puzzle out for yourself how to be gay, how to find a partner, how to make a relationship work, and how to pick up the pieces and go on when it didn't work.

For the last thirty years I have been counseling gay and lesbian couples, participating with them in this process of discovery and trial and error. I have come to marvel at the ingeniousness with which people solve the special problems of same-sex partnerships. I have been excited with my clients at their victories as they fought society, their families, each other, and themselves in their efforts to make their relationships function as effectively as possible. I have ached with them in their disillusionment when the myths and fantasies fell away, leaving them to contend with the bare reality of who they each really were. I have felt their anger and their anguish as they crashed into one another while working through the conflicts that are inevitable in every relationship. I have felt their sadness at separation and their elation at connecting again, with the old lover or with a new one.

I have been heartened by the optimism with which I've seen people go forth looking for love. I have been reinforced in my own optimism by the courage with which these people pursue the elusive prizes of love: trusted companionship, bondedness with another, and the security and continuity of an ongoing relationship.

I have learned a lot from these people who allowed me into

their lives in so open and trusting a way. It is my intention to pay back their gift by sharing what I have learned from them.

ABOUT THIS BOOK

As I write, I am reminded of an experience I had at an art exhibit some years ago. The pieces being shown were by an artist who was known for changing not only his style but also his medium every few years. At this time, he was in his Plexiglas period, and his subject matter was highly erotic. As I stood in front of each picture, I had some difficulty focusing on the figures and what they were doing. The pictures were huge expanses of Plexiglas. Each was monochromatic with many shades of blue or red or gold, et cetera. To actually see what was happening in the picture, I had to stare, then squint, then move my head back and forth. Finally, the figures began to emerge from the background, and I experienced a shock of recognition each time the erotic activity they were engaging in revealed itself. I had an uneasy feeling as I went from picture to picture. It took a while before I realized why.

As I stood in front of each picture, staring into it, there among the subjects at their erotic play was *me*. I was a part of each act, as the Plexiglas mirrored my image back at me. At first I found this quite disconcerting. I wasn't at all sure I wanted to see myself in the midst of all this erotic activity. But gradually I got used to it, and I began to enjoy it, looking forward to where I would fit into the configuration as I moved on to the next picture. Soon I was delighted to be encountering myself over and over.

It is this kind of experience that I hope you will have as you read this book. I hope you will see yourself over and over. It may take some doing, as it did for me, to get yourself in focus. But, if you are able to do this, you will have at least the opportunity to see yourself in a new context, as I did. My experience in the art gallery was frivolous and fun. Yours, in this instance, could yield, I'd hope, some serious information on what you need to do to achieve a more satisfying relationship.

In this book I am going to describe some of the phenomena I have observed, through the years, with regard to gay and lesbian couples who have come to me as a therapist and whom I have known personally. I will also draw on my own experience as a partner in a lesbian relationship. As you read, it is important to try to find yourself in what you are reading. Some of the situations described may feel quite personally relevant, some may seem vaguely familiar, some will be absolutely alien. Think about your own relationships as you read. Put yourself "in the picture" as much as possible.

The very general goals of this book are to enable you to gain perspective on a relationship you may have grown too close to, to identify the particular relationship stressors that may be inhibiting growth in your partnership, and to develop new options for dealing with those stressors.

More specifically, we will be looking at ways of establishing compatibility, learning to diagnose the underlying issues of the relationship, the effects of internalized homophobia, ways to improve communication with your partner, how to negotiate your way out of power struggles, the enlivening effect of constructive fighting, how jealousy can hurt and help your partnership, sexual issues, financial arrangements and legal issues, the role of families in your relationship, having children, and dealing with change in your partnership.

Some parts of this book apply only to gay men. Some parts apply only to lesbians. I strongly urge lesbian readers to read the parts about the issues gay men have to deal with, and the gay male readers to read the parts about lesbian couple issues. A better understanding of each other's lives is something our community can only benefit from.

We are a diverse and complicated bunch, we gay and lesbian people. I have not attempted here to deal with all the diversities or complications. For instance, I have not written about problems related specifically to racially mixed partnerships, or the effects of serious illness on a relationship, or the difficulties encountered by the aging couple or couples living in special circumstances, such as rural areas. I have tried to paint with a fairly broad brush, and I hope that doesn't mean I've left out something that you need desperately to know, but I might have. Forgive me if that is the case.

ABOUT ME

My personal story threads its way throughout this book. I have included it for two reasons. I did not want to write as a dispassionate observer about something so passionately personal. I did want you to know that I, too, have struggled with most of the issues that I have written about here.

FINALLY . . .

There is always the danger of oversimplification when one applies general principles of human behavior to a wide variety of individuals. So much gets left out.

I personally abhor the kind of reductionist thinking that some mental health professionals practice when thinking and talking about the individuals who come to them for help. To believe that one can capture the truth of so mysterious an entity as a complex human being in a diagnostic phrase is self-deluding and invalidates the assertion that psychological exploration is a *quest* for the truth. All too often, it is a gathering of evidence to reaffirm what someone already believes about a particular set of behaviors.

I hope I have not fallen into the oversimplification trap. It is difficult to address effectively the needs of so diverse a readership as gay and lesbian people without generalizing. I have tried to stick to the relationship issues that, over the years, I have heard about and personally experienced most frequently.

Mainly, this book is about reinventing our gay and lesbian relationships. It is about learning to imbue them with all the *solemnity* of marriage without necessarily imitating the heterosexual model. It is about believing even more strongly in the sanctity of the bond with our partners and being willing to do whatever is necessary to preserve that bond.

Haven't we had enough of the cycle of "mate search," falling in love, moving in, getting acquainted, disillusionment, unresolved conflict, breaking up, grieving, and starting all over again?

Gay and lesbian people are not so psychologically different from our heterosexual counterparts. We, too, have the need to affiliate, to have the continuity of companionship that brings true understanding and intimacy. We, too, have the need to be caretakers and to know that there is someone to take care of us if the need arises. We, too, need the stability and tranquility that enables us to compose a life of meaningful activity from a home base that is secure. We have the need. We have the right. We have the personal resources.

In recent years, we have developed the community-wide support for commitment to permanent partnerships that had been missing before.

Now we have couples' workshops, couples' organizations, couple therapy. There are surveys, studies, and seminars on gay and lesbian relationships. Books are written on the subject, movies made, and plays produced. Couples are interviewed on television, written about in mainstream newspapers and magazines. Partners pledge their love in formal ceremonies attended by family and friends. Some professional associations and some insurance companies are beginning to acknowledge officially gay and lesbian couples in their spousal benefits programs.

Now, I believe, we need a concept of permanent partnership for our relationships, a concept that sends the same message that heterosexual marriage does: these two people are bound together in love and in life, functioning as a family unit, mutually committed and invested in one another's future. The integration of such concepts into our thinking about our relationships is the precondition necessary to turn the tradition of failure that we have lived with for so long into a tradition of success. It is that concept and its implementation that this book is about.

1

IT'S TIME FOR A CHANGE

I hadn't seen my old friend Larry in a few years. We were getting caught up with one another. "Bill and Audrey, are they still to-gether?" I asked. He looked puzzled. "Of course," he said. "They're *married*." I had asked the question that way on purpose. I wanted to see how he would respond. Would it be different from the way gay and lesbian people responded to the question, "Are Bill and James still together?" "Is Susan still with Barbara?" We don't look puzzled when asked that kind of question. We are used to hearing it and asking it.

Heterosexuals enter their intimate partnerships with the expectation that they will be permanent. There is much in the couple's life to reinforce that expectation. The union is legally sanctioned, publicly acknowledged, and usually welcomed by each partner's family. Though the statistics on divorce are for-midable, most married couples believe it will not happen to them. They proceed as though their partnerships will be per-manent.

Gay and lesbian people, on the other hand, tend to approach their partner relationships with the hope that these will be long-lasting, even though this prospect is largely unconfirmed by their own experience and that of most of the people they know. There has been much in the natural history of gay and lesbian coupling to reinforce the expectation of failure.

THE TRADITION OF FAILURE

First, there is the *tradition* born of centuries of homosexual pairings not working because homosexuality, as a way of life, didn't work. Gay men met in settings designed for transitory experiences. Frightened of discovery, they made contact under cover of night and returned by day to definitions of themselves that were more tolerable than those which described their true nature.

Lesbians, not having easily identifiable trysting places, met by chance. Some dared to be lovers. Others were too afraid. Many remained in heterosexual marriages and dreamed. For those couples who did somehow manage to build a life together in those dark times, the fear always remained of being found out, ridiculed, rejected, penalized in their careers, or ostracized by their families. Such fear cast a long shadow over the couple's life together. Social taboos made even semipublic displays of affection between two men or two women extremely uncomfortable. Partners learned to disguise their intimate communication. Being in a same-sex relationship required constant vigilance, strategizing, and deception. The need to stop one's self before the spur-of-the-moment kiss or touch of the hand often took its toll in the couple's ability to be spontaneously affectionate, even in private. Love so diminished often did not survive.

Collective relationships seemed to work better and last longer than pairings did. Enclaves of gay men and lesbians provided safe havens here and there in the world. Because these social networks were so insular, they became intricately woven webs of ex-lovers who were ex-lovers of ex-lovers. They were held together partly by intrigue and partly by the profound need to be with one's own kind. All too often, alcohol was the bulwark against a hostile society. It was ruinous, however, for anything resembling a stable emotional life. Beset by conflict from within, surrounded by a conspiracy of silence as to their very existence in the society, gay and lesbian partnerships most often did not endure for long. The tradition of failure in such relationships was established, and persists to this day.

LACK OF LEGAL AND SOCIAL SUPPORT

A second condition undermining same-sex couple life has been the absence of the legal sanctions and social acceptance that heterosexual marriages enjoy. The absence of a legal foundation for the partnership cheats the gay or lesbian couple of insurance benefits, tax breaks, spousal discounts, and other practical rewards that are forthcoming to the heterosexually married couple. Heterosexual newlyweds can usually count on a windfall of gifts to start them out in married life. Not so the gay or lesbian couple, who enter their unions without benefit of ceremony. The celebrations that mark milestone anniversaries of heterosexual marriages bring more gifts. Such celebrations are not common for same-sex couples, though they are beginning to gain in popularity.

Without legal status, the homosexual partner lacks the authority to act on behalf of his/her spouse or, in many places, to visit if that person is seriously ill in the hospital. A well-known jurist commenting on the unfairness of this situation once pointed out that a heterosexual couple married *one hour* had more rights and privileges with regard to one another than did a homosexual couple living together in a committed relationship for twenty-five years. The lack of such legal and social supports represents a constant reminder of society's view of same-sex liaisons as transitory, illicit, and not to be taken seriously. Unfortunately, too often these attitudes become internalized and thus plague the lovers' relationship from within.

Without public acknowledgment of the true nature of their relationship, the gay or lesbian couple must sometimes endure bizarre treatment at the hands of the unenlightened. They might be treated like eligible partners for heterosexual marriage by family, friends, or coworkers. If the person is past forty and not yet heterosexually married, he/she becomes a figure of speculation as to what is wrong. If the person is past fifty, pity for the poor failed "old maid" (male or female) is in order. All of these attitudes would be quite incongruous with what might well be a happily married personal life, though one that is hidden from view.

Because our relationships have not been publicly acknowledged, non-gay people who assume that everyone is heterosexual
have to find an explanation for what is going on between the two
women or two men who are so close to one another. Sometimes
the results are amusing. In my own relationship (of thirty-one
years, at this writing) my lover is seventeen years younger than I
am. We look nothing alike. I am a five-foot tall Jewish person with
blue eyes and curly blonde-hair-going-gray. She is a five-foot, ten-
inches tall, dark-eyed, dark-haired Italian. Yet, presented with this
combination in clothing stores, restaurants, doctors' offices, and
various other venues staffed by personnel apparently unable to
think beyond the heterosexual assumption, they inevitably identify us as mother and daughter. "Come over here and show your
mother how nice this looks on you." "Who gets the check tonight,
mother or daughter?" "The doctor will see you now. Would you
like your daughter to come in with you?"

Once, when I was in the hospital, my lover was adamant that
it be clear what her relationship was to me and that she be accorded all the rights a mate should have. There was a series of Fil-
ipino nurses, struggling with the language, trying to be friendly,
who consistently complimented me on my loving, attentive, and
ever-present daughter. "SPOUSE!!!" she would thunder at them,
"I'm her SPOUSE!" Unable to cope with this announcement,
they would smilingly back out the door, only to be replaced by
still other angels of mercy continuing to extol the virtues of my
very devoted daughter. "Leave them alone," I finally pleaded on
behalf of these perplexed and uncomprehending victims.

Then there is always the drama of the hotel registration desk.
Face to face with the male or female couple refusing the room
with the *twin beds*, the desk clerk, truth dawning, delivers the
death look and completes the transaction in studied silence (unless she or he happens to be gay, in which case we get a knowing
and/or friendly smile). Sometimes there is defiance. "We don't
have any rooms with double beds available. Only twins." I have
found it helpful in this particular situation to fix the desk clerk
with a firm stare, while quietly ordering, "Find one. We'll wait."

Usually it works. When it doesn't, of course we relent and a few minutes later we are into our furniture moving act, pushing the twin beds together while vowing never to patronize this establishment again.

We grow accustomed to such experiences. We laugh about them in retrospect, but they remind us one more time that our relationships are misunderstood, disapproved of, and, in some quarters, reviled.

The refusal-to-acknowledge-the-truth situation that has the potential for creating the most stress for a couple is that in which one partner's family is less than enthusiastic about welcoming their child's lover into the family. In extreme cases, a lover might even be totally persona non grata, as the family plays out its rejection of the truth about their son or daughter's homosexuality. Torn between loyalty to family and loyalty to lover, the individual still willing to put up with such treatment faces a terrible dilemma. The behavior of rejecting families can make a strong statement to a couple about the legitimacy and acceptability of their love in the eyes of people about whom at least one of them cares. This is very different from the experience of the heterosexually married couple, strengthened in their bond to one another as their families welcome and integrate them into their life.

Such are some of the challenges to the fortitude and ingenuity of same-sex couples trying to establish stable and fulfilling relationships. It is no wonder that success so often eludes us and the tradition of failure persists.

WHERE HAVE ALL OUR ELDERS GONE?

A third reason we do not more often have an expectation of permanence in our partnerships is that we do not have much visible evidence of long-term partnerships in our community. We know there are people who have been together for decades. But where are they? They are not seen in the bars. They do not come to political events because they are often still uncomfortable about being publicly gay. Since one tends to socialize in an age group approximating one's own age, the gay or lesbian person in the first two, three, or four decades of life is unlikely to socialize with couples in the fifth, sixth, seventh, or eighth decade of their lives. In a subculture that idealizes youth, being gay and gray does not exactly make one a hot ticket. Older gays and lesbians often relegate themselves to separate and unequal meeting places. Out of anxiety over our own aging, we denigrate their social gathering places as "wrinkle palaces" or "menopause mansions," thereby reinforcing our isolation from them. Effectively we collaborate to hide older gays and lesbians from view, and in the process we are cheated of witnessing their longstanding partnerships.

How different it is in the non-gay world. We see grandma and grandpa enjoying their golden years together, and we are warmed by the sight. It is reassuring to know that people can love and trust and be supportive of one another over a lifetime. We feel good when we come in contact with the visible evidence of such a relationship. Heterosexual married couples picture themselves transformed by the years into grandma and grandpa. It is a pleasant prospect. It gives shape to a life together. It is a goal felt to be attainable because there they are, all those other people who have done it.

And where are our elders in the gay and lesbian world? Certainly not in so honored a role. Certainly not valued and celebrated by their own community. Actually hidden from sight for the most part, not treated with deference but too often with derision. We all lose on this one. They feel diminished and unwanted. We are deprived of the visibility of couples of our own persuasion who have loved and trusted and supported one another over a lifetime. We are stuck with a foreshortened view of what our relationships can be. I look forward to the time when this will not be the case, when it will not be a source of amazement to encounter a same-sex couple who have been together for forty or fifty years. We will have learned to honor our elders and to welcome them into our midst. I hope that this will mean that the gay or lesbian long-term couple will become as commonplace to us as grandma and grandpa who've been together forever, just as we all expected them to be.

THE GAY NATIONAL ANTHEM:
"WHY DON'T WE JUST BREAK UP?"

As though all of the foregoing weren't enough to predispose failure, there is an additional way in which gay and lesbian couples add to the problem. I have come to think of it as the Gay National Anthem:

"Why don't we just break up?"
"This relationship is over."
"It just isn't working for me anymore."
"I think I ought to move out."
"I think you ought to move out."
"I don't need all this hassle."
"I'd rather be alone."
"I'm not even sure I'm gay."

The threat of dissolution is used as a way of dealing with conflict. In most cases the people uttering these words do not mean what they are saying. They do mean to get their partner's attention, to wake him or her up, to have dissatisfaction heard, to strike out, to wound, to get some response, but they aren't really calling for the relationship to end. Nevertheless, impending termination is what they are talking about, and when you have heard it often enough it takes on a kind of ominous reality of its own.

Few things are as destructive to a couple's sense of well-being as this insidious invocation of the power of one partner over the other to bring the whole structure crashing down around their ears. It is a way of flexing muscle. It is a way of turning the screw. It is, all too often, an outer expression of an inner conviction that there is no real legitimacy to same-sex relationships, so easily entered into, so easily gotten rid of. Said often enough, one reinforces one's own as well as one's partner's anticipation of failure.

I have heard so frequently the admission, "I felt I had to hold back for my own preservation. He/she is always talking about leaving. I don't want to get hurt." And when the partner threatening dissolution is questioned about it, more often than not the answer is, "That wasn't really what I meant. I wasn't talking about actually *leaving*, but once he/she started to withdraw so much I did begin to think about it."

One partner threatening abandonment is not the special province of gay and lesbian couples, but because we do not have the social and legal supports that non-gay couples have, our relationships are more at risk. Therefore it is all the more important that we stop singing the Gay National Anthem to each other. We must learn to stop ourselves when the familiar phrase comes to mind. Instead of "I want to break up," how about "I want to tell you what I'm unhappy about," or "I'm unhappy and I'm not sure why." Instead of "I'm leaving," how about "I'm hurt, angry, disappointed, et cetera." Instead of "I don't need all this hassle," how about "I do need you to listen to me." Instead of "This relationship is over," how about "It's time to start talking."

The point is that it's time for a change.

OUR SPECIAL ISSUES

We have tended to accept too quickly dissolution as a solution to relationship problems. We have underestimated our ability to stay in the battle, to make our partnerships work, to build stability and continuity into our lives with our lovers. We have turned away too easily and too often from the hard work of relationship building.

Much of that work, of course, revolves around the same relationship issues that all couples have to deal with, gay or non-gay. Some, however, are unique to our special situation. For instance, the great majority of gay and lesbian people grew up with a terrible secret that affected practically everything we did. Our identity development involved a struggle to integrate something that many people, often including us, believed to be discrediting. Most of us were very much alone with our secret. We couldn't go for help to the people we would usually turn to because we knew, somehow, that they wouldn't like what we had to tell them. They couldn't come to us with help because they didn't know what was happening to us. So we developed our sense of who we were as sexual beings in a context of confusion and self-deprecation.

Add to that growing up gay in an anti-gay society. Just as we knew not to run to Mom and Dad with the good news of our homosexuality, we also knew that the world around us would not welcome the information. In order to protect that information, most of us had to resort to subterfuge and strategy to avoid detection. Sometimes we were afraid that our behavior would be detected. More often it was a fear that someone would intuit what we were feeling, would decipher our encoded communication about ourselves and know the secret.

I believe that these early feelings of conflict about sexuality persist in our unconscious minds and affect the quality of our adult gay and lesbian sexual relationships. I will attempt later in this book to pinpoint some of the consequences of sexual identity conflict in our intimate partnerships. Suffice it to say for now that gay and lesbian relationships differ from those between opposite-sex partners because of this conflict.

You not only grow up gay in an anti-gay society but you also live out your life that way. The degree of homophobia one has to cope with is better or worse depending on how well the gay rights movement is faring and the part of the country in which one lives. The restricted ability to be openly affectionate with your partner in public, to take advantage of the same practical rewards non-gay couples enjoy, to have the approval and support of family—these are a few additional ways in which our relationship issues become different.

The lack of gender-role guidelines for who does what in the couple's everyday dealings with each other is a mixed blessing. It affords wonderful opportunities for creativity and originality. It also produces confusion and conflict when a couple has not adequately negotiated a "division of labor" arrangement that is satisfactory to both partners.

Further complication is often produced by the sameness of the partner's socialization—the complementarity built into heterosexual partnerships has to be developed from scratch in the gay or lesbian couple's life. If men stick only to those tasks they have been socially scripted as males to perform, then who, in a gay male couple, will take on the responsibilities for which they have not been prepared?

Gay and lesbian couples must also deal with many other aspects of their life together that, in traditional opposite-sex relationships, are structured by gender-role expectations. For some couples, these challenges are welcomed and easily coped with. For others too locked into their social scripting, the need to develop a relationship pattern from scratch can prove arduous and cumbersome.

At the very least, these conditions unique to our sexual orientation produce relationship issues that are different from those generated by non-gay liaisons. We do have to work a little harder, and that is one of the ways in which it is time for a change.

THE SEMANTIC DILEMMA

In the case of heterosexual marriage, the terms used to describe the partners in the marriage are models of simplicity and efficiency: "Husband." "Wife." A great deal is conveyed in those two words. You know that these two people are officially and publicly committed to one another. You know that they operate primarily as a unit in social situations (you would not invite one to a social event without the other or without somehow acknowledging that you were doing something unusual). You have some orientation to the roles each partner probably plays in the marriage, though you may not know to just what extent they follow the usual conventions for a married couple. You know their primary sexual activity is with each other, probably exclusively so. You know that these two people most likely expect to spend the rest of their lives together.

We are heavily influenced by labels. An individual is appointed to an important position. It carries a prestigious title. With the assumption of that title the person assumes, in the eyes of others, all the authority and power that accrue to the title. Labels shape our thinking about the people to whom they are attached. They carry a lot of information. Sometimes it is erroneous information. Nevertheless, much of what goes into our attitudes, judgments, and feelings about an individual, as often as not, is more about the labels than the person. Labels are communication shortcuts. Usually they do what they are meant to do—convey a complicated set of data in a quick and simple way.

In the case of gay and lesbian partnerships the terms we use to describe our partners are models of ambiguity rather than efficiency. Rather than clarifying the relationship between the two people involved, they often confuse and mislead. Sometimes they are meant to do that, to be euphemisms designed to disguise the true nature of the relationship because disclosure might carry a penalty. But even when that is not the case, there is an ambiguity, reflective, I think, of the ambiguity that all too often permeates our thinking about what these relationships mean not only to the world, but also to us.

COME TO TERMS

The labels we use for our partners most commonly fall into two main categories—those meant to *conceal* the true nature of the relationship and those meant to *reveal* its true nature.

The concealment list is short: roommate/housemate; friend/buddy; and variations on this theme. These terms, designed mainly for non-gay ears, trivialize the relationship and, if used over a long period of time, may have just that effect. Thus we cooperate with the non-gay society's inclination to undervalue the significance of our partnerships. The problem is that concealment too often is not confined to those situations in which it is felt to be absolutely necessary. It becomes a way of life. We don't mean to, of course, but we do perpetuate a trivialized view of our-selves by reducing the single most important relationship in our life to the status of "friend" or "roommate."

Well, what are we to do? We don't have an adequate name for it even when we are not trying to conceal the true nature of the relationship.

There's "lover." Too sexualized, many say. Has the connotation of a transitory affair. Frivolous. Cheapening. Misleads from the se-riousness of a committed relationship. The term does, however, carry some weight politically. It is the term most gay and lesbian people have chosen to use to describe their nearest and dearest. It is, therefore, self-determining and has value in that regard.

Then there's "partner." Less loaded. Many think it's too neu-tral. Sounds like a business arrangement. Will the non-gay person know that, in addition to sharing the *work* of a life together, we also have a romantic connection, that we make love and enjoy each other sexually? Some choose to stretch it out to "partner-in-life" or "lifepartner." Stilted. Sociological. Does not roll trippingly off the tongue.

How about "significant other"? Now that's a mouthful. It is also pedagogical (which is another mouthful). It's always sounded to me more like a diagnosis than a term of endearment.

"Companion" is nice. Too nice, actually. Summons up an image of the kindly attendant hired to escort someone who is too old, feeble, or demented to take care of him/herself.

Then there are the "halves." "My *better* half" and "my other half." I can't get rid of the sexist connotation. Usually one hears this one from the male side of the heterosexual couple. He doesn't really mean "my better half" when he's talking about the little woman. He usually means "my lesser half who I am gener-ously referring to as 'my better half.' " Also, I don't like the thought that by joining my life to another I give up half of myself.

Then there's the ever-popular "boyfriend/girlfriend." Okay for the under-twenty-one set, but hearing this term from people in their twenties, thirties, or forties makes me feel a little squeam-ish. "Manfriend/womanfriend" seems better, though a bit stern.

"Spouse?" Another term nonspecific for gender. That's good. It does imply entitlement. And, it's very serious. Rather old-fashioned, though. A bit too serious, perhaps. Or, "mate." Jaunty and nautical are my immediate associations. The dictionary says "one of a pair" or "either member of a married couple" or "either member of a breeding pair of animals" (skip that one).

Some people like "lifemate." Accurate enough but a little too kitschy. I hear a heavenly chorus in the background. I see a sunburst of light as my "lifemate" appears on the horizon.

I once asked a couples' group to write down every term they had ever used or heard used to describe the person with whom one is in a relationship. They came up with seventeen terms, but they could not achieve consensus on a single one. A wag of a person I know (Dr. Laura Brown, by name) suggested we might adopt the initials used by the United States Census Bureau to describe "Persons of the Same Sex Sharing Living Quarters," but since that turns out to be PSSSLQ we agreed it was a bit too unwieldy.

So, what are we to do in this semantic dilemma?

I had a fantasy when I began this chapter that I would be able to come up with a brand-new name to use. It would be a label that would be as inclusive, yet simple, as "husband" or "wife." It would be a term that would convey the special meaning of a same-sex partnership. It would be unpretentious, nonclinical, mature, contemporary, equitable, and nondeceptive. Well, I didn't. I, too, am stuck with using the term (take your pick) that seems to fit the needs of the moment best. I find I like to say "lover" the most. I like the self-determining aspect of it. But, then, every act of everyday life cannot be a political statement. Most of us are not that focused, dedicated, patient, and courageous enough to live that way.

The plumber comes to fix the leaky toilet. He is clearly a redneck type. He is in my house. Do I say, "My lover is in the bathroom. She'll be right out and you can go in there"? What chain of associations do I set off in him when I reveal our homosexuality? Is it worth the risk? Do I care about having a more honest relationship with the plumber? No, actually, I'd just like to get the toilet fixed. So, in this instance, my lover becomes "someone" who is in the bathroom or my "friend" who is in the bathroom and in either case, she'll be right out.

As members of an identifiable minority group about which some people have strong negative feelings, we are very much at the mercy of the power of labeling. People tend to relate more to the label than to the person it is attached to when the contact is casual. If the label is an innocuous one—salesclerk, repairman, gas station attendant, bank clerk—this shortcut form of interpersonal relating is unimportant. But, when the label is one that is emotionally loaded it can become a very risky business indeed until one knows with whom one is dealing. There is a tendency toward being overdefined by any label that stirs the emotions. "Gay" and "lesbian" and "homosexual" are loaded terms for many people. When they are attached to a person with whom casual contact is occurring, the result is often overdefinition.

I am many things, but to the person who is the victim of a particularly bigoted upbringing, I am a dyke, pure and simple. I am an oddity, a joke, a threat, an object of derision. If my contact with this person is to be fleeting, I'd just as soon skip their emotional reaction to me as a homosexual and move right along to something that requires less of my attention.

I have a lot of choice about this as an individual. I have less choice when I am a member of a gay or lesbian couple and when there is a need to deal with the nature of our relationship. I want my lover's non-gay physician to know what I am to her. The non-gay insurance salesperson needs to know what our relationship is. Now I must decide which term to use to convey most clearly who we are to one another. I make a judgment call about the person from the information that I have. What'll it be? "My mate"? "My partner"? "My lover"?

The point is, there really isn't an answer. We must tailor our choice of terms to fit the needs of the situation we're in. I hope that we won't be too chicken about it, that more and more of us will take courage from the stalwart among us who *always* accurately identify the nature of their relationship, who are always willing to be known as gay or lesbian and to deal with the consequences of that revelation. Personally, I have determined that I am going to use the term "lover" in as many situations as I can. When that is too uncomfortable, I am going to say "partner." If we are being hijacked by terrorists, she will quickly become my "friend" (I hear they execute homosexuals in some Arab countries). Above all, I will try not to be passive about this, not to take the easy way out every time.

The anti-gay forces in our society would like to keep us invisible and without the ability to effect changes in our status. Like it or not, the battle against bigotry belongs to every gay man and lesbian woman. We are all as much potential heroes in this battle as we are potential victims of the bigotry it is about.

The heroic act might be a very simple one. You will find yourself saying to that inconsequential non-gay person, to whom you have inadvertently given so much power over you, "We are a gay/lesbian couple. My lover and I would like a room with a double bed/to open a joint checking account/to look at the apartment for rent." You'll say it because you are tired, finally, of avoiding, evading, inventing. You will probably be anxious when you do it, maybe even a little excited. You'll be met with nonchalance or surprise, acceptance or rejection, but you will feel good because you will have won a victory over fear. It will be a triumph over inertia, a refusal to remain invisible, a step in the direction of full legitimacy. It is time for that. It is time for that change.

2

BUILDING COMPATIBILITY

SELECTING A PARTNER: WHERE IT ALL BEGINS

I was once asked by a friend, "Describe the person who would be a perfect mate for you." I went through a lengthy inventory of physical, intellectual, and social characteristics. He looked at me bemusedly and said, "You have just described yourself." Startled, I had to acknowledge that he was right. Did this mean that I was so narcissistic that I could not be attracted to someone outside my own skin? Or, was I just articulating what social psychologists have been telling us for years, that relationships work best when the people in them are more alike than different?

Without benefit of social psychological research to guide them in the search for a lover, most people act on the basis of physical attraction and what is happening at the moment of meeting. They like the person's looks. They are shy and the other person takes the initiative. The person reminds them of someone with whom they had a positive experience. Or, the person is just "there."

Many people act on the basis of what they think of as "pictures." More than likely these pictures represent idols of adolescence, the person-I-always-wanted-to-be. When one becomes romantically linked with someone who looks and/or acts like the person-you-always-wanted-to-be, one "borrows" the identity of the admired object and feels completed, at least until the illusion breaks down. I believe this happens more often in same-sex situations than in opposite-sex settings. Your early idols, no matter what your sexual orientation, are usually of the same gender. For those who grow up gay, erotic arousal patterns are often tied to fantasies about these early idols. People get locked into a search for what they come to think of as their "type." They can't be interested in anyone who isn't their "type," which, in the case of the early-idol fantasy, usually means someone who has physical or psychological qualities they wish they had.

The trouble with being guided by "pictures" in the search for your "type" is that the true objective, to find a *compatible* partner, gets lost in the playing out of the fantasy.

For example, the Jewish intellectual high-achiever who has internalized anti-Semitic attitudes revels in the acquisition of a partner who is blond, blue-eyed, and very gentile. But, after a while he/she yearns for someone who understands the Jewish point of view and has the same frame of reference for life. There is no way to search for an ethnic opposite and find a Jewish soul mate at the same time. Compatibility suffers at the hands of fulfilling a fantasy.

Sometimes the fantasy concerns personality traits one lacks. The shy, conservative social isolate is attracted to the vivacious, outgoing, adventuresome Life-of-the-Party. L-O-P likes the quiet stability of the other person. They pair up. After a while Shy-and-Conservative begins to feel oppressed by his/her partner's unending joviality, superficiality, and the pressure to socialize. The misguided notion that being mated with the L-O-P would enhance one's own social skills backfires. The compatibility necessary to successful coupling may never develop.

In another instance of fantasy compromising reality, you court a person who, because of his/her physical attractiveness or prestige, is seen as potentially image-enhancing. "I will be admired for having captured such a prize." But the "prize" turns out to be less than rewarding as a companion in life. Or, the "prize" turns out to attract more attention from others than is tolerable, or the "prize" exploits the partner's vulnerability vis-a-vis the need to be affiliated with him/her, to gain an inordinate amount of control in the relationship. Again, compatibility never develops.

Some people are most comfortable when they are taking care of someone else. They find the wounded birds of the world and develop a relationship in which they can nurture, administer to, or guide their partner's life. Many people are attracted to care-takers, so these relationships work out well—that is, until the caretaker needs caretaking. If the wounded bird is unable to do the physical or emotional taking care of that is called for, the caretaker partner is likely to feel neglected and/or unloved. The relationship works well only under a restricted set of circum-stances.

Relationships based on one partner's essentially taking care of the other often go sour when the caretaker, for some reason, is suddenly unable to fulfill the good mother or good father role. The partner who has grown accustomed to leaning on a care-taker/lover feels deprived and expresses this feeling by withdraw-ing or punishing the lapsed parent/lover. Again, the relationship is in trouble from the beginning because partner selection was based on an unrealistic vision of who the other person was and what the partnership was to be about. None of this is to say that relationships based on any of the above can't work. They certainly can. But they are built on a shaky foundation, and they require a lot of work if they are to get beyond being a vehicle for the play-ing out of the fantasies of one or both partners.

In the "completion fantasies" a partner is selected to supply what the selector feels is lacking in his/her self: good looks, pres-tige, social facility, favored ethnic status, and so forth. The bur-den is on the person selected to cooperate with her/his partner's fantasy. This person may or may not be clued in to the expecta-tions produced by the fantasy. Nevertheless, those expectations play an important part in shaping the relationship. If the expec-tations are not met consistently, the selecting partner's disap-pointment will become a major source of tension between them.

Here is an example of a completion fantasy gone awry. Ken is drawn to Richard because Richard is a doer. He seeks out new experiences. He is up on what is happening and he is always making plans for interesting activities. He likes people and brings them into his life easily. He's a "take charge" person. Ken, on the other hand, is inclined toward inertia. He likes going places once he does it, but he is not inclined to make it happen on his own. Ken becomes involved with Richard. For the first few years of their relationship, Richard does, indeed, do the planning and arranging. He enjoys it. He does it well. Both are quite satisfied with the arrangement. But, as they move further into the partnership, Richard begins to tire of the responsibility of making everything happen in their life together. He begins to feel that he carries too much of the burden for the couple's social schedule. He becomes annoyed with Ken's inertia. Because these men both shy away from talking about their feelings, their reactions to each other tend to get *acted out* rather than *talked through*. Richard acts out by going "on strike." He stops organizing for the two of them. He withdraws from Ken who, in turn, withdraws from him.

Richard is on strike. Ken resents the loss of his social director. He pouts and finds subtle ways to punish Richard. Their social life dwindles, and both begin to feel isolated and full of unexpressed anger. It does not occur to Ken that Richard is trying to tell him something important by his actions. It would be much better, of course, if Richard could communicate directly what he wants changed. By acting out his dissatisfaction rather than talking about it, he creates a whole new set of problems.

Ken, on the other hand, is so overinvested in Richard's usefulness to him as a social director, that he cannot see beyond this aspect of Richard's personality to other parts that may badly need his attention. The relationship deteriorates because they are not able to go beyond its being a vehicle for the playing out of Ken's completion fantasy. They do not talk. They do not explore. They do not understand what is happening to them. They do not confront it and work it through. Their future looks dismal.

Here is another example. Maureen is attracted to Helen primarily because Helen is the "prom queen" Maureen wanted to be and never was. Helen is blond, pert, svelte, and pretty. Maureen, on the other hand, is an astute and accomplished business-woman, and although she is an attractive person, she still carries with her the pain of an adolescence in which she felt different from the others and was ignored by the kids who always scored high in the popularity polls. By affiliating with Helen and her prom queen good looks, Maureen in a sense borrows that aspect of Helen's identity, and the longstanding pain of her teenage years is somewhat ameliorated.

They settle into a relationship, and everything goes well for a while. Then one day Maureen notices that Helen is beginning to gain weight. She jokingly chides her about it. Helen jokes back that she is a happily married woman now and she feels she can afford to relax her vigilance over her figure. Maureen wants to protest but feels guilty because it seems too shallow to care about something like this. Helen continues to gain weight. Maureen continues to be irritated about it. Unaware of the investment Maureen has in her maintaining a prom queen image, Helen soon begins to resent Maureen's jokes about her weight. The relationship is at a critical point. Will it mature into a partnership that supports each member's need to develop as an individual, or will it collapse like a house of cards, which is what a pairing based on fantasy fulfillment can be? What will make the difference will be Maureen's being able to understand the personal significance of Helen's looking a particular way. Maureen has to gain perspective on the real meaning of her fantasy in terms of her own development. She must let go of fantasy with regard to Helen. Maureen needs to see Helen as a separate and unique individual who has needs of her own and who cannot supply, even vicariously, the gratification that was missing in Maureen's own struggle for acceptance and approval as a young person.

In those instances where partner selection was based on a need to have someone to take care of, the symbiotic parent-child arrangement, trouble often comes if and when the child/partner develops too much independence. The caretaking partner is often a person who does not believe in his/her ability to attract and keep a lover without earning it. Deprived of the supporting role, the caretaking partner feels anxious about her/his worth to the lover. "Will she still love me if she doesn't need me?" Sometimes this question results in a subtle sabotaging of the other person's growth or success. Sometimes the caretaking partner acts out the fear of not being needed by pushing the other person away, rejecting before being rejected. If the parties involved do not understand what is happening this dynamic can have damaging or fatal effects on the relationship.

The task at hand, in all relationships in which fantasy fulfillment or the need to caretake serves as the basis for partner selection, is to uncover the underlying need that one partner has for the other. Only when this need has been brought into awareness can the partners go beyond it to begin to establish real compatibility.

Not everyone, of course, is looking for a partner to take care of or complete their personality. How else, then, does partner selection work for gay men and lesbians? Actually, we have both an advantage and a disadvantage over our non-gay counterparts. The disadvantage is that our partner search is relatively unstructured compared to that of heterosexuals. The heterosexual woman is, usually, looking for a marriage partner who is a good breadwinner and who will be a good father to their children. That's for starters. Over and above that she looks for compatibility. The heterosexual man is usually looking for a wife who will be a good homemaker (even if she also has a career) and be a good mother to their children. Breadwinning and homemaking are fairly concrete activities to assess in terms of criteria. Parenting is a little more abstract and, therefore, difficult, but most people carry into marriage a well-developed notion of what they would like from their partner by way of cooperation and support in the parenting role.

Gay men and lesbians, on the other hand, do not start out with such structured criteria in the search for a partner. Lesbian women, accustomed to being self-supporting, usually are not seeking someone to support them financially. Therefore,

income-producing ability is not a major criterion in partner selection. However, some gay men do seek out other men who will
either support them or with whom they can upgrade their
lifestyle. Most simply hope that their partner will at least earn
enough money to be able to afford the same lifestyle that they
enjoy.

Since the majority of gay people are not, at this time, planning for parenthood, one's potential merit as a parent is not
often a significant criterion. So, what are the criteria we use in
making our choices as we scan the room, become acquainted
with, and begin to consider seriously the likely candidates for a
mate? Well, of course, most of us start with looks, whether it's by
comparison to a popularly accepted standard of what's attractive
or to a type that has evolved out of our own fantasy life. We start
there. Unfortunately, many people stop there. It's a roll of the
dice for them. This person whose physical appearance was so appealing may turn out to be the loveliest of lovers or he/she may
turn out to be less than adequate as a partner, perhaps even destructive to self and others.

For those who move beyond physical appearance in deciding
who they want for a partner in life, the following criteria are most
likely to be taken into account: responsiveness to one's self, a
pleasing personality, a semblance of sanity, and some evidence
that the person will like and be liked by one's friends. But *are*
these the qualities that hold up to the demands of a relationship
over the long haul?

These are certainly some of them. But what are the others to
which one should be paying attention? Here's where the advantages accrue to the gay person over the heterosexual, who is tied
into traditional marriage and child rearing for guidance in partner selection. We have much more leeway in our choices.

We can focus on those aspects of a potential partner's personality that are more about being with one another and sharing
a life together, rather than how effectively the roles of husband,
wife, or parent will be played out.

Here are the criteria I believe count, the questions I suggest single gay and lesbian people ask of themselves when they are getting to know someone who may be a potential partner:

Is this a person

• who seems as if he/she will grow as an individual and not become overly dependent on me to make his/her life work?
• who is in touch with his/her feelings, who can talk about them freely, who is comfortable expressing anger as well as affection?
• who doesn't have to run away from conflict, who is willing and able to confront relationship problems and work on them?
• who listens when I talk, who gives me the feeling that I am being heard and understood?
• who can give as well as receive, who would be able to take care of me if I should have that need?
• who can receive as well as give, who is able to ask for what he/she needs, so that a relationship would afford opportunity for both of us to give as well as receive?
• who functions on an intellectual level that is similar enough to mine so that one of us would not be chronically at a disadvantage with the other?
• whose life experience is similar enough to mine so that we can understand and respect each other's values and needs?

Does this person like to do the same kinds of recreational and social things I like, enough to build a life together that would be mutually enjoyable?

Is this person comfortable with his/her sexuality, and are we compatible in our sexual patterns?

Obviously, with most of the preceding criteria, the passage of time is required to develop answers to the questions. Only through interacting over time can one assess the more abstract qualities of another person's character. That is the real purpose of courtship. It provides a period of getting acquainted. Too often, I have found, gay and lesbian couples conduct their courtship after they have moved in together and officially become lovers. In a very real sense, they are having a relationship on two levels. They are getting to know one another on one level and functioning as a family unit on another. Sometimes the demands of those two pursuits are in conflict. In a well-functioning family unit the members know each other's dispositions and habits and are reasonably predictable to one another. If you are operating as a family unit before you really understand your partner, you are probably in for some surprises. The process of discovery occurs best when unhampered by the demands of commitment. It should be a pleasurable experience. Too often, when a couple has rushed the process and moved into a committed relationship before they really know who this other person is, the process of discovery feels more like a rude awakening. When one's best foot is no longer always forward, but both feet are on display (warts, bumps, calluses, and all), the reality of what this relationship will be begins to show. If the courtship is being conducted uncomplicated by the demands of being a family unit at the same time, there is more opportunity, if there is reason to, to question one's choice.

The freedom to reconsider and to extricate one's self gracefully makes the process of discovery and courtship a much more meaningful one. It is then not just a romantic escapade but a true period of assessment as to whether or not this will be a partnership that will be good for life.

If it were up to me, I would require all gay and lesbian couples to spend at least six months in courtship (not living together), insuring that they really know who one another is before they make a commitment to share their life on a permanent basis. I truly believe such a period of courtship would greatly improve the odds against breakups that grow out of learning that the partner who appeared to be one person early in the relationship has turned out to be quite another as time goes by.

So, if you were smart, and lucky, you ended up with a partner who not only suits your fancy but also meets your needs. You have a solid foundation on which to build a lasting relationship. If you weren't so smart and/or lucky, you ended up with a less than perfect match, and you have your work cut out for you.

"ARE YOU CRAZY?"
"NO, JUST DIFFERENT FROM YOU"

My partner and I are about as different as two people can be. I come from a Midwestern, middle-class Jewish family. She comes from an East Coast, working-class Italian Catholic family. My parents are divorced, and I have had five stepmothers. Her parents, on the other hand, were married to each other for over fifty years.

I have struggled with my sexual identity for most of my adult life, coming out after I was forty. She knew she was a lesbian at an early age and has never tried to be anything else. I have had more romantic liaisons with men and women than I can possibly remember. She has had two relationships, one with me and one with her former (female) lover of twelve years.

I am compulsively neat; she lives in a kind of organized disorder, claiming to know exactly where everything is in the mounds of papers on her desk, on her nightstand, in the backseat of her car. I like to become immersed in one project at a time. She loves being involved in many projects simultaneously. She likes to sleep late. I like to rise early. I like to be with people on my own terms, when I want, for well-defined periods, doing what *I* enjoy. She is gregarious by nature, fitting easily into almost any social setting, open to new experience. She would like to have people around much of the time. I like to have people around on a very limited basis. She loves good food, always inclined toward that which is healthy and nutritious. I have learned to love good food, but I'll take a hamburger and french fries any old time. I worry about almost everything. She tends to take everything in stride, worrying rarely, seemingly blind to the multitude of dire possibilities in the world all around us.

Since we are a generation apart, our tastes in music defy reconciliation. I grew up to the mellow sounds and easy to understand lyrics of Glenn Miller and Tommy Dorsey. She grew up with Little Richard, "Long Tall Sally" and "Be Bop a Lula," not to speak of "Da Doo Ron Ron" and "Doo Wop."

She likes to hike and fish and camp out. I tried it once and didn't take to it. She loves opera. I tolerate it. She's never heard of the heroes of my youth. I've never heard of the heroes of her youth. I tend to spend as much money as I make. She is an inveterate saver and investor. How then, in the light of all these differences, do we manage to have a relationship at all?

Well, it has been a long and arduous process of adjustment.

For a long time I felt quite convinced that, in terms of these differences, my way was the right way and she had a lot to learn. I was quite wedded to "my way." After all, I had lived alone for much of my adult life. I hadn't had to make compromises. I maintained maximum control over the people and events I had to deal with. If I wanted to do something unhealthy, unwise, or immoral, I just did it. I had only myself to answer to. I enjoyed almost total freedom to enhance the quality of my life or to allow it to deteriorate. My secrets were my secrets alone. If there was something I didn't want people to know I could hide it quite easily. If I was feeling fragile, I could withdraw to gather strength before emerging to meet the world again. My privacy was my protection, and I guarded it zealously. I knew who I was and what I could do. I experienced myself as a person with a distinct individual identity. I liked myself.

It was fine, just fine, except when aloneness turned into loneliness, when retreat became isolation, when freedom palled, and self-sufficiency only highlighted the absence of a person to share my life with. Certainly the rest of the world seemed to see the coupled life as a desirable goal. I began to long for this kind of affiliation. So, I searched and I searched and, finally, she found me. From the beginning she was clear and definite about what she wanted. From the beginning I was ambivalent and resistant. Is this the right person? Is it too soon? Will she hurt me, hamper me, invade my hiding places? Will she make demands I can't meet? Will I be exposed, judged, rejected?

I held her at arm's length. She waited patiently. I ran away. She followed. I pushed her away. She came back. I was impressed, but I still was not sure. Let her in. Shut her out. Open up. Close down. Yes. No. Maybe. Now. Later. We'll see. I went around and around. I would convince myself that she was too young and too unworldly for me. Then I would watch her move with ease through social situations I couldn't possibly have handled so comfortably when I was her age.

I told myself that she was too straight thinking and uncreative. Then one morning, after we'd argued and I hadn't seen her for a week (we did not yet live together), I awoke to the lovely strains of a chamber music ensemble playing Mozart. Hmm. I must have left the radio on when I went to sleep. I looked over at the radio. It was off. Must have left it on upstairs. (I lived in a hill house and the bedrooms were downstairs.) I went upstairs, checked the stereo. Nothing on. Where was this music coming from? I stood in the middle of the living room. It seemed to be coming from outside. Outside? I opened the front door slowly to find four very serious-looking musicians, seated in my driveway. It was seven o'clock in the morning. They were playing away at a merry pace. They wound their way through the remainder of the piece without looking up or missing a beat.

When they finished, I asked, "What is this?" The cellist, who appeared to be the leader of the group, smiled and said, "This is a gift from an anonymous donor," whereupon she took up her bow and launched vigorously into a Mozart quartet. I pulled up a chair and sat in the doorway for the remainder of the concert, a gift indeed from a "straight thinking and uncreative" anonymous donor. Who would not have been charmed?

Little by little she wore down my resistance. I'd never had anyone go to so much trouble to get my attention. I'd never had anyone offer me love so persuasively and resolutely. Finally, I gave up and gave in. I have never been sorry, which is not to say that I haven't been doubtful, displeased, disappointed, disillusioned, frustrated, confused, resentful, and downright furious, but I have never been sorry.

The primary difference is that the main task regarding the relationship has changed. It is no longer a matter of my making up my mind if I want to be with her or not. It is a matter of acknowledging and accepting the differences between us, rather than seeing them as plots against my sanity or precursors of the demise of the relationship. I know now that there are certain parts of me that she will never understand, no matter how long I talk or what lengths I go to in an effort to introduce her to these corners of my being. I know she will always object to certain things I do because she believes them to be fundamentally wrong, and there are beliefs and behaviors of hers that offend me and probably always will.

We tolerate each other's foibles, but they do not go unnoticed. Humor helps a lot. She tells me, "Since I met you my whole world has expanded. I never knew there were so many things to worry about." This on a morning when some strange-looking birds appeared flying in circles above the long, open deck that ran the length of our hillside house. I didn't know what they were, but they looked like predators to me. I was immediately sure they were going to swoop down and carry away our little dog. "Come inside and close all the doors! These birds might be after the dog." She just stared at me, disbelieving. "I would never have thought to worry about that," she said as she obligingly closed the doors.

On the other hand, I no longer despair when she takes on yet another project, reassuring me it will fit easily into her already overcrowded schedule. I realize now that she is not doing more than she can handle. She is doing more than *I* could handle if *I* were doing all those things. But, I'm not doing them. She is. Leave her alone. She's not crazy, just different from me.

The challenge of integrating the complex realities of two separate and individual human beings into a workable partnership is one of the most exciting and terrifying aspects of being together. That challenge embraces the fear of losing one's identity as an individual, of losing control of one's life, of being misunderstood and mistreated, of having to face up to one's limits and incapabilities while still maintaining a perspective as a worthwhile and lovable human being.

The tough task in all of this is recognizing, acknowledging, and dealing constructively with the differences between you and your partner.

Most of us are most comfortable when we are with people who are similar to us. Similarities enable predictability, which enhances our feeling of being safe in the presence of another. Some people have a higher tolerance for unpredictability in their lives than others. They are the lucky ones, I think. A certain amount of unpredictability is required to make life interesting. The question is, how much? Living with another person, becoming increasingly known and vulnerable to that person is threatening enough for most people. When the person is significantly different in some important ways, the job gets harder, anxiety rises, uncertainty about the wisdom of continuing the relationship is likely to increase.

I have found it particularly helpful for partners in intimate relationships to learn to identify their differences as just that. Too often a perceived difference in one's partner is ascribed to a character defect at best and a derangement at worst. In reality, what is being perceived might be nothing more than a different way of viewing the world and coping with problems than the perceiver is accustomed to. I believe, therefore, that learning to identify differences, and acknowledging and appreciating them as such, is one of the most important tasks a couple must attend to in the beginning of their relationship.

It might be helpful for you to think about the ways in which you and your present (or a past) partner are different. Are some of the differences more threatening than others? Do you know why? Have you been seeing the differences as just that—differences between you—or have you been thinking of them as evidence that your partner is (or was) impaired, or inferior to you? Is there anything you, or your partner, might do to make the differences between you less bothersome? A discussion with your partner about the issue of differences could be helpful.

MYTHS AND FANTASIES

Intimate partnerships are, in one very important aspect, a never-ending process of the falling away of our myths and fantasies about love and intimacy. We all have them, these idealized versions of what The Relationship will be like, what The Lover will be like. We bring these images, and the expectations attached to them, into our partnerships and wait to be fulfilled or disillusioned.

The sources of these myths and fantasies are many and varied. They color our thinking, our feelings, and our behavior. While they are always operating they are usually not conscious; thus, they are hard to get at to analyze or to dispel. After many years of questioning gay and lesbian couples as to where they got their ideas of what a lover relationship would be like, I have come to think of the following as the major kinds of fantasy that we bring into our same-sex partnerships.

The first two categories we hold in common with our non-gay counterparts. We begin with the Father-Knows-Best, Ozzie-and-Harriet, My-Little-Margie, Perfect-and-Harmonious-Family Fantasy. In this fantasy everyone is open, honest, and mutually supportive all the time. Every conflict situation has a happy ending. Motives are pure and uncomplicated. The world is a clean and pretty place. Life is easy and usually goes according to plan.

The influence of this fantasy makes the real world of unresolved conflict, complex motivation, competitiveness, power struggles, unpredictable problems, and an endangered and polluted environment even more difficult to live in. When partnerships produce conditions antithetical to the Harmonious-Family Fantasy, such relationships are unduly faulted and often dispensed with. Why can't things at our house be like things at their house? I must be with the *wrong partner.* There must be something wrong with *me.* If one or the other were not true this wouldn't be happening.

Next, we have the Candlelight-and-Roses, Love-Is-A-Many-Splendored-Thing, Relationship-As-Romance Fantasy. In this one, the major portion of the couple's time together is spent in romantic ecstasy, gazing into each other's eyes, gently caressing, sweetly kissing, lost in the obsession of love, each at the center of the other's thinking at all times. It is, indeed, a wonderful fantasy, fueled forever by novels, movies, songs, and folklore, not to speak of the great American industrial machine that sells romance in the form of every conceivable kind of commercial product and service. The fantasy is hard to get away from. It is so seductive. It feels so good when it's happening. Why can't it be like this *all the time?* Why does *harsh reality* have to intervene? The main problems generated by this fantasy occur when partner Number One has invested in the fantasy and partner Number Two has not. Then the relationship might feel very flawed and partner Number Two might feel very inadequate, often enough so that the partnership is abandoned.

Then we have the Steamy-Sex, Conquering-Hero, Warriors-Together Gay Male Fantasy. This fantasy has its origins in the fictionalized world of pornographic films and publications. In these depictions men are together primarily in terms of their physicality. They are victor and vanquished to one another as they play out the drama of the hunt, first one, then the other as conquering hero. Young, handsome, and well built, they are undistracted by thoughts of inadequacy or fear of failure. They are warriors together, flexing the muscle of their male power and prowess.

When this fantasy is brought to a relationship, both partners are expected to have high sexual desire. Their erotic encounters are expected to be frequent, steamy, and athletic. Body building is considered a central activity of the couple's life. Images of hot sex scenes from sexually explicit films and magazines guide the couple's lovemaking behavior. Because many gay men cut their sexual teeth on these depictions, this fantasy is a commonly held one. The problem with it is that it gives rise to so many reductionist myths: 1. Men need and want sex as often as possible. 2. Good sex is hot sex. 3. Ideal partners are young, handsome, hunky, and hung. 4. Sex is about performance.

Two men together operating from this fantasy version of what intimate partnerships are all about are in for a lot of stress as they try to keep the fantasy alive. Sometimes body building becomes obsessive, crowding out shared activities that might give the relationship more depth and psychological richness. The overemphasis in this fantasy on looks is necessarily diminishing to those not blessed with great physical attractiveness. It might create anxiety and insecurity far out of proportion to the significance of this aspect of human existence.

Role behaviors in the Conquering-Hero Fantasy can become exaggerated and overscripted. Can the conquering hero also ask to be held like a baby and rocked to sleep in his lover's arms? Can warriors talk about their fears, express feelings of inadequacy, let their tears be seen when old emotional wounds are touched? Is it all right to be fragile, embarrassed, shy, confused? Is it all right not to care anymore if one's chest loses its definition because going to the gym has become just too enervating or too boring? In the context of this fantasy, what happens when sexual desire is blocked, sexual performance is off, the body just wants to rest? What happens when the soul needs soothing more than sex? What happens when life intervenes and, stress inhibits sensuality so that it is not even accessible to the person, much less to his partner? What happens when alcohol or drugs impair the body's ability to function sexually? What happens when age and/or experience in the world broadens one's perspective so that sex loses its importance as a central organizing force of one's life? Does the partnership now begin to lose its luster? Yes, for many plugged into this fantasy it does. They interpret any diminution of sexual activity in the relationship to mean that they are no longer in love with their partner or he with them. A heavy investment in this fantasy usually impedes the individual's ability to move into the more mature kind of broad-based love a relationship offers in its later stages.

Finally, we have the Equality-In-All-Things, Universal-Sisterhood, Politically-Correct-Lesbian Fantasy. In this fantasy, the two women are never aggressive with one another. One never tries to dominate the other. They don't compete with each other. Neither cares to impose her ideas or wishes on her partner. In other words, neither partner thinks, feels, or acts "like a man." In this fantasy, the partners share a common heritage of abuse by a patriarchal society. Therefore, they are extra careful never to behave with each other in any way that might suggest that one has more power in the relationship than the other, or wants to have, or ever will have. Sexually, they always give the other woman's pleasure at least as much attention as their own. Mutuality is the order of the day, and no matter how much time it takes they persevere in their decision-making process until each party is perfectly satisfied that her wishes have been taken into account. Of course, they believe that a significant amount of mutuality is built into their relationship simply because they both are women. They respect and trust each other to be gentle, nurturing, and life-giving by nature.

It is a most appealing fantasy. It eliminates some of the main sources of conflict in any couple's life, or at least it attempts to do that. The problem is that there are aggressive women and dominating women and women who want to be dominated. There are women who are competitive and who have the courage of their convictions to the point of believing it the right and kind thing to do to share their convictions with others, aggressively. There are women who are "male identified" because doing so has enabled them to get ahead in ways that are important to them. And, there are women who are drawn to other women who exhibit the competitive, assertive, take-charge behaviors that we usually associate with the male of the species.

When any of these kinds of women find themselves in relationships strongly influenced by the Equality-In-All-Things Fantasy, they tend to take one of two paths. They either deny the aspects of their personality that come in conflict with the fantasy, or they see their relationship as not working because it lacks the degree of equality and mutuality that the fantasy promised. In either case they are likely to be angry and/or disillusioned. Feeling stifled in the expression of who one really is produces resentment against the person or force that is perceived as causing that feeling. The partnership suffers. Sometimes the effect is fatal to the partner's ability to move beyond the fantasy.

It can be crucial to the success of a relationship to be able to identify the particular fantasies that might be operating to inhibit growth in your relationships. There are others, of course, than the ones I have described.

Think about the myths and fantasies that you have brought into relationships at various times in your life. Do any stand out as having a counterproductive effect on the relationship you are (or were) in?

3

FEELING GOOD ABOUT BEING GAY

Insofar as you have problems with feeling good about being gay, no matter how subtle, they will show up in your same-sex intimate partnerships. After all, being in a primary relationship with another person of the same sex is ground zero for being gay or lesbian.

Because the relationship to your own gayness can be so critical to success in a relationship, I will deal here, at some length, with the issue of how gay/lesbian identity forms. I will then describe some specific ways in which conflict about being gay can affect the couple relationship.

I believe the process of gay identity formation has been most effectively chronicled by the Australian psychologist, Vivienne Cass.* From her observations, Cass has produced a "model" of what happens, typically, as one moves from a sense of self-as a heterosexual person to a sense of self as a homosexual or gay person. As you read what follows, think of your journey from first awareness to where you are now in your gay/lesbian identity.

---

* Cass, Vivienne C. "Homosexual Identity Formation: A Theoretical Model." *Journal of Homosexuality* Vol. 4 (3), Spring 1979.

THE CASS MODEL

A "model," in this use of the word, is a *representation* of something that happens in the real world. In this representation, the events described are arranged in such a way as to produce insight into the process by which these events come to occur as they do.

The model presented here is based on Dr. Cass's clinical observations and on her research data involving gay and lesbian subjects in Western Australia. It is a tribute to her astuteness that many psychotherapists and social scientists in the United States find her formulations to be as accurate in describing American gays and lesbians as they are in describing her Australian clients, subjects, and friends.

According to this model, the identity formation process occurs in six stages beginning with the individual having a sexual self-portrait that is heterosexual. Let us say, for example, that we are talking about a male. He sees himself as heterosexual. He sees his behavior as heterosexual. He sees others viewing him as heterosexual. His sexual self-portrait is consistent, or *congruent* for heterosexuality.

Then at some point in his life a change occurs. It might happen in childhood, in adolescence, in early adulthood, in middle age, or even very late in his life.

Stage I: Identity Confusion

Occurs when there is continuing personalization of information regarding homosexuality.

The change begins with the conscious awareness that information regarding homosexuality is somehow personally relevant. When the continuing personalization of this information can no longer be ignored, the individual's sexual self-portrait now feels inconsistent, or incongruent. The process of gay identity formation has begun.

The person now begins to privately label his/her own behavior (or thoughts or feelings) as possibly homosexual. The person maintains a self-image as a heterosexual and perceives others as maintaining the same image.

In order to deal with the incongruity that has been introduced in the sexual self-portrait, the person adopts one or more of the following strategies.

The Inhibition Strategy

Here the person regards the definition of his/her behavior (thoughts, feelings) as correctly homosexual but finds this definition undesirable and unacceptable. The actions taken may be one or more of the following. The person

- *restricts* information regarding homosexuality ("I don't want to hear, read, or know about it.")
- *inhibits* behavior ("It may be true, but I'm not going to do anything about it.")
- *denies* the personal relevance of information regarding homosexuality ("It has nothing to do with me.")
- becomes *hypersexual* (heterosexually)
- becomes *asexual*
- seeks a "cure"
- becomes an *anti-gay moral crusader*

The Personal Innocence Strategy

Here the person rejects either the *meaning* or the *context* of the homosexual behavior so as not to have to own it. He/she then redefines the meaning or the context of the behavior.

REDEFINING MEANING
Example: In our society genital contact between males is acceptable in a variety of situations without the individuals participating being defined as homosexuals. Little boys have "circle jerks." Men confined for long periods of time without access to women have genital contact with one another, and

they are not necessarily defined as homosexuals. The shift occurs when males develop emotional attachments to the other
males they are having sex with, or when they have repeated
contacts with the same male, increasing the possibility of emotional involvement.

For females, in this society, just the opposite is true. Girls can
be inseparable, experience deep emotional involvement with one
another, spend more time with each other, even into adulthood,
than they do with the men in their lives, and they are not defined
as homosexuals. The shift occurs when they have genital contact
in addition to their emotional involvement. That is considered to
be homosexuality.

Therefore, an individual in Stage I adopting this strategy
would be careful to do the following:

Male—keep sexual contacts free of emotional involvement
and avoid repeated contacts with the same person.

Female—keep relationships with women strictly nonsexual, no
matter how emotionally involving they are.

REDEFINING CONTEXT
Here the individual disowns responsibility for his/her homosexual behavior by redefining the context in which it occurred:

- "I was just experimenting."
- "I was drunk."
- "I just did it for the money."
- "I did it as a favor for a friend."
- "It was an accident."
- "I was taken advantage of."

I have heard from several people that their early sexual experiences during adolescence occurred in the context of the
game "Dare." Accepting a *dare* to do something is different from
taking responsibility for doing it because you really want to do it.

If the inhibition strategies employed are completely successful in enabling the person to inhibit, or redefine, or disown re-

sponsibility for homosexual behavior, there will be a foreclosure of gay/lesbian identity at Stage I.

Success in the use of the inhibition and personal innocence strategies depends on the individual's ability to avoid provocative situations and to employ the psychological defense of denial. Nevertheless, it will probably be impossible to avoid erotic dreams or physiological responses to persons of the same sex to whom the individual is attracted. In this instance, these strategies will be only partially successful and the individual may very well experience the beginning of a negative or self-rejecting sexual identity.

The Information-Seeking Strategy

The person is likely to adopt this strategy if the meaning attributed to his/her homosexual behavior is perceived as correct, or at least partially acceptable: Now the individual seeks more information—in books, in therapy, in talking with anyone who might have expertise or experience related to this topic. The question being addressed is, "Am I homosexual?" This strategy of seeking more information moves the person along to Stage II.

Stage II. Identity Comparison

Occurs when the person accepts the possibility that he/she might be homosexual.

Now the individual begins to examine the wider implications of being homosexual. Whereas in Stage I the task was to handle the *self*-alienation that occurs with the first glimmerings of homosexuality, the main task of Stage II is to handle the *social* alienation that is produced by feeling different from peers, family members, and society at large.

A particularly troubling aspect of relinquishing one's heterosexual identity is the giving up of behavioral guidelines and the expectations for one's future that go with them. If marriage and family are not in one's future, what is? What will there be to give

form and structure to one's life? With the letting go of a perception of a self that is clearly heterosexual, one can experience a profound feeling of loss. As with any loss, the way to move beyond the
grief is to acknowledge and express it. That means talking about
it. Expressing grief over the loss of one's heterosexual status and
all the fantasies about the future that went with it has not been too
popular a topic for dialogue in the gay and lesbian community.
But, at this stage of identity development, grieving the loss of that
heterosexual blueprint for life is an inescapable part of what is
going on. The more it is acknowledged and talked about, the
sooner it can be worked through and prevented from becoming a
chronic, underlying theme in the person's intimate partnerships.

Certain conditions heighten the feeling of alienation from
others. For example, if the person is geographically isolated, with
no gay people or resources available, the feeling of being different, of being the only one can be especially anguishing. Or, if the
person comes from a family that is deeply religious with strong
convictions about homosexuality as sin, the feelings of alienation
from family can be particularly distressing. How do people deal
with these experiences of alienation? In her model, Cass describes three approaches most often taken:

1. *The person reacts positively to being different and devalues the importance of heterosexuals in his/her life.*

Positive reactions to being different occur because:

• the individual has always felt different because of (unla-
beled) homosexual feelings and now it is a relief to know that
there are others who have had the same experience, and that one
might get support and understanding from them
• the individual has always been nonconforming regarding
interest in marriage or parenting
• the individual finds being different special and exciting

Devaluing the importance of the heterosexuals in one's life
works if the person is able to avoid negative confrontation from
heterosexuals regarding one's homosexuality. In other words,

one needs to be able to "pass" or pretend heterosexuality. This passing strategy works if the person can:

• avoid threatening situations, such as social gatherings where one is expected to be accompanied by an opposite-sex partner (or have such a partner available)
• control personal information, as in dressing and behaving carefully to avoid being typed as a homosexual
• deliberately cultivate and present a heterosexual image (the supermacho man, the ultrafeminine woman)
• disassociate from anything homosexual

2. *The person accepts the homosexual definition of his/her own behavior but rejects a definition of self as homosexual in order to feel less alienated from important heterosexuals in his/her life.*

Here are four strategies the individual may employ to reject homosexual self-definition while continuing homosexual behavior:

• *Special Case.* The person characterizes what is happening as the product of the liaison with this person and this person only— "If it were not for Walter I would be heterosexual."
• *Ambisexuality.* This person says he/she "can do it with anybody." It doesn't matter what gender the other person is.
• *Temporary Identity.* Here the individual regards his/her homosexuality as only temporary—"I could be heterosexual again any minute."
• *Personal Innocence.* This person "blames" his/her homosexuality on anyone or anything else—"I can't help it. I was seduced into this. It's Connie's fault I'm this way."

In all of the above strategies, the individual tends to compartmentalize sexuality, keeping it separate from other aspects of life.

3. *The person accepts self and behavior as homosexual but so fears negative reactions from others that overt homosexual behavior is inhibited, homosexuality is devalued, heterosexuality is given much positive weight.*

The most common example of this strategy at work is with

the gay male who is heterosexually married and seeks anonymous sex under covert conditions. He participates in these surreptitious activities with the "not me" part of himself.

Or, the person reduces the fear of negative reaction from others by moving to another city or country to remove him/herself from the scrutiny of particular heterosexuals about whom there is concern.

When any of the above strategies for dealing with social alienation are employed successfully, sexual identity is likely to foreclose at Stage II. If any of these strategies are only partially successful, a self-hating identity is likely to be perpetuated. The person is neither here nor there, not seeking further information and experience, not accepting of the information he or she already has. The person is most likely to move into the next stage when any of these strategies break down.

Stage III: Identity Tolerance

Occurs when the person has come to accept the probability that he/she is a homosexual and recognizes the sexual/social/emotional needs that go with being homosexual.

With more of a commitment to a homosexual identity, the individual is now freed from the task of managing the confusion and turmoil that accompanied previous identity states. There is more time and energy to pursue social, emotional, and sexual needs. Doing this, however, accentuates the *difference* between the person and heterosexuals even more. In order to deal with this increased social alienation, the person seeks out gay people and the gay subculture. Involvement with the gay/lesbian community has distinct advantages in terms of the individual's movement toward a more positive gay/lesbian identity. It contributes:

- a ready-made support group which understands and shares the individual's concerns
- opportunity to meet a partner
- access to positive gay and lesbian role models

• opportunities to practice feeling more at ease as a lesbian or a gay man

How successful this experience will be in moving the person along to a further stage of development depends on the quality of contacts with people in the new subculture. If these contacts are perceived by the person as positive, he/she is likely to develop a more positive sense of self. If the contacts are negatively perceived, there is likely to be a devaluation of the subculture by the individual and, therefore, less to be gained from it.

Positive or negative perceptions, of course, are very individualistic. For example, one person may find gay or lesbian bars exciting and exhilarating. Contacts made in these establishments will most likely have a positive connotation. Another person may find the same bars depressing and degrading, and contacts made there will have a predictably negative connotation. If this person gets no further into the community than the bars, he/she is likely to reject the entire subculture as a context for rejecting further exploration of his/her sexual identity. Positive contacts are made more difficult if any of the following are true. The person:

• has poor social skills
• is very shy
• has low self-esteem
• has strong fear of exposure (of sexual identity)
• has a fear of the unknown

So, people who are uncomfortable meeting others socially, or who are fearful of trying something new, or who fear their gayness will be discovered outside the community are likely to limit their contacts to such a degree that positive experiences will not come easily. Much also depends on the people encountered. If they are gays or lesbians who are still employing the inhibition and denial strategies of Stages I and II, contact with them will probably be experienced as negative. These lesbians and gay men will be perceived as unhappy, self-rejecting individuals with whom one would not want to be affiliated.

On the other hand, if the people encountered are accepting of their gay or lesbian identity, they might become confrontational with regard to one's continued employment of inhibition and denial strategies. In either instance a shift occurs during this stage of identity development. The significant others for the person are now becoming the *homosexuals* in one's life rather than the *heterosexuals*. Who these gay people are, what they do, and what they think of you, are now what is beginning to matter the most.

If the contacts made are experienced as negative, it is probable that there will be a reduction of involvement with gay subculture, resulting in foreclosure at this third stage of Identity Tolerance. If contacts are perceived as positive, it is likely the strategies employed have broken down and that you will want to explore further. This breakdown of strategies will result in movement into Stage IV. In any case, the commitment to a gay identity is now sufficient for the person to say, "I am a homosexual."

Stage IV: Identity Acceptance

Occurs when the person accepts rather than tolerates a homosexual self-image and there is continuing and increased contact with the gay/lesbian subculture.

The individual now has a positive identification with other gay people. The questions of earlier stages ("What am I?" "Where do I belong?") have been answered.

Critical at this point are the attitudes toward their sexual orientation of the gays or lesbians with whom the person becomes associated. If these individuals regard being gay as partially legitimate (being gay is okay in private, but being public about it is not okay), then the person is likely to adopt this attitude as his/her own philosophy, and to live a compartmentalized, "passing" gay life. In order to reduce the stress involved in interfacing with a homophobic society, the person has less and less to do with heterosexuals. There is some selective disclosure of gayness to non-gay family, friends, and coworkers, but as much control as possible, is exercised over the potentially discrediting information. The emphasis is on fitting into society and not making waves. If this strategy is successful, the person forecloses at this Identity Acceptance stage.

If, on the other hand, the person comes to associate with people who regard being gay as *fully* legitimate (in private and in public) this attitude is likely to be the one that is adopted. Feeling that being gay is legitimate tends to increase the distance the person feels from a society that is still, for the most part, anti-gay. Homophobic attitudes are now particularly offensive. In order to deal with the anger toward the anti-gay society, in combination with the increasing self-acceptance that is occurring, the person moves into Stage V.

Stage V: Identity Pride

Occurs when, accepting the philosophy of full legitimization the person becomes immersed in the gay/lesbian subculture and has less and less to do with heterosexual others.

The world is now divided into those who are gay and those who are not. As identification with the gay/lesbian community deepens, pride in accomplishments of the community increases. However, daily living still requires continuing encounters with the heterosexual world and its homophobic attitudes. These encounters produce feelings of frustration and alienation. The combination of anger and pride energizes the person into action against the heterosexual establishment and creates "the activist."

Confrontation with the heterosexual establishment brings one more into public view, and the earlier strategies to conceal sexual orientation must be increasingly abandoned. Doing so precipitates disclosure crises with significant heterosexuals such as family and coworkers. (Better to tell the folks yourself than to let them hear that you are gay as you are interviewed on the six o'clock news.)

What becomes critical at this point is whether those significant heterosexuals in your life react negatively to the disclosure as expected, or whether they react positively. If there is a negative reaction, confirming the person's expectations that it would be so, the view of the world as being divided into gays (who are okay) and non-gays (who are not okay) gets reinforced. In this instance the person forecloses at the Identity Pride stage. If, on the other hand, the reactions of the heterosexuals to whom one discloses are positive and *inconsistent* with the person's negative expectation, the person tends to change those expectations, which moves him or her into Stage VI.

Stage VI: Identity Synthesis

Occurs when the person develops an awareness that the "them and us" philosophy, in which all heterosexuals are viewed negatively and all homosexuals positively, no longer holds true.

The individual now acknowledges that there are non-gay people who are as supportive of his/her gay identity as other gay people are. The anger of Stage V is still experienced but not with the intensity of the previous stage. Since heterosexuals as a class are no longer seen as hostile, it is no longer necessary to sustain the high level of anger of Stage V. Increasing contact with supportive non-gays produces more trust. (Unsupportive non-gays continue to be devalued.) There is no longer a need to dichotomize the world into gays who are okay and non-gays who are not. The gay/lesbian aspect of one's identity can now be integrated with all other aspects of self. The identity formation process is complete.

SEXUAL IDENTITY FORMATION AND RELATIONSHIP PROBLEMS

It is my belief that certain problems that regularly surface in gay and lesbian relationships are born of the unworked-through residue of the strategies employed early in the identity-formation process to inhibit and deny one's homosexuality. I believe this happens even though the individuals involved may be functioning, generally, at an advanced stage of gay/lesbian identity development. It is what's left over, what didn't get resolved, the unfinished business of the struggle to make sense of unacceptable thoughts, puzzling emotions, and behavior that sometimes felt out of control. For some people, a positive gay identity may develop, but parts of that identity seem stuck in earlier stages of the process. For instance, a strategy to inhibit feelings, thoughts, and actions that might be labeled homosexual can have a very powerful effect on a person's ability to be comfortably gay in an intimate relationship later in life.

Let's look at some specific possibilities for early denial strategies producing relationship problems. Stage I denial strategies require the person employing them to be able to cut off his/her reaction when erotic arousal toward someone of the same sex is involved. Cutting off feelings in that way over and over eventually has an effect on the person's ability to be spontaneously sexual and affectionate. The inhibition that results may range from a blunted emotionality with very reserved sexual behavior to serious sexual dysfunction. If one needed proof that this is true, one would have to look no further than the widespread (pre-AIDS) use of drugs to enhance feeling and sensation in gay male sex. In my practice and among my friends I have known many men who have been having drug-enhanced sex much of their adult lives. In the service of developing healthier regimes to protect their immune systems they have given up these drugs and must face the sexual and affectional inhibitions they feel without them. This reliance on drugs has often been true even with partners who've been together a long time. This is a time for gay men to be particularly supportive of one another by talking together about what is happening to them, by helping each other to reshape the sexual bond so that it offers solace instead of threat, validation instead of challenge.

I think it is always best when understanding and comfort come from those who are closest, but not everyone is fortunate

enough to have a partner who is available in this way. If that is
your situation and if you believe yourself to be experiencing the
kind of inhibition I have described, I strongly urge you to get professional help. There are now many competent, talented psychotherapists in the gay and lesbian community. In addition, in
many cities clinics and counseling services have been set up primarily to deal with the problems of gay people.

Another example of an early coping strategy that might later
cause relationship problems is that of redefining the *meaning* of
homosexual behavior (Stage I) so as not to have to think of one's
self as homosexual. Here we have the little girl who had crushes
on her female teachers and friends, who was inseparable from
her closest girlfriend of the moment, to whom it was a catastro-
phe if her beloved friend showed favor to another girl. The little
girl becomes the adolescent and then the young woman who continues to lose her heart to other females rather than males. She is
not ready, however, to think of herself as a homosexual so she de-
fines her preoccupation with women in terms of strong friendship. She does not have any genital contact with these other
women. For the most part she does not even allow herself the in-
dulgence of sexual fantasies. When she feels in danger of such
fantasies occurring, she blocks them and reminds herself that this
is her *friend* she is thinking about.

Let us say that at some point the strategy stops working because the need for deeper involvement with women asserts itself.
The young woman comes to regard herself as a lesbian. She enters
into a relationship with a lover. In the beginning they are very
much in love and are often sexual with each other. But, after time,
passion wanes and the old programming returns. She feels deeply
attached to her lover but finds she has less and less interest in
being sexual with her. Soon, sex between them stops altogether.
This young woman has no trouble thinking of herself as a lesbian
now, but there is some residue of the early strategy that once *protected* her from unwanted feelings. Now it *deprives* rather than protects. She misses out on a fully loving partnership, and she
deprives her partner of the opportunity to express herself eroti-

cally with the person she loves. If this woman is able to understand what is happening to her, she has the best chance of changing it. In the best case scenario she can talk to her partner about what is occurring between them and together they can explore the reason it is happening and the remedies available to them.

This same "redefining meanings" strategy can cause a different kind of problem for gay men in relationships. Take the little boy who enjoys circle jerks with his friends. Everybody was doing it. No big deal. In adolescence he was still doing it. Now he was aware, however, that he was having *feelings* toward the other boys. He was attracted to them on an individual basis. He dealt with the idea that he might be queer by being careful never to show any emotional attachment to these boys, and he did not show emotional attachment to any of the young men he "experimented" with later in adolescence.

When this individual grew up to be gay, he had difficulty forming a relationship. He felt unable to sustain sexual interest in his partners for very long. On the other hand, he functioned just fine in sexual situations that were casual with no demands beyond the moment and with no emotional involvement. He did not function well in relationships in which he was expected to show affection and demonstrate commitment to his sexual partner. He had learned too well the lessons of detachment. Here, again, the task is to understand the reasons for his behavior, hopefully through an exploration in which he is joined by a caring partner. Once the reasons are understood, the task is to reprogram himself to abandon the no longer needed denial strategy and replace it with an acceptance of his sexuality and an appreciation of the pleasure sex-in-relationship can bring.

These strategies deal with altering behavior to maintain a nonhomosexual self-image early in identity development. Another kind of strategy that can cause problems in relationships is that which involves a way to maintain a heterosexual *self-image* without altering homosexual *behavior*. The "temporary identity" strategy described in Stage II enables individuals in their early identity formation process to hold on to the idea that they could be heterosexual again any time they choose. The person may go on year after year living a gay life but never really committing to it. When this person enters a relationship, the same principle applies. He/she thinks privately, "I'm not sure if I should be in this relationship because I'm not really sure that I'm gay." This thinking enables the avoidance of commitment to the relationship. This person not only threatens abandonment with regularity but also throws in, "I don't even think I'm gay," or, "I think I'd really like to be straight and get married and have children." Giving up the strategy means embracing the truth of one's sexual orientation and the potential it has for offering fulfillment.

As one moves along in the identity formation process, a clear theme emerges. Continuing exploration of the meanings of being gay or lesbian enhances one's ability to develop further in that direction. After a certain point that exploration must progress from personal, private experience to contact with the gay/lesbian subculture. If that contact is with the more positive aspects of the subculture (that is, the organized gay/lesbian community), the likelihood is that the person will evolve an identity that is a positive one. One of the strategies the individual who is in conflict about being gay uses to avoid further involvement is to devalue the organized gay and lesbian community (Stage III). These people decry parading in the streets, open activism, or "flaunting" of any kind. They are embarrassed by the activities of gay and lesbian activist organizations. They prefer not to call attention to themselves, and they wish that other gay people would do the same. They try to maintain the position that all this "carrying on" has nothing to do with them.

When both partners in a relationship are dealing with their unresolved identity issues in this way, they isolate themselves from the organized community. They usually socialize only with other couples who also disassociate themselves from the community. They reinforce each other in their negative orientation to being gay. They cooperate to insulate themselves from a movement they are threatened by but which, in reality, exists to make their lives better. They deprive themselves of the opportunity to enhance their individual growth and their growth as a couple.

Then there is the couple who are totally in the closet, who do not even have other gay friends. They are each other's sole confidants. They depend on each other for everything, which has the potential for overburdening the relationship to the point of collapse. I am pained when I see such a couple, so motivated by fear of exposure, living in isolation from all that is positive about being gay.

The clues for remedying these unresolved sexual identity issues are embedded in the process of identity formation itself. One moves forward in establishing a self-accepting gay/lesbian identity through a willingness to search for new information, new meanings, new ways of being. That search is best conducted in the context of the organized gay and lesbian community, where opportunities for positive and affirming experiences abound.

4

"WHAT'S GOING ON HERE?"

I call it the "theater of the relationship." It usually happens when a couple has been together for a while. Problems have developed that they don't want to deal with or don't know how to deal with. Unaddressed, these problems cause continual tension. The couple then attempts to deal with the tension by going through a kind of routine—that is, they launch into an exchange about something one or both is dissatisfied with. It's a topic or set of topics that can always be counted on to get a rise out of the other person. They've been through it dozens of times before. It is as though by now it were scripted. Each partner knows his/her lines. The script seldom varies. It never goes anywhere, and there is no resolution because the real problem underlying the discussion is not even touched upon. The energy is in the routine. Of course, they don't think of it as a routine. They are deadly serious about it. Tempers flare. Voices rise. The routine builds to a crescendo. Then it's over. But it's never *really* over. They will come back to it and do it again and again. You can depend on it. It serves a very important purpose: it *masks* issues that are too frustrating or too painful to confront.

As long as a couple stays in the "theater" of their relationship and does not deal with the underlying problems between them, they will indeed be as actors on a stage playing out a drama with a predictable outcome. Just as the actors do not change the lines in pursuit of a new and different ending at each performance, so the couple sticks to the familiar dialogue, insuring that their outcome also will be predictable. It is relationship by rote, leaving little room for improvisation or discovery or innovation. The real drama waits to unfold beneath the surface of the relationship.

Following are three examples of couples who, with the help of therapy, were able to move beyond the "theater" of their relationships to deal with their underlying problems.

JERI AND HELEN

Jeri and Helen have been together about ten years. Both are in their late forties. Jeri is a very successful attorney, earning a sizeable income. She is opinionated, strong willed, and accustomed to having her way. Helen is soft spoken and rather shy, with a quiet sense of competence about her. She had been an executive secretary when she and Jeri first met. Helen didn't particularly like her job and after she and Jeri had been together about six months, she quit. Jeri was very happy to have Helen stay at home, taking care of the house, the pets, and her.

For a few years Helen felt quite satisfied doing this. Then about five years into the relationship she began to grow restless. Looking about for something of interest to occupy her, she decided to take scuba diving lessons. She found diving to be quite interesting, and she became more and more involved in it. She went on diving expeditions, and having achieved a level of significant skill, she began to teach diving. She got a job as a part-time instructor at the school where she had taken lessons. She was quite good as a teacher and soon she went to work full-time. This meant that she was away from home much more than she had been for some time. She no longer cleaned the house, but they hired a housekeeper to do that, so it didn't matter too much. Though once she had done most of the cooking, Helen now cooked less and less. Jeri had never learned to cook, so they went out for most of their meals. Then Helen began to pay a lot of attention to her body. She lifted weights and did aerobics, and she went on a very strict diet, which made it very difficult for her and Jeri to share many meals. Jeri began to complain about this, but Helen told her that physical conditioning was very important to being a successful diver and she intended to continue her regimen no matter what.

The tension between them grew. Jeri began spending less and less time at home. She developed a relationship with another woman, whom she saw quite regularly for a period of years.

She and Helen continued to live together, though they now occupied separate bedrooms. From time to time Jeri would suggest that she and Helen try to do something about their relationship because she believed they really loved one another. Helen agreed that she did love Jeri, but she felt distanced from her. This exchange would lead into a discussion of what was going on between them.

In these conversations Jeri always proceeded to list all the wonderful benefits Helen had been the recipient of during the years she stayed at home. She then would remind Helen that she did not need to work because there was plenty of money. At this point Helen would become tight-lipped and retreat into silence. She knew that Jeri wanted her to stop working and stay at home. She felt frightened of Jeri's ability to overpower her, so she avoided any real discussion of her side of the story. She wanted to work. She enjoyed her job. She loved having some independence from Jeri. But she was afraid to present her case because she didn't trust her own verbal skills pitted against Jeri's. So she withdrew and quietly went about her business.

After a couple of years, Helen found out about the other woman. She felt hurt and angry, but she kept these feelings to herself because she didn't want to face what might get stirred up in a confrontation. Her resentment built until one day, when Jeri was pressing her to be intimate again, she exploded at her, "You seem to have solved that problem on your own." And she told Jeri what she knew about the other woman.

Jeri was very cool, responding, "I had to do something. You had become so unavailable to me. But I really love you, and I want us to be lovers again in the way we were before."

Helen answered, "I'll consider that only if you give up that woman."

Jeri replied, "That's not so easy to do. She has become a very important friend to me."

"Then why don't you just go and be with her?"

"I don't want to do that. I want to live with you. I want things to be the way they were before. I want us to be lovers."

"How many people can you love at once?" Helen scoffed.

"More than one, I'm sure," Jeri replied.

"Well, you'll get nothing from me as long as you're seeing her!"

"I will continue to see her as long as I'm not getting what I need from you!"

And round and round it went, that time, and the dozens of times they had this exchange in the ensuing three years. Eventually they both tired of their mutual war of nerves. They came into therapy together. They sat opposite me, each looking as if a battle cry was ringing in her ears.

"What do you see as the main problem in your relationship?" I asked.

"She is involved with another woman," Helen volunteered. "She has been for some years now, and she won't give her up."

"She won't let me touch her," Jeri answered. "She won't give me any affection. So, of course, I had to go elsewhere to get it. The problem is that she is so cold and rejecting toward me."

Helen said, again, "The problem is that she is having an affair with another woman and she won't stop."

For the first two months of the therapy, no matter where we headed, we always ending up doing business back at the same old stand.

"Give her up."

"I will when you start giving me some affection."

"I'll give you affection when you give her up."

Then I began to see how predictable it was that they would

get into this routine. It was a set piece, right down to the dialogue. And, as is true in any scripted drama, their interaction was
structured by the script, leaving no room for the unexpected. I
began to think of what they did with each other as the "theater"
of their relationship. It was a scene that could be cued up any
time, always ready for a rerun. And it never went anywhere except
back to the beginning, to be replayed the next time.

Occasionally they played it a little differently. Jeri would say,
"Okay, I'll give her up. I won't see her anymore." Then they would
go along for a while, warily in détente, until Helen would discover
that Jeri had not given the woman up at all. There was always the
inevitable trail of bread crumbs, left by Jeri, leading to the discovery. Then Helen would return to her former position and her separate bedroom. They would move silently around each other in
the house until Jeri was ready to "try to patch things up again." She
would reach out to Helen, asking for affection. Helen would refuse for you-know-what reason. She would deliver her ultimatum
regarding "the other woman." Jeri would deliver hers and they
would be at it again. It was a long-running show and both were
tired of it, but they didn't know how to get off the stage.

One day, in my office, they started in on their routine once
again. "STOP!" I said. "From now on you are no longer allowed
to discuss this matter in this office." I told them that they could
talk about anything they wanted to except Jeri's affair and
Helen's lack of affection.

Eventually they did begin to talk about other issues in their
relationship. Jeri wanted a wife. She wanted Helen to stay at
home and take care of her. She also wanted to be at the center of
Helen's existence. In return she was happy to earn a lot of money
and provide for Helen. She wanted an old-fashioned marriage,
the kind her own parents had. She could not understand why
anyone would not want the easy and protected life she was offering Helen.

Helen did not want to be Jeri's wife. She wanted a career and
an identity of her own. Once she rejected the role of Jeri's wife
and gained a measure of independence, she felt she had to guard

jealously her position. She could not allow herself to be vulnerable to Jeri, so she all but abdicated from the relationship. No sex, no affection, no acknowledgment of feelings that might compromise her defense against what she felt to be Jeri's power over her.

Because Jeri and Helen had never developed a very effective way of communicating about what was going on between them, they had not been able to get to the basic, underlying issues that troubled them about their relationship. An essential first step for them was to see how they used the theater of their relationship to avoid dealing with the complex problem of who they were in relation to one another.

Eventually they were able to identify and abort their routine and talk about what each needed from the other. As a result they were able to reshape their expectations and build a partnership that more realistically accommodated each person's needs, including those that were in conflict.

Jeri learned to respect Helen's need to strive for recognition in her work. She came to see the importance of supporting Helen's agenda for her own life rather than trivializing it, as she had been doing. She let go of her need to control Helen's identity, and she readjusted her vision of what their relationship should be. And, yes, she did give up "the other woman."

Helen, gaining the understanding and support she needed, began to feel valued by Jeri as a person. Consequently, she felt stronger, more independent, and increasingly like an equal partner in the relationship. She was able to drop her defensiveness and allow the feelings she had for Jeri to find expression. They resumed a sexual relationship and were able to show each other the affection they both felt.

BARRY AND SAM

Barry and Sam had been together for four years. It was the first relationship for Barry, who had struggled against being gay all through his twenties. He'd had few sexual partners before Sam.

Barry was now thirty-five. Sam, on the other hand, had spent many years enjoying sex with other men, mostly casual, one-night stands. He'd had a few brief relationships, none lasting more than a few months. At thirty-eight, he was glad to be settling down. Barry and Sam shared many interests. They both liked competitive sports. They were interested in politics. Both were history buffs. They liked to work out together at the gym. They sailed in the summer and skied in the winter. Both liked hiking, backpacking, and camping out. They had an active and busy life. They also enjoyed being at home in their apartment, which they were gradually fixing up. Their areas of disagreement were few, but consistent, mainly about money and just how sexually exclusive their relationship should be.

Their agreement about sexual exclusivity was ambiguous, at best. Sam insisted on the freedom to have other sexual partners on a one-time basis, though he infrequently took advantage of this option. Barry had readily agreed to the arrangement, primarily because he believed this was the correct way for gay men to be in a relationship. He had never, however, taken advantage of the option.

In spite of his agreeing to the arrangement they had, Barry found that every time Sam had sex with someone else, he was extremely jealous. He would punish Sam by ridiculing his taste and suggesting that he pursued these sexual adventures only to prove his dubious manhood. Sam would be infuriated by these attacks and would retaliate by going on drinking and cruising sprees. The longer Sam stayed away, the more angry Barry would become. He would go looking for Sam, and when he found him there would be a nasty scene, sometimes erupting into violence. The period following these episodes would be one of silence and coldness between them. Then, gradually, there would be a thawing, and they would resume enjoyment of their life together. They would be cautious with each other at first. It always took a while for trust to be reestablished.

In the area of finances, they had a running battle. Both agreed that they should split everything down the middle. They spent an inordinate amount of time totaling up who owed what to whom. Often they disagreed as to the balance. One or the other was often miffed about being taken advantage of or being falsely accused of avarice. In the fifth year of their relationship, the arguments seemed to be taking over their life. Between Barry's jealousy and Sam's acting out in response to it and the seemingly endless bickering over money, their good times together were becoming fewer and farther between. They didn't understand what was happening to them and decided to seek help. In my office they spent a great deal of time in the theater of their relationship. Barry verbally battered Sam, referring often to his "whorish" activities. Sam accused Barry of being possessive and overcontrolling. Each accused the other of being too acquisitive and caring too much about money.

After a month of listening to them, I was able to call a halt to the theatrics. Then they began to speak of other concerns.

Sam said he felt confined by the relationship. It felt unnatural to him to have to depend on one person for so much. Eventually he was able to say that it scared him to be so deeply involved with someone, that he wasn't really sure he even knew how to do that. He said he wanted to trust Barry completely, but it was hard to let his guard down. He was afraid that he'd lose himself. It was as if he had to fiercely defend his individuality and his masculinity all at once. A man was supposed to be strong, independent, and self-sufficient. That's what he'd learned in his family.

To Sam, giving in to the idea of commitment to Barry felt like giving up what amounted to the prerogative of his manhood, the ability to be strong and independent. Admitting to needing someone felt like weakness to him. It compromised his sense of himself as a man. He was actually quite disturbed about his conflicting feelings. He loved Barry and wanted a closer relationship with him. He also wanted to maintain the distance from Barry he felt he needed to be the self-sufficient male he was brought up to be.

Barry had similar concerns, but his struggle with accepting his gayness was very much at the center of his conflict regarding the relationship. Sam validated his gayness by having casual sex with other men. For Barry this epitomized being gay at its worst. It was almost intolerable for him to be associated so closely with someone who indulged in promiscuous sex with men. For him that had been the dragon at the gate of his homosexuality. He had so feared falling prey to that temptation (and thereby becoming gay) that he had mobilized himself to resist any attraction to such casual sexual activity. The ease with which Sam indulged in this kind of sex threatened Barry's defense against it.

Talking about these feelings, Barry came to see the conflict for what it was, a product of his own sexual identity struggle, rather than Sam's trying to destroy him and the relationship. He worked on his homophobic feelings until he had a better perspective on his sexuality. He could then give up some of his need to control Sam's sexual behavior.

Understanding better just how operative his resistance to being gay was, Barry could then see how it got played out between him and Sam. Somehow he had broken through his own defenses to establish the relationship with Sam. Having accomplished this, he had felt a great need to bind Sam to him. Sam was, paradoxically, his protection against being involved sexually with other men, an aspect of being gay that he had been so afraid would engulf him. Barry was able to see that he did not need to continue to use Sam in this way. If he did not wish to engage in sexual activity with other men he didn't have to, whether Sam was doing it or not. Realizing that cleared the way for him to think about whether he really wanted to share his partner with others, a different issue altogether. He decided that he did not want to do that and called for a renegotiation of their sexual exclusivity agreement.

Both Sam and Barry came to understand that their problems with money management reflected their problems with being comfortable in a committed relationship with another man. When they were able to make progress with that important underlying issue, the matter of how they dealt with their money seemed much less problematic. They stopped bickering and decided on a pooling of their money that made it unnecessary to calculate fairness at every turn. The pooling of their money symbolized commitment and a new level of trust for one another. That enabled each of them to open his heart to the other, to give up still more control, to tolerate vulnerability to another, and to experience the more tender aspects of being with the person you love.

Eventually Sam and Barry clarified their agreement regarding sexual exclusivity. They decided to be monogamous for a variety of reasons, AIDS not the least among them. Sam now also felt that his masculinity was not compromised by being emotionally dependent on someone. That made it possible for him to discover the different kind of sexual expression that a deeper love can produce. Both felt very satisfied with their new arrangements.

SUSAN AND LORI

Susan and Lori have been together for three years. Both are in their late twenties. Susan is a nurse, and Lori teaches English in a small college. Susan is a rather laid-back, congenial person. Lori is high strung, competitive, and an overachiever.

Lori is an only child from a troubled family. Her father's numerous affairs were an ill-kept secret. He was rarely at home. Lori's mother was a long-suffering victim of her unsatisfying marriage. She was depressed and emotionally unavailable much of the time that Lori was growing up.

Susan comes from a rather ordinary, well-adjusted family. Her parents loved and respected one another. Her sisters and brothers enjoyed each other's company. The family was a source of strength and comfort to everyone in it.

Susan and Lori care a great deal about each other and they have a good life together. Their one major source of contention is that Lori constantly pushes for "more romance" in the relationship. She asks to be touched, held, kissed, and courted, incessantly. At first, Susan was tolerant of these demands. She, too,

felt the need for a lot of physical contact and time spent expressing affection. But now, three years later, she has become impatient with the intensity of Lori's demands on her.

If Susan forgets to kiss Lori when she comes home, Lori pouts
for hours. If Susan does not tell Lori she loves her before they go
to sleep at night, Lori lies awake and eventually wakes Susan to
ask her if there is anything wrong. When they sit together watching television Lori wants to be held. If Susan moves away from
her, she looks hurt and worried.

Periodically, Susan has had enough of this, and she tries to
talk to Lori about it. These conversations do not work very well.
Susan says, "Lori, you know I love you. I wouldn't be here with
you if I didn't love you. You are so easily hurt by things I don't
even know I'm doing."

Lori answers, "I don't think it's too much to ask to have a little affection from your own lover."

Susan says, "A little affection? You are a bottomless pit. No
matter what I do it isn't enough."

Lori says, "That's not true. If you would just loosen up this relationship would be more fun. Don't you believe in romance?"

"Sure I believe in romance, but I also believe in reading and
washing dishes and seeing friends and talking on the telephone
and cooking and driving the car. Life is not just about sweet talk
and holding hands and kissing and hugging. We're not a couple
of moon-eyed teenagers."

"You are really cold."

"No, I'm not. I'm just not a full-time smoocher like you. I'm
a regular grown-up with lots of different interests."

"Oh, and I suppose I'm not."

"Of course you are, but your main interest seems to be playing lovebirds. Enough already."

Lori begins to pout. "I guess it's obvious. You don't love me as
much as I love you."

Susan erupts, "I love you. I love you. You, the person. I do not
love the bottomless pit."

Lori is now angry, hurt, and frightened.

Susan is frustrated and resentful.

They have this conversation many times. It is the theater of their relationship.

When they came to me, I asked them what the problem was. Lori said, "The problem is that Susan is an uptight person and she can't give me the kind of affection I need from a lover."

Susan said, "The problem is that Lori is too much of a romantic. She doesn't realize that there is more to life than lovemaking."

Neither is correct, of course. Susan is not uptight; she is quite capable of loving Lori adequately. Lori knows there is more to life than lovemaking.

Susan and Lori go through their routine in my office until I stop them. Then they begin to go more deeply into what is happening between them. Lori comes to see that she has brought the unfinished business of her childhood into her adult relationship with Susan. She has cast Susan in the role of the all-embracing, caretaking parent. When Susan plays out the role imperfectly, Lori is very disappointed. She brings the frustration of a deprived child (which she was) to the situation with Susan. Lori's complaints about Susan are really complaints about her parents, who were too busy making each other miserable to meet her need for affection. She now presents Susan with this need. Susan, of course, could not possibly make up for the love and affection Lori did not get from her parents. In this respect Lori is indeed a bottomless pit.

As Susan and Lori are able to talk it becomes clearer to both of them why Lori behaves as she does. Lori learns to separate Susan from her parents in her mind. She can soon make the distinction between what she needed from her parents when she was a child and what she needs in her adult relationship with Susan. The ability to make this distinction helps her to catch herself when she begins making demands on Susan that really belong to her relationship with her parents.

Susan learns to read Lori's signals more accurately so she is better able to give her the reassurance she needs periodically, that she is not being emotionally abandoned, as happened with her parents. Together, they are able to build a relationship in which both are more realistic about who the other person is.

In these three examples, the couples were able to identify the underlying issues causing them trouble but only after they were willing to relinquish the stage of the theater of their relationship. That is, they developed the ability to resist falling into the routine arguments that they came to depend on to avoid dealing with the more difficult, if not painful, issues underlying them. You do not have to be in therapy to learn to identify the unproductive routines you have come to depend on to avoid tackling the tough relationship issues. Just be alert to the dialogue between you and your partner that sounds all too familiar. If you've been over this territory countless times and you never seem to make any progress with it, there is a good chance you are into one of your routines.

UNDERLYING ISSUES

The concept of underlying issues can be a confusing one. In an effort to clarify it, I have identified two main categories of underlying issues that I see individuals bringing to their gay and lesbian relationships most. They are Child-Within-the-Adult issues and Gender-Role Conflict issues.

CHILD-WITHIN-THE-ADULT ISSUES

Each of us carries within us what has been called our "inner child of the past."* This child is never completely finished with the drama of childhood, always seeking to complete the unfinished business of parental and sibling relationships. If your mother and father loved you and valued you and understood you and trusted you to take care of yourself when the time came, you had wise and

---

* W. Hugh Missildine, M.D., *Your Inner Child of the Past.* (New York: Simon & Schuster, 1963).

caring parents and letting go of childhood was relatively easy. If you were not so fortunate to have had such parents, you probably have unfinished business with your childhood, and letting go of it is not so easy. For many in this predicament, it can become a life-long mission to find the love, understanding, trust, and valuing that didn't happen sufficiently in the parent-child relationship.

It should not be surprising that this unfinished business gets played out in intimate partnerships, where many of the same dilemmas regarding love and trust, understanding, and valuing are at issue. Since none of us likes to think of ourselves as child-persons with needs over which we have little or no control, the issues involved are often disguised as easily explainable matters common to any adult relationship. But therein lies the rub. How many times have you said, "What are we arguing about? Neither one of us cares that much about this." The other person may agree, yet the argument goes on. In those instances, most likely, it is the child-within pressing its agenda. Unless that child and his/her issues are addressed, the dissonance between the adult partners is likely to continue. The child-within is persistent. If it doesn't get the attention it needs this time, it will seize upon the soonest opportunity to present its need again, you may be sure. So long as the response is directed to the rational adult, the child-within remains unsatisfied and is reinforced in its need to try again to be heard.

One of the major reasons intimate relationships are so complicated is that they take place on several different levels at the same time. Perhaps you are a parent-figure to your lover. He/She plays out unfinished business with his/her own parents through you. Much of that business, inevitably, involves power and control issues, which crop up in *your* transactions over and over again.

Conversely, you may be child to your lover-as-parent-figure. Sometimes you are stubborn. You want to do something your way, even if you know that your way may not be the best way. Your lover asks you to listen to reason. You see that request as an effort to control you. You resist. You pull on your end of the rope. Your lover pulls on the other end. You are locked in a tug-of-war, stuck in position until you are able to refocus—allowing the other to emerge into the foreground of adult consciousness. Only then do you begin to see the other person clearly, not as an adversary from the past but an ally in the present. You do not have to pull against your lover. You let go of your end of the rope. You let go of your ghosts from the past. You are ready to move on collaboratively with your partner.

The most effective way to work out of this kind of cycle is to learn to listen for the underlying issues that belong to the child-within and to speak to those issues. Doing this will yield positive results only if the persons involved are interested in continuing and improving the relationships they are in. Also, some people, for one reason or another, are too filled with sadness or anger to respond to any effort to nurture them. In these instances, listening for underlying issues might be an exercise in futility. Hoping for the best, however, let us proceed to the issues. I have divided the child-within-the-adult issue into two categories: Unfinished Business with Parents and Unfinished Business with Siblings.

Unfinished Business with Parents

I have posed these issues as questions. I will list them first and then elaborate on them.

- Do you really love me?
- If I show you who I really am and what I need from you, will you continue to love me?
- If I open up to you, will I be able to handle the degree of intimacy that might produce?
- Can I trust you not to abandon me?

Do you really love me?

If you are this person, you came away from childhood feeling undervalued. For one reason or another your parents did not pay sufficient attention to you and/or other siblings were favored by them over you.

As an adult, you are very sensitive to the quality of attention you are getting from other people. You often think your partner is not *listening* to you, even when that is not the case. You need frequent updates on the status of your relationship, or you fish for compliments and expressions of love from your partner. Arguments are often about not getting enough sex, not getting enough affection, not being listened to or not being important enough to your partner. The child-within is asking for reassurance that he or she is worthy of love.

If I show you who I really am and what I need from you, will you continue to love me?

If you are this person, you probably came from a family in which no one talked about feelings. Everyone was "strong," never letting pain or anger or sadness show. You were told such things as, "Don't cry." "Get that sourpuss look off your face." "Don't raise your voice to me." "Calm down." "You can take it." "Don't give in." "Be brave." The underlying message appeared to be, "We don't want to hear about your feelings. We don't want to know about what you are experiencing. We just want you to do as we say, be as we are, and please us."

You were trained to hide your feelings. As an adult you rarely let others in on what you are experiencing inside, and that includes your partner. You have come away from childhood with the conviction that talking about feelings just makes trouble, so you don't talk about them, but periodically you blow up. You act out what you are feeling in some dramatic way that enables you to communicate anger or distress without having to take responsibility for *talking* about it. The frustration of having to deal with your feelings, once removed, and having to guess what it is you are trying to say with your actions, puts a strain on your partner and on the relationship. You are confused yourself about all this, and you struggle within yourself to go against your conditioning and talk about feelings, but it is very hard to do. The question for you is, "If

I show you who I really am and what I need from you, will you still love me?" The answer seems to be yes, but why? How is this relationship different from the one with your parents? Is it really? Can you afford to take a chance and break your deeply ingrained rule? This issue underlies every conflict you have with your partner.

If I open up to you, will I be able to handle the degree of intimacy that openness might produce?

If you are this person, as a child you may have had a parent who made demands that frightened you. You felt your parent's need, but you didn't know what to do about it. You've carried this fear into your adult relationship, where you hold back, not trying because you're afraid you won't measure up to the other person's expectations. You present yourself as someone who just doesn't care for the "touchy-feely" way of life. You keep your partner at a distance. When you are troubled, you withdraw into yourself. You don't want to give anyone an opening they might push through, into the soft, vulnerable part of you. Arguments are often about your inaccessibility, which you interpret as normal in contrast to what seems to you to be your partner's abnormal need for closeness and affection. The child-within wants closeness and affection also but is frightened of *failing* once again in an important relationship.

Can I trust you not to abandon me?

If you are this person you have either experienced parental abandonment, physical or emotional, in childhood, or abandonment was threatened often enough to make you believe it could happen at any time.

You grew up feeling powerless to hang onto anything that mattered to you—jobs, lovers, possessions, the admiration and friendship of other people. You believe abandonment is your fate and that people will stay with you only until they find someone better to take your place. You are very jealous. You get upset when your partner pays too much attention to anyone else. Most of your arguments with your partner are about his or her alleged be-

trayals of you. Your partner is discouraged because no matter
what reassurances you are given, you do not seem to be able to
feel trusting and secure.

Many other relationship issues have their origins in the parent-
child experience: "Can I count on you to understand what I
need?" "Will you be able to meet my needs?" "If I give you more
access to me, will you try to control me?" "Will I be able to
maintain my individuality in this merging of our identities?"
And so on.

These are some examples of the kinds of underlying issues
the child-within-the-adult brings to intimate relationships. Insofar
as these issues are the result of unfinished business with parents,
the severity of the childhood experiences that produced them
varies greatly from person to person. I have described some of the
more severe conditions. Such need not be the case for these issues to emerge. You may come from loving, attentive parents
whose child-rearing mistakes were quite minor. Nevertheless, you
bring into your relationships concerns about how lovable you are,
how competent you are as a partner, how interesting you are as a
person, and how desirable you continue to be to your lover. It is
as though a part of us never grows up, never finishes with the
fears and insecurities of childhood. And what better place to
bring those fears and insecurities than to a lover with whom there
is always the promise, at least, of everlasting affection, understanding, and acceptance. Adult intimate relationships do offer
opportunities to resolve many of the insecurities of childhood,
but only if the child-within is listened to and his/her issues are
taken seriously.

Unfinished Business with Siblings

The unfinished business of your child-within may be with sisters
or brothers. It may involve envy or unresolved rivalry. Envious
feelings can be directed at almost anything your partner has or
gets that you wish you had or were getting. Since envy is not the

most laudable of emotions, we sometimes deny to ourselves that we are feeling it at all. In that case it often simmers beneath the surface of a relationship, occasionally erupting into outright antagonism, the source of which is usually not clear.

About four years before the writing of this book, I decided to retire for an indefinite period from my almost full-time ten-year involvement in gay and lesbian community activism. I went to a great deal of trouble to extricate myself from the various boards of directors of which I was a member, from organizational responsibilities, from training and consulting activities.

I did it because ten years of placing my personal and professional life second to my activist life seemed enough. I needed more balance.

I also did it because the number of people available to be involved as activists, minuscule in the 1970s, exploded in the 1980s. Activist ranks were now swelled with eager, energetic, talented newcomers—as it should be.

My retirement took about six months to effect. The phone, that had rung all the time, slowly became very quiet. Soon it hardly ever rang at all except when family or friends called. Ahh. Peace.

But no. My younger lover, who had watched, helped, observed, and gradually replaced me in many of my roles and activities, now seemed to be getting very busy in her own right. Her telephone (different number, same house) began ringing and ringing and ringing. She was being asked to conduct workshops and do training programs and join committees and serve on boards and be the keynote speaker. Wonderful, I thought. She likes it. She does it well. She's having a good time.

Rooms were filled with never-ending telephone conversations, gossip, planning, plotting. There were also the urgent calls that interfered with dinner, sleep, sex, being together.

At first I thought, I'm glad it's not me. Then I began to think, Wait a minute, it might as well be me. It's all around me. I don't like it. But still I said nothing. It wouldn't be fair. After all, I had encouraged her to do this. It would be petty to object now. I lived with it, wincing every time her phone rang, resenting the seemingly interminable, avidly involved conversations. Then I would explode about something else, some lapsed responsibility around the house, criticism about the way she miscalculated the time necessary to get things done, her "adolescent love affair with the telephone"!

Eventually I was able to face it directly. I was envious. I was envious of her "popularity." I used to be the "popular" one. I was envious of her importance. She was right in the middle of the exciting and newsworthy events happening in our community. I used to be in the middle. I used to be the important one.

My phone was silent. No one called me anymore. And I resented it, even though I had carefully arranged it. It would have been so much easier if she weren't around. Let her have her celebrity, her importance, her popularity. I wouldn't care. But having it in my face every day was becoming unbearable. I felt the urge to start up again myself. I could become very active any time I wanted to. I didn't want to. I really didn't. But how was I going to cope with my resentment?

The answer came when I was ready to face the truth of my envy. It all felt very familiar. I have a younger sister, my only sibling. Since I had been an only child for ten years, I resented her coming along. Then, to add insult to injury, she was the best little girl in the world, didn't make trouble for anyone (except me), minded well (I was always rebellious), and she had beautiful straight brown hair (I had rather frizzy, no-special-color hair). She was pretty (I was passable), and she was extraordinarily healthy (I was often sick with some real or imagined malady). Everybody liked her. My reviews were mixed.

Now I am an adult. I have this lover. She is younger than me. She is prettier. She, too, has beautiful straight brown hair. She, too, is extraordinarily healthy. And now she has "usurped" my role in the community. I am furious. But at whom? My lover? My sister? My parents?

The trick is to sort it all out, to get to those issues produced by my early experience that continue to underlie my interaction with my partner in the adult relationship.

My anger at my sister is long since gone. As adults we have become good friends. I love her, and I am *very* glad that she did come along. But what about the child-within? My child-within, I'm afraid, still harbors those feelings of resentment and envy. If there are conditions in my contemporary relationship that sufficiently mimic my earlier relationship with my sister, the same old feelings of envy and resentment are likely to get stirred up. An issue that otherwise might be minor becomes major because feelings about it match up with similar feelings of an earlier period. It's unfinished business. And it's a psychological axiom that that which is incomplete will continue to press for closure, in one way or another.

When I am able to see these connections I can begin to separate which feelings belong to my lover, and her behavior, and which belong to a time long gone. That new perspective enables me to experience whatever feelings I am having regarding my lover without the contamination of past feelings. I can remind myself that I am no longer a powerless child with a cruel fate being imposed on me. I am an intelligent and resourceful adult. I have a brain. I have a mouth. I have interpersonal skills. I know what to do—and I do it.

I sit my lover down and explain all this to her. Together, we figure out how her activities can be conducted so as to interfere with our life together minimally. Now that she understands what is happening, she begins to find all kinds of ways to address my feelings in relation to her community activities. I soon find the sting has been removed. We have dealt with the issue underlying my problem with her behavior. The envious child-within has been quieted.

Unresolved Rivalry

Some people bring their unresolved rivalry with a sibling into their adult relationship with a partner. These are the very competitive people for whom much of life with a lover is a contest. Who's a better breadwinner? Who makes friends more easily?

Who has more friends? Who is a better driver? Who is a better planner? Who is smarter, sexier, more sensitive, has better taste, manages money more effectively, understands the world better? You name it, these individuals are ready to compete for it. They are still locked in battle with the sister or brother of their childhood whom they needed to best to prove something about themselves.

In the extreme, this competition as a way of life can be exhausting. Even in its milder forms it takes a toll. But, most important, it is a barrier to intimacy. One does not open up and become vulnerable to one's competitor. What one does with one's competitor is to play it cool, exercise control, and focus on winning, none of which is likely to contribute to the growth of an intimate partnership. Two people together dealing with the unresolved rivalry of childhood can turn what might have been a loving relationship into an adversarial nightmare.

Here the child-within is moved by one all-consuming passion: I must win in order to feel safe, whole, and content. It becomes the issue underlying many of the transactions this person has with a partner. As with the issue of unresolved envy of a sibling, the remedy here is to explore the origins of the rivalrous feelings and to sort out what belongs to the past and what belongs to the present. Hopefully, if this is done successfully, it will be a relief to lay the contest to rest, to let go of the need to win, to come to see one's partner as ally rather than adversary.

Again, you don't need a therapist to guide you toward the real underlying issues in your relationship. You can learn to identify them for yourself with a little effort. It will be effort well spent.

GENDER-ROLE CONFLICT ISSUES

Roles are clusters of behaviors that are associated with some identifiable aspect of a person's life. For instance, there are "occupational roles" referring to the behaviors and functions usually associated with one's vocation. There are "family roles" referring to the behaviors and functions usually associated with position in the biological family, such as mother, father, daughter, son. And, there are "gender roles," referring to behaviors and functions usually associated with being male or female.

These clusters of expectations are very important in guiding us as we play out our roles in life. Unfortunately, as with anything that is in danger of becoming so institutionalized as vocational, family, and gender roles, there is a point of diminishing returns in how helpful expectations can be. That which brings clarity at one time overcomplicates at another. There is no better example of this than the confusion that can be caused by gender-role expectations when they are out of sync with what one's life is all about.

We are all "taught" from childhood what is expected of us and what we can expect for ourselves as a result of being a male or a female. Gender-role training is a very strong theme in our society. In many situations, one's worth as a human being is judged by how "manly" a male is, or how "womanly" a female is.

Many of the specifics of gender-role expectations are based on the assumption that males and females will grow up to pair up, to produce children. Therefore, the male-female pair bond encompasses the behaviors thought necessary for bringing up baby. The female of the pair is considered to be the primary caregiver. She is expected to make the home and to provide for the practical and emotional needs of husband and children. In order to accomplish this she is trained to be nurturing, emotionally expressive, and skilled in homemaking. In order to keep her at home, she is conditioned to be submissive and dependent. Even if she does happen to work outside the home, she is still expected to fulfill her homemaking and maternal duties.

The male, on the other hand, is considered to be the primary provider of the material support that makes the female's caregiving possible. He is expected to be assertive, in control of his feelings, independent, and in charge.

Their roles are supposed to complement one another. She fulfills the functions at home that enable him to go out into the world to earn the money to support what she is doing at home—a neat and efficient scheme that once worked a great deal better than it does now. The world has changed and the possibilities for living and loving configurations have changed with it.

Males and females do indeed still pair up and have children, but often the female partner also has to work outside the home in order to maintain a desired lifestyle, or just to survive economically. Someone else takes care of the children. Sometimes the male partner does a significant amount of the caretaking of the children. Sometimes, no one takes care of the children.

Some males and females pair up and don't have children. Some males and females pair up, produce children, and then abandon the nuclear family arrangement. Some males and some females don't pair up at all. Some of these have children anyway.

Some males pair up with other males. Some females pair up with other females.

Now we have not only gender-role behaviors that are redundant, we have people paired up in ways that negate and make unnecessary the complementary role behaviors built into the male-female pair bond. How does anyone know who is supposed to do what, with whom? Who is the breadwinner? Who is the homemaker? Who is the nurturer? Who is in charge? Who cooks? Who cleans? Who takes out the trash? Who fixes the car? Who initiates sex?

When the obligations and prerogatives of each person in a relationship are not allocated according to gender, how are they allocated? The dilemma produced by this question can be a major source of problems underlying gay and lesbian relationships, especially if the couple is practicing denial that any role-playing is occurring at all. Such denial is often the product of political or philosophical beliefs growing out of the feminist or new gay rights movements, with their emphasis on breaking down stereotypes. "No role-playing in gay and lesbian relationships." "No more butch and femme." Indeed, younger gay people do not typically assume husband-wife roles as was once the more common pattern in same-sex relationships. But I think we have gone overboard in protesting the very existence of gender-role behaviors in our partnerships.

The truth of the matter is that we have had to learn how to be in an intimate relationship from somewhere. The most common sources up to now have been our own heterosexual parents, other heterosexual couples in our environment, and depictions of heterosexual couples in movies, books, magazines, and on television. Like it or not, we internalize what we read and see. A lifetime of internalizing heterosexual relationship models inevitably produces, at some level of consciousness, an orientation that is patterned on the complementarity of male-female role behaviors. The question now becomes, by what process do the roles in a same-sex relationship become allocated to one partner versus the other? And, the question that follows that is, how satisfied is each partner with the resulting arrangement?

The fact is that there are gay men who are very male-identified in their self-image, and there are gay men who identify more with being female than male. There are lesbians who are super feminine, and there are lesbians who are quite male-identified. And, there are a lot of folks in between.

When a very male-identified gay male and a female-identified gay male get together, the roles played out in their relationship are most likely to be based on the gender they identify most strongly with. When a male-identified lesbian and a female-identified lesbian pair up, their roles vis-a-vis one another will likewise tend to arrange themselves around the gender with which each identifies most strongly. For the most part these situations are not problematic. Everyone involved understands what is happening and why. What we are more concerned with here is the instance in which partners find themselves locked into gender-role patterns, not knowing how they got there, not liking it, and not knowing what to do about it.

In the early 1980s, the *Journal of Homosexuality* published an article* in which the authors put forth some very interesting ideas about how certain responsibility patterns tend to develop in same-sex relationships. They hypothesized three different ways in which these patterns might develop.

The first possibility, they suggest, involves pragmatic factors, and occurs in two stages. Initially, pragmatic factors would lead one partner to assume certain tasks or responsibilities in the relationship. Subsequently, additional behaviors that are part of the same gender-role as the initial behavior will also be assumed by this partner. For example, differences in partners' work schedules might lead one of them to take responsibility for the preparation of dinner. Meal preparation is part of a cluster of behaviors including housework, decorating, and purchasing household supplies. Thus, assuming responsibility for cooking might imply assuming responsibility for these tasks as well.

In addition to the practical matter of who gets home first as a basis for becoming the meal preparer, the authors also cite "skill differences" (some cook, some don't) and "income disparity" as pragmatic determinants of who assumes this task. The partner who can't contribute as much monetarily as the other might make up for it by taking on certain household responsibilities, and then find that related tasks are assumed. Thus a pattern develops that may never have been intended.

The second possibility for pattern development involves power issues and is described by the authors as follows:

> [It] rests on the observation that the masculine role is more valued and more rewarded than the feminine role. Thus, it might be that the claim to the masculine role is the prerogative of the partner who is the more powerful member of the couple. This power could be based on such personality traits as domi-

---

* Jeanne Marecek, Stephen E. Finn, and Monda Cardell, "Gender Roles in the Relationships of Lesbians and Gay Men." *Journal of Homosexuality* Vol. 8 (2), Winter 1982.

nance or ability to influence others. Alternatively, it
may be based on the higher status afforded by such
factors as greater age, higher income or greater educational attainment.

The third possibility involves "gender identity":

> Gender identity refers to how "male" or "female" one
> feels. . . . There is considerable variation among mem-
> bers of each sex in the extent to which individuals iden-
> tify with that sex. . . . For example, both partners in a gay
> male couple may be male-identified but if one is ex-
> tremely male-identified, he may assume masculine-role
> behaviors and functions exclusively. His less-strongly
> male-identified partner may have to assume complemen-
> tary feminine role behaviors.

The problems arise when one partner becomes dissatisfied with
his/her role. This dissatisfaction seems to occur when the role
one finds one's self in is that of the "wife."

This reflects the attitude of a society in which masculine
endeavor is taken more seriously and is more highly valued
than feminine endeavor. I have known male couples who took
all their meals out because neither partner wanted to "be the
wife," that is, do the meal preparation. Fortunately such couples are in the minority, but concern about this issue underlies
many an argument about whose turn it is to do what in the
kitchen. Of course, a gay man cooking dinner does not mean
he really wants to be a woman. It usually means he's hungry
and needs to eat. By the same token, a lesbian fixing her car
does not mean she really wants to be a man. Most likely it
means she is tired of paying could-care-less mechanics to keep
her car running.

The real problem is about patterns getting set and then becoming doorless rooms from which there is, it seems, no exit.
What began as a practical necessity becomes an oppressive obli-

gation when it is taken for granted by another. Take, for instance, the following couple (who happen to live in Hollywood).

HAROLD AND PETER

Harold and Peter have been together for five years. Harold is a physician who earns a considerable amount of money. Peter, who is younger, is a struggling actor. Sometimes he works, more often he does not. He takes acting lessons and singing lessons, he visits his agent, and he goes to auditions. Because Peter has a lot of unscheduled time, Harold expects him to take care of the house, the dogs, the yard, and the everyday errands. In the beginning Peter readily agreed to take on many of these responsibilities as his contribution to their life together. He soon discovered, however, that he didn't like doing most of these things. He felt stuck.

As his acting career demanded more and more of his time, he began to slack off on his household duties. He forgot to pick up the cleaning, to take the dogs to the groomer, to resupply the kitchen cupboards. Harold complained, and they slipped into what has become a familiar argument.

HAROLD: Peter, the dogs are beginning to look like the Loch Ness Monster. When are you going to take them to the groomer?

PETER: I'll do it, I'll do it. On Friday.

HAROLD: That's what you said last week.

PETER: C'mon, Harold. You know I had to go to that audition last Friday.

HAROLD: And what happened to Saturday, Monday, Tuesday, Wednesday, and Thursday?

PETER: You know, Harold, I do have a few other things in my life besides this house and these dogs.

HAROLD: You know these are your dogs, and this is your house, too.

PETER: No, Harold. This is *your* house and these are *your* dogs.

HAROLD: You live here rent free. You don't have to pay for anything. You don't even have to buy your own food. And I can't get you to do a few simple things around the house.

PETER: I have a career, just as you do. Just because it isn't as lucrative as yours right now doesn't make it meaningless. It's important to me, and it takes time.

HAROLD: Great. So, who's supposed to take care of this house and the dogs and the yard in the meantime?

PETER: I don't know. I guess I'll have to do it. I'll find the time. Don't worry about it.

You may be sure that Harold and Peter will have this conversation again. They did not get to the real issue underlying their tension, which is Peter's resentment of the role he has been assigned in the relationship. Rather than confronting the issue so that it might be renegotiated, Peter has, in a sense, gone on strike. This condition is likely to persist until the underlying issue is addressed. Peter took on certain domestic responsibilities because he had more free time than Harold and he wanted to contribute his share. Soon he found that Harold expected him to take on many of the other duties associated with those responsibilities, behaviors that clustered with other behaviors to make up a role.

Peter feels himself to have been pushed into a role he doesn't want. He resists the role, and everything involved suffers as a result. Peter and Harold must confront this underlying issue of their relationship. Only then can they begin to restructure the partnership so that the emphasis is not so much on their role conflict as on a consensually arrived at plan to maintain their home and relationship in good order.

A last word on gender-roles and gay and lesbian partnerships. If a couple wants to get into a complementary gender-role pattern, it should be their business, and no one else's. The key is to be sure that each partner is doing what he or she *wants* to be doing. For those who do not wish to get into such a pattern, division of labor should be designed according to the interests, skills, time available, and inclination, in a given instance, of each partner. Care should be taken to avoid becoming locked into patterns from which there is no escape. Needs and interests change and a growing relationship accommodates the changes.

5

"ARE YOU LISTENING TO ME?"

My partner and I were out for our morning walk. I was in a complaining mood. I was listing all the things I had to do that day and lamenting the lack of time to do them. She listened for a time and then suggested I was working too hard and should give myself a little more time to relax. That annoyed me. Already pressured, should I stop what I'm doing, sit down with a magazine and relax? The thought made me more tense.

"What do you mean, 'relax'?" I said. "What kind of thing is that to say to a person? Can't you be more specific?"

"Okay," she said. "Strike a balance. Do some things that will balance out all the work."

"That's what you call *specific*? That's specific? Can't you be more concrete?"

She looked exasperated. "You know exactly what I mean. Why are you pretending you don't?"

"I'm not pretending. I don't know what you are talking about. You use vague terms like 'relax' and 'strike a balance.' That's like saying 'shape up' or 'feel better.' Who in the world knows what that means?"

She continued her admonitions about "balancing" and "relaxing." I said to myself: Give up. I walked in silence while she went on and on. I tuned her out. I concentrated on the vegetation, the architecture of the houses we were passing, the debris in the gutter. After a time her voice pierced my reverie. I had no idea what she'd just been saying.

"Well, say something," she insisted.

I looked at her blankly.

"I give up," I said.

"Have you heard anything that I've just been saying?"

"No," I answered honestly.

"You're impossible," she said.

"Uh-huh," I said.

We continued our walk in silence.

I thought about it later. Why did I just give up? There were many things I could have said to explain to her just why I was feeling so pressured. I could have responded to her wish to be helpful even though she wasn't doing a very good job of it. She meant well. Actually, I'd been saying the same things to myself. What did I want from her? I thought about it.

I realized I wanted more interest in what I was *feeling* rather than advice on altering my behavior. I wanted her to understand, without benefit of explanation, why I was feeling as I was. I think her advice giving annoyed me. It made me feel as though I didn't have the sense to know what to do for myself. (Forget for the moment that I didn't in that instance.) I didn't like her response, so after very little effort to communicate what I was feeling, I just gave up. I shut her out. I shut myself off. I aborted real communication. I closed the door on a conversation that might have helped her know me better and helped me get some support for my feelings. I know better. In that moment, I just didn't care.

We all have that experience at one time or another. Some people have it uncomfortably often. If you are a person who is afflicted with the "I give up" syndrome when your partner is not meeting your needs in a given situation, I encourage you to take a second look at your behavior and your reasons for acting as you do.

Good communication is the pathway to intimacy in a relationship. To allow another person access to your inner reality, to the hopes, the dreams, the fears, and the doubts that motivate

your life is to make the most intimate kind of contact with another. It is what distinguishes love from infatuation and real partnership from romantic illusion.

This chapter is about communication in the context of an intimate partnership. It is about the ways two people talk to one another that either enhance or inhibit their collaborative
arrangement. It is about what they say and what they don't say in
the service of becoming closer or resisting becoming closer. It is
about the common communication we require to get through
the day and the uncommon communication that lifts conversation out of the ordinary and transcends what was expected or
what went before.

It is also about the special problems with communication that
I see occurring in gay and lesbian relationships, some having to
do with habitual secretiveness about one's life, some having to do
with male and female socialization. That socialization becomes
especially telling when there are *two* people having trouble with
the same relationship skill, such as two men unable to collaborate
successfully because of their underlying competitiveness.

People in relationships sometimes use communication, or
the withholding of it, to control their partners. Some never let
their partner finish a sentence. Others allow that to happen, giving away their power of self-expression easily but resenting it inside. Then there are people who withdraw into silence whenever
they are troubled about something personal or something in a relationship. They isolate themselves, keeping their partners at bay
and, in the process, ensuring that a desired emotional distance is
maintained. Sometimes they are following examples set by their
own families. Sometimes they have the need to demonstrate to
themselves that no one really can care about them, or that they
are the strong, stand-alone, sufficient-unto-themselves adults they
were brought up to be.

The reasons for bad communication in relationships are as
various as the forms it takes.

I have known people who never talk about what is bothering
them but act it out, as though they did not possess the power of

speech when strong emotions are involved. They deal with their anger by striking out physically, or by indirect sniper attacks, or by displacing it onto something or someone else, or they clam up or remove themselves altogether, thereby canceling out any possibility of resolution of the conflict.

Some people act out their sad or hurt feelings through their bodies, punishing themselves and others around them with their illnesses, through which they are saying, "Don't hurt me." "Take care of me." "Love me."

Then there are those who communicate through the excessive use of alcohol or drugs. The messages vary: "I don't need you." "I don't have to *feel* anything if I don't want to." "I am punishing you by putting myself out of your reach." "I am punishing you by making a mess of our lives." "I can't help myself." "I am sick, and I need your help."

A danger in communication that is acted out rather than directly expressed is that the true messages might be lost in the camouflaging action. "I am angry at you, and this is why . . ." is much clearer than sniper attacks or deadly silence or flight.

"I feel hurt by what you did" is much clearer than illness that makes you inaccessible or silence that does the same or rage that covers up the hurt. Again, the true message is lost, the opportunity to effect some desired change is missed. The tension is unrelieved.

I have been utterly astonished, on occasion, at what people withhold from their partners of five, ten, twenty years.

"Why," I ask, "have you never told your lover this?"

"I didn't think he would understand and that would devastate me."

"I was afraid she would stop loving me if she knew this."

"It didn't seem important at first, then I couldn't tell him because I waited too long."

"I didn't want her to know too much about me. That would have given her too much leverage."

And so they live with their imperfections or indiscretions which turn into closely guarded secrets. Such secrets are like barnacles on the side of a ship. If enough barnacles collect, the ship

sinks. An intimate relationship that has collected too many secrets is similarly in danger of going out of business. Secrets in an
intimate partnership are dangerous. They burden the foundation
of trust. They compromise the ability to disclose freely the self, a
necessary condition for the growth of understanding and compassion between partners. Such disclosure is also the ultimate act
of faith in the relationship. Anything that inhibits it should be
carefully reviewed and readjusted. But enough of warnings and
misgivings. Let's get to the crucial question.

WHAT IS GOOD COMMUNICATION IN A RELATIONSHIP?

The elements of good communication involve what the sender
does and what the receiver does.

As the sender:

• You are direct. You are saying what you have to say rather
than acting it out or disguising it. Your meaning is immediately
understandable. It is not a message that needs to be decoded to be
understood. If you are talking about feelings, you identify them,
"I'm angry." "I'm hurt." "I'm pleased." "I'm envious." "I'm lonely."

• You say what you need or want, even if there is risk involved. You don't swallow your needs or deny that they exist. You
don't consistently defer to the other person out of a conviction
that your partner wants that or because it's just easier that way. If
you need more attention, you say so. If you need to be taken care
of for a while, you say so. If you want something that you are not
getting, you say so. You don't take to your bed or take a drink or
take to the road to express your needs and wants.

• You say what you don't want. You don't just put up with
conditions that upset you. You don't just silently resent your partner's behavior. You don't go along with plans and programs that
are not to your liking. You say no when that's how you feel and,

in the best of all possible worlds, you will tell your partner exactly why you are saying no to his/her wishes.

As the recipient:

• You check it out when you are not exactly sure what your partner is saying to you. You don't guess or just let it go by if it's unclear. If there is any doubt in your mind, you make sure that you understand what your partner means.

• You don't give unsolicited advice when your partner is trying to tell you what happened to her/him. Giving unsolicited advice cuts off the opportunity your partner needs to talk about feelings. As long as you are giving advice, your partner can't talk about whatever it is that he/she needs to get out.

• You don't problem-solve when your partner is trying to talk about a troubling experience. If you are asked to problem-solve, fine. But, if your partner is trying to get his/her feelings out to relieve the tension of a frustrating or frightening experience, you are cutting off communication when you move too quickly into problem solving. By doing so you cheat your partner out of one of the most precious assets an intimate relationship has to offer: a willing and receptive companion who understands and cares about you enough to share the experiences of your life.

With premature problem solving or the giving of unsolicited advice, you are saying to your partner, in essence, "Don't tell me your feelings. Listen to what I have to tell you." The effect can be as inhibiting to your partner as if you'd said, "Stop. I don't want to hear anymore." Inadvertent as it may be, such a statement may produce a deeply felt loneliness in the other person, especially if it happens often.

• You don't give false reassurance in an effort to make the person feel better. This, too, makes the statement, "I don't want to hear anymore," though that may not be what you want to convey at all. For the person who needs very much to be listened to, a rush of reassurance is as good as saying, "You'll be fine, and that's enough of that."

• You are listening carefully to what your partner is saying. You are listening from as deep a place as possible at a given time. You are focused on your partner's words, and you are listening for the feelings that underlie those words.

• You are asking questions to draw the person out, particularly questions about feelings.

• You are speaking from your own experience to convey that you understand, being careful not to divert the discussion so that it is more about you than about your partner.

• You are acknowledging the feelings that are being expressed, conveying to your partner that you are interested in more than just what happened. You are interested in her/his personal experiencing of what happened.

Most of all, in any or all of these ways, you are communicating to your partner that you care and you understand.

All too often I have watched the most well-meaning people dispense advice in an effort to be helpful, and it has pained me to see the person on the receiving end lapse into defeated silence. That person didn't want advice. He/she wanted not to be alone with his/her experience.

We sometimes rush to reassure, I think, because we want to deny the pain inside ourselves. We don't want it stirred up. "Don't worry, it will be all right."

If I reassure the person I will lessen the chances that I will have to witness/feel any more of this pain/anger/sadness. I will lessen the chances that I, too, might have to get in touch with such troubling feelings. It's like the old "Don't cry" admonition from childhood. The parent doesn't want to feel the child's discomfort or doesn't want to be bothered or perhaps can't cope with the frustration of not being able to help effectively. The parent then, out of his or her own need, says, "Don't cry," thus cutting off expression that is important to the discharge of tension associated with the child's physical or psychic pain. If it happens often enough, this child becomes the adult who will go to any length not to cry in front of others, even after suffering great sorrow or discomfort. This person still hears the plea of the frightened or impatient parent, "Don't cry." "Don't cry *in front of me.*" So this person spends the rest of his/her life trying to comply. It's bad enough to have suffered this cutting off of emotion as a child; we shouldn't continue to do it to each other as adults.

It is not weak to cry with another person, as some people think. It is a gift. It says, "I trust you enough to be vulnerable with you." It is a compliment. It can be a bonding experience. And, if it does happen to embarrass the other person because of their own flawed upbringing, feel compassion for that, but don't cut yourself off because of it.

Another way in which I often see people cutting each other off is by agreeing too quickly to stop, start, or continue doing something that their partner is expressing feelings about, as in the following example.

Jerry and Ken had a relationship in which communication was often abortive. Usually, the pattern was that Ken would try to talk about something: an impending decision, a possible purchase, a recently made plan. Immediately upon Ken's raising any question at all about the matter, Jerry would throw up his hands and declare, "Okay, we won't do it!"

Ken would then become conciliatory. "No, no, I didn't mean we shouldn't do it. I just have some second thoughts, and I want to talk about them. That doesn't mean we shouldn't do it.!"

Jerry is now in high gear. "No. It's over. We're not doing it. I don't want you to do something you don't want to do."

Ken now has several choices. He can give up: "All right. I guess we won't do it."

Or, he can persist in his effort to communicate to Jerry what he wants to do.

"Look. I'm not saying I don't want to do this. If I do make the decision that I don't want to do it, you'll be the first to know. Right now I want to tell you what my thoughts about it are. And, I want you to listen, not to argue with me, not to cut me off. Just listen."

Ken then says what he has to say. He asks Jerry what he thinks.

If Jerry begins to cut off the discussion again, Ken doesn't let him do it. He insists that Jerry respond to him, that the discussion go on, that they give themselves the opportunity to work their way through to a decision that is mutually satisfying.

SECOND GUESSING

For every person in an intimate relationship, there is the reality of who the other person is, and then there is the embellishment on that reality, supplied by one's fantasies about who the other person is. These fantasies evolve out of the need for the other person to be a particular way. Perhaps the need is for the person to be very similar to one. Perhaps it is a need for the person to be what one is not. Perhaps it is a need to deny something about the person that is undesirable. Whatever purpose the fantasies serve, they generate a set of assumptions about what the other person needs and wants from us. These assumptions may or may not be true, but we usually treat them as if they are true. We second-guess our partner's needs and proceed with a kind of surety that we are doing just what we should be doing. If, indeed, we are doing what is desired of us, everything turns out well. If, on the other hand, our second-guessing is a product of our fantasies more than our grasp of the person's reality, we are probably in trouble.

Here is an example from my own life: It was early in our relationship. My lover had just finished graduate school. She was about to present her first paper at a social work convention to be held in her hometown, Boston. At the time, we did not live together and it was not taken for granted that if she traveled, I would most likely travel with her. I was quite busy at the time, and I was not eager to interrupt my schedule to go anywhere. But I began to think about what it had meant to me to present my first paper at a professional meeting. It had been many years before. I remembered clearly how nervous I was. The paper was scheduled for 7:30 A.M., a time slot reserved for presentations not expected to shake the world. About half a dozen people attended, among them a professional acquaintance, Dr. George Bach, who was, by then, a well-known psychologist. George sat down next to me, took my hand and assured me that I was going to do just fine and that this, no doubt, would be the beginning of a long career of presenting professional papers in public.

As it turned out, he was right, but at the time the prospect of a long career of experiencing such anxiety did not seem attractive. As I presented my paper, George smiled reassuringly from the audience. It had a calming effect on me. His presence (especially at that ungodly early hour) meant a great deal to me, and I never forgot it. He had done this as a friend. Surely it was the least I could do for my lover. I decided to accompany her, to be there for support as George had been there for me so many years ago.

When I suggested that I might come to Boston with her, she was delighted. Aha, I thought, she is nervous though she isn't saying so. Her enthusiastic acceptance of my offer confirmed it. I knew she was as nervous as I had been.

In the weeks that ensued, whenever I thought about her presenting that paper, a wave of anxiety would pass over me. I was glad I was going to be there to hold her hand, if need be, to smile reassuringly at her, to give support in any way that was required. I would be her stalwart ally.

In our conversations about the impending trip, I watched her closely for signs of anxiety about the paper. There weren't any. She was handling it very well, I thought.

Then, one day, as we were developing our actual plan for the trip, she said to me, "You know, you don't really have to come to hear my paper."

What was this? Was she so terrified that she didn't want me to be present to witness the disaster? "No," I said firmly, "I will be there!"

A few days later she brought it up again. "I don't see why you want to come to hear my paper. You've already read it. It's going to be early in the morning. Why don't you just sleep in that day?"

"Well," I said, "it defeats the purpose of my going to Boston if I'm not there to hear your paper."

She looked puzzled. "Defeats the purpose? What purpose?" she asked.

"I thought you wanted me to go to Boston with you," I said.

"I do, very much. What's that got to do with my paper?"

"But that's why I'm going. I know you are nervous about it, and I'm going to support you. That's the *reason* for my going."

She looked astonished. "I'm not in the least bit nervous about giving this paper. I feel fine about it."

"Then why," I asked, "did you want me to go with you on this trip?"

"Well," she said, "I thought we'd have fun together in Boston. I'd show you where I grew up and all that. I just wanted us to enjoy ourselves there."

"You're not nervous . . . at all?"

"Not at all."

And, she wasn't. I had made assumptions about what she needed that were based on my fantasy about who she was. I had assumed that she was just like me and that she would have an experience just like mine. I didn't check out my assumptions. I took it for granted that they were true. I second-guessed her, and I was wrong. As it turned out, I did go to Boston. I went to hear her paper because I wanted to be there. She wasn't nervous at all. And, we did have a good time visiting the settings in which she grew up.

Now, after all these years, we still second-guess each other. The odds are better that we will be right, but there continue to be those wrong guesses. I think every couple does this. You go to an event that you really don't want to go to because you believe it means a lot to your lover and actually, it doesn't. You put up with people you don't like, you go out of your way to buy that special something, you give up what you want for what you think he/she wants, and then you find out that you guessed wrong. You didn't have to do any of those things. Sometimes you find out much later, after you've been putting up with, and putting out, for a very long time, that it was quite unnecessary in the first place.

Your lover tells you that when you do something you don't really want to do, your martyrdom is more than apparent. You don't really believe this. Of course, you're sure you pull it off quite graciously. This is the rub in second-guessing. Selective recall aside, most of us are not very good actors. We send out subtle messages of discontent to our partners. When we are second-guessing and doing something we don't really want to do, the message of discontent may be received, but the basis for that feeling may not be clear. We may have created a whole new source of tension: you didn't want to go to that party. You went because you were certain that your partner wanted you to. You didn't check it out. You were just so sure. You resented going. You showed it at the party. You were grumpy on the way home. Not knowing that you had gone under protest, especially since you *insisted* on going, your lover is puzzled, and wonders what he/she did to upset you. You don't want to tell your lover why you're grumpy. The two of you are at a communication impasse.

The treatment of choice here is clear communication. If I don't want to do something but I think you do, I might save myself a lot of time and trouble by asking you to tell me honestly how you feel about it. Then, I might return the favor by telling you honestly how I feel about it. If I find that I am doing a lot of second-guessing with you, I would do well to examine the fantasies I have about you. Are they so compelling that I can't give them up for the reality of who you are? What are these fantasies? What purpose do they serve for me in our relationship?

GIVING ADVICE AND PROBLEM SOLVING

Individuals whose occupational roles thrive on their ability to solve other people's problems often don't recognize that there are alternative ways to relate to a person who is troubled about something. When that person is their lover there may be an accumulation of unexpressed resentment toward the problem solver, who seems more interested in giving advice than in hearing what the partner is going through.

Take this transaction between Paul and George, for instance. Paul arrived home in a very disturbed state. He is glad to find his lover there. He really needed to talk about what happened to him at work today. George gives him the lead-in. "You look very upset." Paul threw himself down on the couch and launched into a description of the day's events.

"The day got off to a really rotten start when my boss came in to tell me that the project I'm working on has been canceled and I'm being transferred to another department. Wouldn't it be nice to have a little warning? Wouldn't it be nice to be consulted about where I might *want* to work rather than just being told, 'Pack up your stuff, you're moving'? It isn't as if I just joined the company. Wouldn't you think five years on the job would entitle a person to some say in what happens to him?"

Paul shakes his head. "I don't believe it. I just don't believe it. Then, two hours later, I hear from one of the other guys that because business has been so bad they are probably going to fire some people. Then I have to start worrying about whether I'm getting the ax, too. I ask my boss about this. He says he knows nothing of people being fired. I say, 'So, can you reassure me that I will have my job next month?' He says, 'I can't reassure anybody about anything right now. I just don't have information about any individuals being fired.' So, now I'm up the creek. I'm angry. I'm scared. I'm frustrated."

George leaned toward Paul. He spoke resolutely. "You know what you have to do? You have to get yourself out of this victimized frame of mind. That's first. Then, you have to strategize just what you'll do in response to anything they might do. You have to fight."

Paul closed his eyes for a few seconds before he spoke. "You know, I have tried so hard on this job. I really wanted to be successful. I've pushed myself more than I ever have before. How could they do this to me?"

George stood up and began pacing. "Now, here's what you should do tomorrow morning. You have to get as much information as possible about what's going on. You have to talk to a lot of people. Then you can begin to develop your counterplans for anything they come up with. Information is your ammunition in this fight."

Paul said, "You know, George, I think this makes me feel worse than anything that's ever happened to me in a work situation. I feel so devalued."

George stopped in front of Paul. He leaned close to him. "You can beat this if you go on the offensive. You'll not only be showing them that you care about the company and the job, but you'll be demonstrating that you have the kind of strength they need working for them at a time like this."

Paul just stared at George. "Yeah, well, I guess it'll all work out."

"Paul, I'm telling you, you have to fight it!"

Paul sighed. "I'm not exactly in a fighting mood right now, George."

Paul got up and walked into another room. George watched Paul walking away. He shook his head. "I try to help him and he doesn't even listen to me."

It should be obvious that Paul needed to talk about his feelings. He tried. George virtually ignored him. Paul tried again. George did not get the message. He was too caught up in advice giving and problem solving.

If George had been better able to read his partner's message about what he needed, he might have responded to Paul's initial comments by saying something like the following.

"What a blow. Sounds like you've had the wind knocked out of you." To which Paul might have said, "Yes, I really feel terrible." Then he would have gone on to say how much he wanted to be a success on this job and how he's pushed himself. George might have responded to these comments with "I see you are feeling really disappointed and discouraged."

When Paul said that he felt devalued, George might have conveyed that he knew how that felt and acknowledged that he understood how painful this experience was for Paul. It is most likely then that Paul would have wanted to tell George more about what he was feeling. This would have provided Paul with an opportunity to get his feelings off his chest and in the process, with George listening and being sympathetic, Paul would have felt supported and attended to. Rather than being turned off by George, Paul would have felt "embraced" by his lover at a time when that was what he most needed. Later, Paul might have asked for George's thoughts about a plan of action. Then it would have been appropriate for George to offer his advice.

THE SILENT TREATMENT

Sometimes a couple's communication problem is about what seems to be the lack of it, as in the following example.

She was a rather pretty woman about thirty-six, neatly attired in a skirt and jacket. She carried herself stiffly, her face set in a scowl. When she sat down it was as if she were sitting at attention. Her partner, on the other hand, was somewhat loose-jointed, sprawling rather than sitting on the couch. She wore blue jeans, a T-shirt emblazoned with a political slogan, and long, dangling earrings.

It was their first visit to my office. I wasn't sure which one I had spoken to on the phone.

"Maxine?" I inquired.

The T-shirted one answered. "That's me. This is Sally."

"Hi, Sally." Sally nodded, almost imperceptibly. "Well," I said, "tell me why you are here."

There was a brief silence, then Maxine said, "She doesn't communicate."

I looked at Sally. She was staring straight ahead, her face now expressionless.

"Tell me what you mean," I said, "when you say, 'She doesn't communicate.' "

Maxine fixed me with an are-you-kidding look.

"She doesn't communicate. Look at her. She's been like this for a week. She doesn't speak."

I looked at Sally. She continued to stare, expressionless, at the opposite wall.

"Well," I said, "she may not be speaking, but she certainly is communicating something."

"Pissed is what she is," Maxine said, "but she won't communicate."

"You mean she won't talk to you about her anger."

"She won't talk to me about anything. She won't communicate," Maxine insisted.

I decided to try Sally. "Sally, are you angry at Maxine?"

Sally responded by turning her head slightly away from Maxine's direction. She continued to stare at the wall.

Maxine shouted, elated at this demonstration. "You see, she doesn't communicate."

I quietly repeated, "She is communicating. She just isn't speaking."

Then I asked Maxine to tell me what she understood about why Sally was angry. There followed a tale of sexual infidelity, betrayal, and promises broken (Maxine's) and angry recriminations, threats of abandonment and, finally, violent retaliation (Sally's). Maxine told me of the clothes thrown out the door and the telephone ripped off the wall. Sally's communication was, if nothing else, intense and dramatic. It just wasn't verbal. She was acting out her anger rather than talking about it. Her partner was left to decode the messages she was sending through her actions. In the case of the clothes and the telephone, that decoding was not hard to do. Sally was indeed pissed. And Maxine certainly knew what she was angry about, but now, locked into her silence, Sally was communicating a complex of feelings, leaving her partner frustrated as to what they were.

Maxine asked, "Come on, honey. I just want us to be together. I made a mistake, but it's over now. It will never happen again, I swear. I want us to be happy the way we were before. Talk to me."

Sally sat, silent and impassive. What was her silence saying? Was she angry? Was she hurt, disappointed, demeaned? What did she want to happen? What did she need? What did she want Maxine to do now? How did she want things to be different between them in the future? By acting out her feelings through her chilling silence, she effectively punishes Maxine, but ineffectively communicates her feelings. She does gain the upper hand, but to what advantage?

Mutely, Sally stares down the wall, her only truly readable message, "I am not available." It is a particularly maladaptive way of communicating, though it is most certainly communication.

If I could have rewritten that session with Sally and Maxine, I would have Sally expressing her anger toward Maxine in *words*. She would tell Maxine exactly what she is angry about, just how angry she is, and specifically what she needs from Maxine now, and in the future. Maxine would allow Sally to have her anger. She would listen carefully to what Sally had to say about what she needed. She would supply that need in the present and convey that she understood what Sally wanted from her in the future. In future sessions, they would talk through what had been happening in their relationship that might have led Maxine to do what she did. They might express feelings they had not expressed before. They would each say what they needed and were not getting from the other person. They would work out, together, alternatives to what each was doing that troubled the other. They would, in other words, allow one another a deeper knowledge of who they were. They would, in the end, strengthen the foundation of their partnership.

This is a very different story from what I saw. Sally never emerged from her stony silence, then, or in the two subsequent sessions I had with them. Maxine finally gave up and left the relationship. Sally decided to stay on in therapy and was able to explore the experiences of her early life that made it so difficult for her, as an adult, to talk about her feelings. Sally's parents had paid very little attention to her as a child. When she talked they didn't listen, so she stopped talking. No one was interested in her feelings so she concluded, in her child's way, that she should try to ignore them also. She had grown into an adult who had never learned to talk about feelings and, often, did not even know what her feelings were. She had trained herself well. But, she had been pained by her experience with Maxine and she realized that she needed to learn to communicate better. As she was able to un-derstand the reasons for her inability to express feelings directly, she was gradually able to gain more access to her own emotional life and to verbalize what she was feeling rather than having to act it out.

TALKING ABOUT CHILDHOOD

I have often been surprised, talking with couples who have come to me for help, to learn that they know relatively little about each other's childhoods. "Why is that true?" I ask. "We never talk about it," they answer. "Why not?", I ask. "It never occurred to us," they answer. The slow unraveling of a person's early history can often fill in the necessary missing pieces in the jigsaw puzzle that our partner's personality presents to us: "Ah, this piece fits here—the reticence to do this or that which I have never understood, and that piece fits there—the tendency to do that particular thing in a way that I have always found to be so unusual. It all becomes clearer now."

The process of discovery enlightens and provides a backdrop against which the person you thought you knew stands out, with added dimension. It helps to know what those early dreams were, those early illusions about life, the fantasies that shadow present reality. Talk about one's childhood can be superficial, but in-evitably those lingering images emerge to tell the tale of who the child really was. If you talk long enough about it, the deeper emo-tions attached to childhood experience surface and can be brought into the adult relationship to enrich the emotional bond that is already there between partners. Talking about childhood is a vehicle for communicating intimate aspects of who one is. I recommend it for couples interested in becoming closer.

We have all, at one time or another, been willing conspirators in maintaining the silence that has surrounded "our secret love." This is particularly true for people who lived any significant part of their gay or lesbian life prior to the 1970s, when concealment of one's sexual orientation was almost universally accepted as being necessary to the survival of one's career, family relationships, and standing in the community at large. We covered up the truth about our personal lives. We hid our relationships from the world. Any self-disclosure had the potential of being dangerous because there might be a slip, the discrediting reality being revealed. Self-disclosure was carefully monitored, and for many the ability to be self-disclosing came to be seriously inhibited as a result. Avoiding self-revelation became habitual. It didn't stop with how the self was presented to the world outside private life. It permeated even the most personal of relationships. I believe it continues to be a factor in the communication of many gay and lesbian couples, especially if they were adults prior to the contemporary gay and lesbian rights movement. If, for instance, you remember the reasons people gave in chapter 4 for withholding something important from their lovers, they sound exactly like the kinds of reasons people give for not disclosing to important people in their lives that they are gay. "I didn't think she would understand, and that would devastate me." "I was afraid he would stop loving me if he knew this." "It didn't seem important at first, and then I couldn't tell her because I waited too long." "I didn't want him to know too much about me. That would have given him too much leverage."

If this describes you, you would do well to consider a possible connection between the style with which you had to communicate from the closet and the style with which you communicate in your partnership. I believe this connection, where it exists, can be broken.

What is required is a special willingness to give up the relative safety of keeping your most personal thoughts and feelings to yourself and a special effort to communicate with your partner in more self-revealing ways than you have in the past.

6

"WHO'S IN CHARGE, NOW?"

THE ALPHA-WOLF ROLL-OVER

I must admit I was appalled the first time I was instructed to execute the "alpha-wolf roll-over"* on a one and a half pound puppy.

"Don't worry," the kindly Puppy Lady said, "we aren't going to hurt them."

The Puppy Lady, as we called her, had been hired to train us and our two ten-week-old Yorkshire Terrier puppies to something resembling a collaborative partnership.

"Now, first," she said, fixing us with a determined stare, "you must show them who is boss in this relationship. You must *dominate* them. Dogs, you see, are descended from wolves. In the social structure of the wolf pack the leader is the alpha-wolf. He maintains his place at the top of the pecking order through certain dominance rituals, one of which we are going to borrow to show these little wolves who's in charge here. You are the alpha-wolf and you are going to roll these puppies over onto their backs, exposing their soft underbellies. You are then going to hold them in this vulnerable position, looking them right in the eyes. They will soon look away from you, signaling that they sub-

---

* A training method originally recommended by the Monks of New Skete in *How to Be Your Dog's Best Friend* (Boston: Little, Brown & Co., 1978).

mit to your greater power. With the roll-over, you will have established that you are the alpha-wolf, that you will lead, and they will follow."

She then placed tiny Minnie on her back, encircled her two-inch throat between thumb and forefinger, and covered Minnie's abdomen with a broad palm. She kneeled beside the floored and flattened Minnie and stared into her tiny eyes.

"You'll have to learn who's boss here." And with that, she shook Minnie's little body while emitting a loud and guttural "PFUI!!!" (I later learned that "pfui" is a German exclamatory word frequently used by dog trainers.)

Minnie stared in astonishment at the Puppy Lady and went limp, promptly averting her eyes in the centuries-old gesture of submission understood immediately by other canines, writers of dog training books, and puppy ladies.

"Ha!" the Puppy Lady said. "You see how easy that was. Now she is ready to be trained. Now she knows who is giving the orders here."

The Puppy Lady released Minnie and picked up her sister, Max. She rolled Max over onto her back, encircled her tiny neck and flattened her palm against Max's abdomen. She fixed Max with a piercing gaze, gave her little body a shake and shouted fiercely, "PFUI!!!" Max screeched in protest and began to wiggle from head to toe.

"PFUI!!! PFUI!!! PFUI!!!" the Puppy Lady shouted. Max stopped wiggling for five seconds, looking for all the world as if she were going to open her mouth and say, "What is with you, lady?" She then began to squirm and kick and squeal without stopping for a good five minutes. The Puppy Lady persevered, alternately shaking Max and bellowing, "PFUI!!! PFUI!!! PFUI!!!"

Half an hour later Max was still staring defiantly into the Puppy Lady's eyes and squirming, kicking, and squealing.

"I don't know what's the matter with this dog. I've never seen a dog resist this much. This is amazing." The Puppy Lady was quite breathless by now. Max appeared to be just getting her second wind.

"They have to be dominated, you know, or it will be very difficult to train them. You're going to have to spend time each day dominating Max until she submits. She has to know who is in charge. It's for her own good."

The Puppy Lady took advantage of a momentary respite in Max's battle against domination.

"There," she said, letting go of the dog. "That isn't good enough, but it will do for right now."

Max stared her straight in the eye, obviously proud of herself. The Puppy Lady stared back at the one and a half pound dog. Clearly it had been a draw. She then picked the puppy up in a gentler, but no less effective expression of dominance and brought Max's face opposite her own. Max's tiny tongue flipped up and down against the Puppy Lady's nose.

"You see, she has no hard feelings." She nuzzled Max and cooed appreciatively at Max's kisses.

The Puppy Lady always left us with written instructions for the week's training assignments. The first day after her visit I stared at what she had written. "Dominate Max every day for at least half an hour."

I couldn't believe I was going to do this to my poor little dog, but I remembered the Puppy Lady's words: "It's for her own good."

I proceeded to roll Max over onto her back, encircled her neck, flattened my hand against her abdomen and pressed down gently, saying "Pfui!" Max, with an oh-no-not-this-again look began squirming and squealing. I pressed harder. I made my voice more stern, "Pfui!" Max wiggled. I leaned in close, stared into her eyes, shook her hard, and shouted, "PFUI!!!" Max wiggled. I thought, I have to dominate this dog. I am a fully grown adult human being, and this a one-and-a-half pound puppy.

Max squealed, squirmed, and kicked her little legs up and down. She twisted her head from side to side. She flailed her forepaws in the air. After ten minutes I began to feel desperate. I was getting nowhere, but I couldn't give up. I envisioned fifteen years of ongoing combat with this dog. I persisted and quit only when saved by the clock. Half an hour was enough for both of us. Max retired to her puppy pen and I to a deep chair to contemplate the meaning of it all.

Little dogs are devoid of the knowledge of the world that they need to protect them from a myriad of dangers. They are therefore dependent on their human owners to supply that protection. In order for the owners to carry out their responsibility, there must be established a kind of dominance hierarchy that can be activated at any moment. The dog must know that the human is in charge. The dog must be programmed to follow any order forthcoming from the human. It may very well be the command that will save its life. When that is the case there is no time for rebelliousness or battles for independence. The order of the day is immediate obedience. Dominance training sets the stage for that. It is clearly for the dog's own good—an understandable rationale for what may seem like a rather harsh and unfair piece of business.

DOMINANCE RITUALS, HUMAN STYLE

Thinking about all of this brought to mind the many kinds of dominance rituals human beings perform with one another in their everyday lives, particularly in their intimate relationships. What is the rationale here, I wondered? The issue of protection from the dangers of the world does not apply with two adult women or two adult men in a consensual relationship. There is no clear-cut reason for one partner in such a relationship to have dominance over the other. And yet, the amount of time and energy that often goes into rituals of dominance between intimate partners is impressive. Usually these battles for dominance are benign and are carried on as a subtext to the conflicts that arise out of the couple's everyday life together.

Sometimes, however, they are of a more prominent order, seriously impacting on the dominated partner's sense of self-worth. Typical of such dominance rituals are the following:

- The affluent member of a couple regularly reminds the nonearning or low income partner of the inequality of his/her financial contribution to the relationship
- The much-in-demand successful professional partner never lets it be forgotten how important his/her work is and the priority it must take over practically everything else in the relationship
- One partner relishes the wonderful surprise trips given to a cherished lover, who is never consulted or given a choice but always expected to be delighted and grateful to be so well treated
- The partner with the well-advertised strong sex drive insists on having sex at any time of the day or night, without regard for the state of mind or body of his/her partner

Why do some people need to go to such lengths to demonstrate power over their partner? Why do we all need to struggle so often with issues of control in our personal life?

THE INFLUENCE OF EARLY EXPERIENCE

The struggle for mastery over our fate begins at the moment of expulsion from the warm comfort of the mother's womb. We squawk in protest, but it is too late. From that moment on life is a battle to exert enough control over our environment, in one way or another, to get our needs met.

Our early experiences are important. They shape our expectations for what is to come in relationships for the rest of our lives. In the beginning, our survival depends on the fallible people who are our parents, or parent substitutes. If these people do a creditable job of meeting our needs, it is likely we will grow up to believe that the people on whom we become dependent are trustworthy and of good will. We will be individuals who do not have an excessive need for control of the people around us because we trust their caring and conscientiousness. Our early models taught us to be able to do that.

If, on the other hand, our early models were not able to meet our practical and emotional needs adequately, we are likely to grow up preoccupied with issues of power and control, which become equated with survival. Who will feed me, change me, pay attention to me evolves into who will respond to me sexually, care about what happens to me, attach to me, love me? These individuals often find partners on whom they allow themselves to be dependent because these partners are relatively controllable. Deep down these people seriously doubt that they are worthy of the love and attention they seek. After all, their early messages, inadvertent or not, told them they were not important or not lovable enough to be attended to in the way they needed to be. They usually compensate for this by making themselves in some way compelling and powerful to the people around them. Paradoxically, it is this very exertion of power and control that often gets them into trouble and results in the rejection they so fear will happen again. If, however, they are able to find a partner whose need is to be controlled, the relationship may be quite workable and enduring. The problems occur when the fit is not so complementary, or when the dominance-submission needs of either partner change and the pattern of the relationship is not modified to accommodate to that change.

CONTROL ISSUES ARE UNIVERSAL

The issues of power and control, phantomlike, invade our relationships and occupy their territory. I say phantomlike because they are so often an invisible presence in our transactions with our lovers. The surface issues may be money, sex, division of labor, decisions about with whom time is spent, house rules, degree of commitment, or where to go on vacation, but the underlying questions are, "Will we do it my way or your way?" or "Who's in charge here?"

We all struggle with issues of control in our relationships. How much control do you need to hang onto in order to protect your individual identity, your freedom, privacy, ability to make self-determined choices? How much control is it safe to give up with any particular individual?

You think, "If I give up control over my money and material goods to my lover, will he squander them, cheat, steal, ruin me?" "If I let down my defenses, will she take advantage of me or hurt me?" "If I give him my love, will he cherish it?" "If I let her know what I need from her, will she understand and respond?" Tiny choice points. We pass them everyday. We return to them over and over. New versions, new questions, new levels of concern, but always back to the same issues of how much control am I willing, able, ready to give up? How much control do I need to maintain in order to protect myself, to protect my partner from myself, to keep our relationship viable?

Sometimes we overcontrol, taking too much responsibility for decisions, fostering unwanted dependency. When we over-control in the relationship, we are in danger of choking off spontaneity and growth. The overcontrolled partner might give up, become passive (maybe aggressively so), stop trying to influence outcomes.

John is a traffic manager in a large shipping firm. He loves his work so much that he goes right on doing it after he gets home. He decides where he and his lover will go to dinner, what trips they will take for vacations, and which friends they will see on social occasions.

John's partner, Doug, is an agreeable type, rather passive, and somewhat in awe of John's perpetual ability to make plans and implement them. If John plans something that Doug doesn't like he never says anything about it. He either finds a reason not to participate, or he goes along halfheartedly, his lack of enthusiasm being attributed to anything but his dissatisfaction with John's planning.

Doug has long since given up even trying to make choices in his relationship with John. It's just much easier to leave everything to John. Actually, Doug feels somewhat stuck in his life, but he is not inclined to put any energy into figuring out why he feels that way.

John, on the other hand, has grown weary of always being in charge of the couple's life. He asks Doug where he would like to go to dinner. Doug says, "I don't know. What do you suggest?" He asks Doug where he would like to go on their next vacation, Doug says, "I don't know. Wherever you want to go." So John goes right on making all the decisions. It comes naturally to him to do so. Neither John nor Doug is really happy with the arrangement, but neither is willing to give up doing what is most comfortable to him.

Sometimes control is abdicated *too* easily by one of the partners, causing the other to resent having to carry so much of the burden of decision making. Often this person is a natural leader, accustomed to being in control, doing it almost automatically, perhaps. But, how often I have heard just such a person protesting that he/she is tired of always having to make all the decisions for what happens in the couple's life.

THE INFLUENCE OF CULTURAL CONDITIONING

How we relate to issues of power and control in a relationship is a function not only of individual development, but also of cultural conditioning.

In our society, dominance of one person or one group over another is highly valued. It is praiseworthy to be the boss, the leader, the captain, the chief, the chairperson, the president. Men dominate women, the haves dominate the have-nots, whites dominate nonwhites, the educated dominate the under-educated.

We speak of people as winners or losers. There is unremitting emphasis on winning. "Who won?" we hear repeated over and over. It could be the game, the prize, the ratings, the business, the war. Competition is a way of life in our society. We are conditioned to see life as a contest and other people as our adversaries. The competitive ethic is greatly prized. We are trained to it. It is built into our educational system. Competitiveness does prepare us for the contests of life. But how well does it prepare us for our intimate partnerships?

The competitive ethic, so prevalent in society, is actually the poorest preparation for the kind of trust-building that real intimacy requires. It is antithetical to the most important aspects of successful participation in an intimate partnership: the ability to open up and become *known* to another person, the willingness to be *vulnerable* to another, the valuing of *equality*, the commitment to *collaborating* rather than competing.

We grow up with the cultural imperative to be strong, to win, to be in control. Real intimacy requires use of the ability to be soft, to surrender, to relinquish our defenses. It is particularly tough for two men to go against their cultural conditioning. I am amazed at—and sometimes despairing of—the lengths to which many men will go to avoid the very conditions that will make their relationship work: openness, vulnerability, equality, and collaboration. They are following their cultural conditioning and making their partnership an uphill climb, which it shouldn't have to be.

Another way in which intimate partnerships are affected by culturally determined attitudes toward power and control derives from the transfer of prerogatives many people make from their occupational roles to their home life. For instance, physicians tend to be particularly controlling with their partners, especially if those partners are in less prestigious occupations. The same is true of successful professionals, executives and people who wield authority, hold the fate of others in their hands, take major responsibility for decision making in their everyday work life. These people tend to carry over their "take charge" attitude and behavior into their relationship with lovers. They are so accustomed to solving other people's problems and to giving orders that they just go right on doing it after hours as though the only transition between office and home was one of geography. They have a hard time making the transition from authority figure to peer.

The less dominant partner might be a willing conspirator to this arrangement. Sometimes, the ability of the professionally successful dominant partner to provide an elaborate lifestyle is compensation enough for giving up the prerogatives of equal partnership. Perhaps having a dominant partner who acts *in loco parentis* (in place of the parent) is just what the person wanted.

The problems come when an affluent lifestyle no longer compensates for the inability to participate fully in decision making about the couple's life, or when the dominated partner no longer needs a parent figure. If the partners involved are able to recognize what is happening and renegotiate the balance of power in their relationship, a deeper and richer union can result. If they are not able to do this, they are in trouble. The dominated, dissatisfied partner may retreat into alcoholism or drugs, or illness, or transient love affairs. Or, he or she may just retreat, unable to confront the more powerful partner.

VICTIM POWER

Often an underground power struggle develops that becomes the subtext to much that goes on in the couple's life together. If the power struggle is not out in the open, it might involve bids for control that are more covert than overt: for instance, the power of the victim who gets others to do his/her bidding out of pity or guilt. These people do not directly demand control, but they shape other's responses to them by being needy, helpless, put upon, or in some other way victims of life. Victim power is especially difficult to deal with in a relationship because of the contradiction it sets up in terms of what is required of the partner to avoid becoming the victim of the victim. To have one's life controlled by the excessive needs of one's lover is oppressive enough. To have to hold back on loving behavior because it can reinforce a partner's inclination to be the victim is doubly draining.

For instance, Alice has accidents. She doesn't mean to. She doesn't want to, but, with some regularity, she meets disaster of one kind or another. Alice is an "accident-prone" person.

Once, Alice threw her back out carrying her German shepherd to the vet. The dog had a thorn in his paw. He was okay the next day. Alice was in bed for a week. Martha, her lover, had to wait on her hand and foot.

Another time, Alice crashed her car into a light pole on a traffic island, because she was trying to write down something interesting she'd heard on the car radio. She wasn't injured but it took weeks to get the car repaired during which time Martha had to drive her to and from work.

On other occasions, Alice burned and cut her fingers while cooking, hammered her thumb black and blue while putting up some bookshelves, and sprained her wrist trying to imitate a shot-putter she'd seen on television. Alice used a boulder that was too large and too heavy for shot-putting.

All of these injuries prevented Alice from being able to function in the kitchen for weeks at a time, making it necessary for Martha to do all the cooking and the dishwashing.

In the beginning of their relationship, Martha was very sympathetic toward Alice when she had her "accidents," but after several years of chauffeuring Alice to work, doing double duty in the kitchen, and playing nurse to Alice's patient, Martha came to see the pattern in Alice's behavior. When Alice was having a hard time in some department of her life, rather than asking for a little extra attention, she had an accident. Then Martha had to take care of her and the need that Alice had for tender loving care was met, but always at a cost to Martha. Martha became the victim of the victim. She decided to do something about it. She tried to talk to Alice about her insight, but Alice brushed her off, saying that no such thing was happening, that it was all in Martha's imagination.

Then, Martha took action, or, more accurately, she stopped taking action. When Alice had an accident, Martha virtually ignored it, which was not always easy since Alice usually made it very clear that she was suffering and needed attention. Martha had to hold back whatever feelings of sympathy she had. She didn't like behaving in this way, but she felt sure that her solicitousness and caretaking in response to Alice's accidents were encouraging their occurrence. Martha resented it every time she had to inhibit her natural feeling of compassion for a person close to her in trouble, but inhibit she did.

Alice continued to have accidents. Sometimes Martha would make the observation to Alice that her accidents seemed to come at times when she was particularly stressed about something. After a while Alice admitted that this did seem true. Martha encouraged Alice to *tell* her when she was troubled about something rather than having an accident to get the attention, she needed. Alice said she would try. Martha also tried to be as sensitive as she could to what Alice was experiencing in her life so she could give her the extra attention she needed at those times. Eventually, Alice's accidents diminished, much to the relief of both partners.

VETO POWER

Another covert means of control in a relationship is through use of veto power. The less powerful partner may veto sex, affection, plans, even conversation, anything that requires his or her cooperation in order to make it happen. I watch the guerrilla warfare that goes on with a lot of the couples I work with when one partner has more of something significant—money, prestige, visibility, or influence—than the other. The have-not partner uses her/his veto power over the intangibles in the relationship—sex, affection, understanding, acceptance, support—in order to to equalize the power balance.

The veto is all-powerful. No matter how much *overt* power one partner may have due to wealth, superior intelligence, accomplishment, physical attractiveness, or professional status, the application of *covert* control in a relationship can more than even things out when it comes to *de facto* decision making. The only remedy for this frustrating situation is to bring the power struggle into the open so that a rebalancing can be directly negotiated.

CONTROL AS A DEFENSE AGAINST INTIMACY

Often when couples are locked in a power struggle that permeates their relationship, I find it useful to ask them to imagine what their relationship would be like if they did not spend so much time trying to control one another. Of course, they must first be able to see that there *is* a struggle for control. Then, when they explore what a relationship free of such a struggle might be like for them, they very often acknowledge anxiety about increased intimacy. They might be dealing with a fear of becoming too vulnerable, of not being able to handle more closeness, of becoming known to another in a way they never have to anyone before. It is difficult for men together, less so for lesbians. Lesbians, in general, seem much better prepared through their early conditioning as women to trust the bond of relationship, to open themselves to one another, to tolerate growing intimacy, to form a collaborative unit based on affection and trust. Male couples have to work harder at it, their competitive conditioning predisposing them more to a dominance-submission model of relating.

THE PARTNERSHIP OF PARITY

I would like to focus now on what I see as the major alternative to the dominance-submission model for two people in an intimate partnership. It is the *partnership of parity* in which *democratic rights* hold at least as high a priority for the partners as their need to compete, or their need to be in control.

In the partnership of parity, *negotiation* is the mechanism of choice for correcting power imbalances, for resolving conflict, and for the continual updating of the couple's mutual goals and objectives. Parity means equality. A partnership of parity is one in which there is always willingness to negotiate change if either partner feels the need for such change.

In the 1970s, a creative and enterprising group of behavioral scientists at San Francisco State University's Center for Homosexual Education, Evaluation and Research (CHEER) undertook a large-scale study* of the abridgment of the civil rights of gay and lesbian people.

One aspect of that study dealt with the conflict between democratic rights versus psychological needs in two-person, same-sex relationships. The researchers suggested that there were democratic rights that needed to be protected in relationships between two people, just as such rights needed to be protected in relationships between a person and an institution, such as a government. They defined these rights as follows:

Participation in Decision Making is the right of each party to make and implement decisions and rules that govern the relationship.

Equality is the right of each party to the same opportunities in the relationship.

Dissent is the right to disagree, criticize, and protest.

Due Process is the right to hear and answer charges of wrongdoing before punishment is considered or imposed.

It is inevitable in the two-person relationship, as it is in the relationship between a person and an institution, that certain psychological needs will come into conflict with these democratic rights.

In the CHEER study, the psychological needs deemed most likely to conflict with democratic rights were the needs for power, dependency, and competition, defined as follows:

Power is the need of one person to control the decisions and actions of another person.

Dependency is the need of one person to submit to the decisions and actions of another person.

Competition is the need of one person to attract more attention or gain more favor than another person.

While the CHEER study was only exploratory and did not produce conclusive results, it did provide a rather interesting way of

---

* John P. DeCecco and Michael Shively, "A Study of Perceptions of Rights and Needs in Interpersonal Conflicts in Homosexual Relationships." *Journal of Homosexuality* Vol. 3, no. 3 (Spring 1978).

looking at the needs versus rights problem in couple relationships. For instance, one person's need to be the powerful person in the relationship, to control a partner's actions, might seriously compromise that partner's right to equal participation in decision making or to the ability to dissent effectively or to defend adequately against charges of wrongdoing—power *needs* versus democratic *rights*.

Paradoxically, one person's need to be dependent on another could make it very difficult for a partner trying to maintain a democratic climate in a relationship. The dependent partner might fight being an equal participant in decision making, might avoid dissension even when it is in order, or might even refuse to defend against charges of wrongdoing. The refusal to address problems ensures that nothing different will happen, which is then used to reinforce the dependent individual's conviction that he or she is powerless to effect change. The clash of one partner's dependency needs with the other partner's democratic rights can be as insidiously undermining to a relationship as that caused by the clash of power needs with democratic rights.

The same is true of competition needs. If one or both partners has a strong need to compete, to "do it better" than the other partner, it can make it very difficult to maintain equal participation in decision making. One will need to go further, to win, to have the final word. Equality will not be enough. Dominance will be the objective sought. The psychological *need* to compete compromises the democratic *right* to equal access and collaborative decision making with regard to the opportunities for fulfillment in the relationship. If my predominant need is to win over you, I am more likely to block your opportunities for equal participation, effective dissent, or due process for defending yourself.

Think about your own relationship. Have there been instances in which the psychological need for power, dependency, or competition, on either person's part, has come into conflict with the other person's democratic right to participate in decision making, enjoy equality of opportunity, dissent, or have access to due process in defense against accusation? If you can identify clear instances of such conflict, it might be helpful to talk with your partner about your thoughts on these issues.

NEGOTIATION

In the partnership of parity the democratic rights of participation in decision making, equality, dissent, and due process are held in high esteem. When psychological needs clash with these rights the mechanism of choice for dealing with the conflict is negotiation.

Negotiation is the process by which parties to a conflict define the issues about which they are in conflict, and trade proposals for resolution of that conflict. In successful negotiations, solutions are developed that satisfy each party's needs sufficiently to enable them to continue their relationship in the same or an improved way.

More often than not, negotiation involves change. Somebody doesn't like the way somebody else is doing something. What are they going to do about it? If the people involved are able to agree on the definition of the problem and are able to talk about what they want to happen, they have a chance to achieve resolution. Sometimes when I talk to couples about improving their negotiating skills, they object to the very idea of negotiation. "Too cold," they say, "too antagonistic." They think of negotiations between labor and management, or governments in conflict. They don't want to think of their relationship as one of two parties-in-conflict. However, unavoidably, on occasion any partnership becomes two parties-in-conflict. The more directly and openly the conflict is dealt with, the more workable the alliance is likely to be when there is no conflict occurring.

I believe the ability to negotiate well, in a relationship, is crucial to a couple's well-being, and this is particularly true when there is a power imbalance of any order. I have, therefore, developed the following guidelines for good negotiating. As you read these guidelines, imagine yourself negotiating with your partner about something in your relationship that one of you would like to see change.

GOOD NEGOTIATING MOVES

If You Are the Person Asking for Change:

Spend some time thinking through, as specifically as possible, what you want by way of change.

"I just want to be treated more like an equal" won't cut it. You are more likely to get the equal treatment you want if you can spell out the specifics. Whether you want time, money, attention, more to say about decisions, or recognition of the importance of your endeavors, you enhance your negotiating position by being specific about the change you'd like to see.

Tell your partner directly what you want to see changed, why, and how you feel about it.

One is more likely to be taken seriously and responded to positively if requests for change have been clearly thought out, reasons for wanting change explained, and the effect on one's emotions shared. Such a thorough and rational approach can set the tone of the negotiation to be one of reasoned discussion. Too often people convince themselves that they are going to lose this battle, or that their partner is going to get angry at having the boat rocked. They go into the negotiation feeling defeated, betrayed, put down. They are already angry at the partner and express this anger even as they present their proposal for change. The partner then feels under attack and responds to that more than to the proposal being made. Or, the person is so frightened of what might come of the confrontation that he/she goes " 'round Robin's barn" trying to make it. The resulting lack of directness leaves the partner on the receiving end confused about what is going on.

If your partner appears not to understand what you want, clarify your proposal.

Don't jump the gun and assume you are being met with rejection if there is not immediate agreement. Ask if there is anything you've said that isn't understandable and be prepared to elaborate if necessary.

If your partner rejects your proposal, be prepared to modify it.

While you may feel like punching her/him out, or running screaming from the room, don't. At least, not yet. Give your partner, and yourself, a chance to work through whatever objections there are. Be alert to how you can compromise your position and still get much of what you want. THE IMPORTANT THING HERE IS NOT WINNING; IT IS EFFECTING CHANGE THAT WILL MAKE YOUR RELATIONSHIP WORK BETTER IN THE LONG RUN.

Stay targeted on the issues you have identified and the changes you want to see happen.

Resist the temptation to get into recriminations about past behavior when it feels as if things aren't going your way. Don't get into a contest about who is the most stubborn and unyielding, or stupid, or crazy. Don't let the discussion slip into territory that is safe but irrelevant to your proposal. If that happens, gently bring the discussion back to what you are trying to get changed.

Stay with the negotiation.

No matter how frustrated, discouraged, or angry you feel about how the negotiation is going, try to elicit counterproposals from your partner. Listen to what he/she is saying to you. Compromise. Modify. Counterpropose. Try to stay with the discussion until you have reached a resolution that is satisfactory to both of you.

If You Are the Person Being Asked to Change:

Listen carefully to what your partner is saying to you. Get the full story before you begin to react.

Ask for clarification if there is anything you don't understand about what your partner is proposing.

We all get a little defensive when confronted with the dissatisfaction that someone close to us feels with us. What else could it mean but that we are doing something wrong? We may be, but there is life after confrontation. That is what we are interested in here. Try to keep your mind as well as your ears open and ask for clarification if you feel as if you are missing something in what is being said to you.

Make a counterproposal if what is being asked of you is unacceptable.

Show your partner that you have heard what's been said and you are willing to be reasonable about it even if the proposal being made is unacceptable to you. Be willing to make a counterproposal that addresses the *need* that is being expressed. You may not wish to sell the house and move to a sheep farm in New Zealand, but you can respond to your partner's need to have a change of scene in his/her life in some way. Travel more? New friends? Less time devoted to work? Perhaps a couple of woolly sheepdogs will do it. (But don't knock yourself out with your own humor. There is probably a serious need being expressed here and you should take it seriously.)

You, too, should be willing to modify your counterproposal if it is unacceptable.

Don't get into a contest to see who can be the most stubborn. You'll both be the winners if you can reach a mutually satisfying compromise. There are no prizes for winning by holding out here, only detriment to your life as a couple.

Stay targeted.

There is no time to drag in everything that has been bugging you about your partner for the past six months. It is also no time to start a discussion about what happened to you at work today, or who's going to talk to the new neighbor about his all-night parties. Stay targeted on the issues.

Stay with it.

It is so easy to run away from the tough transactions of our lives. That way we never find out if we were up to doing what was being asked of us. We all need to be a little braver, about sticking it out and working it through in our relationships. Stay with the negotiation.

BAD NEGOTIATING MOVES

With the hope that you will be able to identify your own bad negotiating moves, I offer the following descriptions of such moves that I find to be most common with couples. (They are not mutually exclusive, and often overlap.)

Being indirect about what you want.

People do this in the hope that they can get some kind of reading from a partner on how acceptable their proposal is going to be without actually making it and having to take responsibility for it. This move usually leads to confusion and an aborted effort toward change since the information is too incomplete, or too indirect, to convey accurately what is desired by way of change.

For example, Rona wants to stay home alone more with her partner, just the two to them, no other people around, but she's afraid to bring it up to Caroline because she knows that Caroline loves being around a lot of people. So Rona decides to "test the waters."

"You know, I really envy Pam and Paula. They seem to have such a wonderful time together, just being alone with each other."

Caroline says, "I can't believe they don't get bored with one another, spending all that time together. Thank God *we* have a stimulating social life."

Rona tries again. "Then there's Marilyn and Karen. They party so much. They must never be alone with each other. I'll bet there's not much depth in their relationship."

Caroline responds, "Whaddya mean, 'depth'? They have a good time. They know some very interesting people. They are deeply involved in their social life. There's some depth for you."

Rona is getting irritated. "You are just being contrary."

Caroline says, "Contrary to what? We have two different opinions, that's all."

Rona, angry: "That's not all. I really believe Pam and Paula have a much better relationship than Marilyn and Karen."

Caroline shrugs her shoulders. "So? You're entitled to your opinion."

Rona is getting nowhere fast because she is being indirect about what she wants. She knows what she wants. She "floated" the idea, and it sank out of sight. Caroline never really had a chance to respond to Rona's need to spend more time alone because Rona never made the proposal. Of course, we would all like our partners to be so finely tuned to us, so open to our needs, and so smart that they could always be relied upon to know what we *really* mean even when we don't say it straight out. But, alas, they usually are tuned to another station, oblivious to our inner rumblings, and not psychic enough to decipher the edited-out part of our messages. Being indirect is a bad negotiating move.

Getting locked into an adversarial position.

This means digging in one's heels, becoming more involved in winning than in reaching a resolution. This often occurs as a result of what has been called the "fixed-pie bias"* which assumes that there is only a fixed amount of the "pie" to divide up, and whatever one person gains, the other person loses. This bias most often dictates a distributive solution to problems. "I gain this much, which means that you lose that much," thereby designating a "winner" and a "loser."

For example, Jack wants to go to Europe for two weeks on the couple's next vacation. Fred says, "We can't afford to go to Europe. We need a new roof on the house."

Jack says, "To hell with the roof. We haven't been any place really interesting for ages. Let's go to Europe."

Fred shakes his head in disbelief. "Do you realize that the rains are coming? Do you want to be rained on in your own living room?"

"Yes," Jack says jauntily, "I have always wanted to be rained on in my own living room, since I was a little boy. C'mon, Fred. We'll put buckets around to catch the rain. We'll wear pots on our heads. At least, we'll have something interesting to talk about while we're being rained on."

---

* Max H. Bazerman (Graduate School of Management, Northwestern University), "Why Negotiations Go Wrong." *Psychology Today* (June 1986).

Fred bristles. "That's not funny, Jack. When you own a house you have to be prepared for these things. The roof has to come before a trip to Europe."

Jack's jaw is out now. "Well, I refuse to have the roof fixed this year if it means I can't go to Europe."

Fred pleads. "We can't do both. We don't have enough money."

"Then Europe it is. I refuse to spend one dollar on that damn roof."

"I refuse to go to Europe. I'm doing the roof."

Jack smiles. "Great. I hope you and your roof will be very happy. I am not going to spend my vacation money on a roof."

These partners have posed themselves against one another and gotten locked into adversarial positions that ensured they would get nowhere with their negotiation. The more productive alternative would be the *integrative* solution in which the needs of both parties are integrated into the solution. Win-win, rather than win-lose.

For instance, this discussion might have been more productive if Jack had acknowledged Fred's (legitimate) point of view, instead of making jokes about it. Jack's jokes cause Fred to become more stern in his lecture about the responsibilities of home ownership, which, in turn, causes Jack to become more defiant. At the point when Fred refers directly to the issue of their limited funds, Jack might have said something like, "Let's sit down and figure out just how much we can spare and how much each of these things would cost. Maybe there's a way to do both, like we could get a loan and pay off the roof over time and still take the trip to Europe."

The search for integrative solutions requires a willingness to consider the mix of issues all at once rather than looking at them one at a time. It also requires a willingness to relinquish being the victor in favor of being a partner in a collaboration.

Falling into the escalation trap.

This involves increasing demands in order to keep negotiations open or holding out too long on current demands to save face. Let us say that two partners are negotiating a new financial arrangement for their relationship. Henry would like to pool all their money. Dan would like to keep his money separate except for the "household account," to which both would contribute a fixed amount.

Henry suggests, "If we put our money together we won't have to have those nasty arguments anymore about who owes what to whom."

Dan says, "We don't have to have arguments. We just have to do more careful bookkeeping."

Henry frowns, "You are so business oriented. This isn't a business. I thought you agreed that we were going to show our trust for one another in this new arrangement."

Dan throws up his hands. "All right, I'll agree to put a significant amount of money into the household account and keep just enough in my personal account for miscellaneous expenses."

Henry asks, "Like what?"

Dan answers, "Like getting my clothes cleaned. Like buying toiletries. I don't know. Like . . . whatever."

Henry says, "No. You don't understand. All that comes out of the household account."

Dan says, exasperated, "That leaves me very little for my personal account."

"Well, actually, the way I have it figured," Henry answers, "you don't need that personal account at all. You can write yourself a household account check at the beginning of each week for your personal expenses. That will be your 'walking around money.' I'll do the same. That way we'll just need one account between us."

Dan is obviously troubled by this. "I think I'd better do it the other way around. I'll keep most of my money in my personal account and write a check once a week to the household account."

"Oh no you don't. That's just back to the present arrangement. You don't need a personal account at all."

Dan says, "I don't care for you telling me what I do or don't need. I think I don't even want a household account. Let's just keep our money completely separate and each pay his own way."

As with the "fixed-pie" bias, escalation tends to reduce the ability to problem-solve and to find the integrative solutions that are most productive.

If Henry had been listening more carefully he might have heard that the personal checking account had special importance to Dan. He might not then have been so quick to suggest that Dan didn't really need this account. When Dan objected outright to Henry's suggestion, Henry stepped up his insistence that the account be done away with. This caused Dan to want to abandon the negotiation altogether.

Their discussion might have been more productive if Henry and Dan had taken time to talk about Dan's feelings about not wanting to give up his personal account. Dan might then have felt less pushed and more understood and he might have been willing to work toward a compromise. Also, if Henry had been able to temper his position somewhat Dan might not have felt that he had to protect himself against what seemed like a significant loss to him. He might have been freer to consider Henry's reasons for what he was proposing, enabling a more thoughtful pursuit of a mutually satisfying solution.

Framing the outcome of the negotiation in terms of loss rather than gain. How you "frame" possibilities or outcomes in your mind can strongly influence what the outcome is. If I am fixated on what it will *cost* me to make concessions to you, what I will *lose,* I am less likely to make those concessions. If, on the other hand, I frame possible outcomes in terms of what I will *gain,* how I can *profit* if I make concessions to you, I am more likely to be open to integrative and productive solutions.

Mary and Judith are trying to negotiate a plan for a trip that will include a visit to Judith's family. Mary does not like Judith's family and would rather not visit them.

Judith says, "Look at it this way. It's only a few days and we'll be together."

Mary protests, "Sure, together under your mother's unblinking stare. I wonder if your mother closes her eyes when she sleeps. She stares at me constantly. It makes me very nervous."

Judith says, "Look, she's working it out. She's getting used to you. The more you go there the easier it will become."

Mary shakes her head. "If I go there I will be giving up a big chunk of my much needed vacation to be stared at by your mother."

"Think about how much pleasure you'll be giving me by making it possible for me to visit my family and still be with you."

"I'll be spending all that money to go and have your mother stare at me for four days."

Judith, ever hopeful: "We can take rides out in the country and see things we never see here in the city."

Mary, looking forlorn: "I'll be losing four days of my vacation."

Judith says, "You'll be making me very happy."

Mary answers, "I'll be a nervous wreck for the rest of the trip. I'll be throwing my vacation away." While Judith continues to frame her side of the negotiation in terms of what Mary would be gaining from the trip, Mary focuses only on what she would be losing. She is locked in, therefore, to her need to make no concessions to Judith. This negotiation goes nowhere.

Abandoning the negotiation.

This is the worst move of all.

In reading the following examples think about my guidelines for negotiating and the bad negotiating moves just described.

JEANINE AND MATTIE

Jeanine loved people. Having grown up in a large family, she felt most happy when her house was full of people. Before she met Mattie she had always entertained a lot. Her friends felt comfortable dropping in unannounced. She encouraged them to do so whenever they felt like it. She liked impromptu parties, as well as those that were planned elaborately. She often had houseguests, and being the gregarious person she was, she made friends wherever she went. She had a friendship network that spanned the country, and whenever anyone in it was headed her way they expected to stay with her. With all this socializing, Jeanine spent a significant amount of time on the telephone, planning, inviting, and arranging the events that filled her social calendar.

One Sunday afternoon, one of Jeanine's friends brought Mattie to a gathering at Jeanine's house. Jeanine was instantly attracted to the tall, dark-haired woman with the deepset eyes. Mattie seemed to like Jeanine also. They talked a long time about interests they had in common, and Jeanine invited Mattie to have dinner with her the following night. That was the beginning of a month-long courtship that culminated in Mattie's moving in with Jeanine.

At first, the constant flow of people in the house was interesting to Mattie. She had grown up as an only child, and she had always been something of a loner. Surrounded by Jeanine's friends, immediately accepted by them, she felt as if she had acquired an instant family, and it felt good to her. She enjoyed the parties and the out-of-town guests. There was always something new happening, always a lot to look forward to and a lot to talk about.

It wasn't until she had lived with Jeanine for about six months that Mattie began to realize that she didn't know her lover very well. Someone had asked her a question about what Jeanine was like when there weren't other people around, and Mattie found that she didn't have anything very cogent to say. They weren't alone that much. That realization started her thinking about their pattern of nonstop socializing. The more she thought about it, the more empty she felt inside. Though she knew Jeanine loved her, she felt as if she experienced that love in a rather shallow way. Jeanine was kind, thoughtful, and attentive, but their conversation was usually about people and events outside their relationship. They rarely talked about what was happening between them. There was not the curiosity about who she was that Mattie had felt from previous lovers. Jeanine just seemed to accept her as she experienced her, and that appeared to be enough. So, questions about her feelings, how she experienced life, what she thought about and how she felt about herself were never asked.

Mattie began to feel quite alone. The feeling grew over a period of months. She no longer enjoyed the people or the parties. She tried many times to get Jeanine to say no to prospective houseguests, to leave evenings free for just the two of them, to plan trips they might take alone. She was unsuccessful. Jeanine always had a reason for this special person to stay at the house, that important party being given, the need to include particular friends in the vacation being planned. Finally, Mattie brought her concern up with Jeanine.

"Honey, I think we need to look squarely at what is really going on in our lives. I am very unhappy because I never get to spend time alone with you. I have to share you with so many people. I feel as if I hardly know you."

Jeanine was obviously irritated. "Oh, come on, Mattie, we spend a lot of time together. What is all this nonsense about not knowing me?"

"We spend time together but not alone. There are things one just doesn't talk about with other people around."

"Mattie, that's ridiculous. We're all one big happy family. You can talk about anything in front of our friends."

"No, that isn't true. At least it isn't true for me. I need time alone with you. We have to figure out a way to make that happen, because I can't go on just being one of the 'family.' "

"Mattie, honey, you know me. I love people. I'm friendly. I'm outgoing. That doesn't mean I love you any less."

"I understand that, but I want us to live our lives a little differently. I want us to plan time to be alone. Is that so much to ask of a lover?"

Jeanine put her arms around Mattie. "Why, of course not, you just aren't as outgoing a person as I am. I understand that, but you are getting better. It just takes getting used to. You'll probably like it as much as I do before long."

Mattie pulled away from Jeanine.

"Jeanine, you're not listening to me. We have to figure out how to do this differently."

"Fine," Jeanine said. "I'm willing to do that. I want you to be happy."

"All right," Mattie answered. "Now I propose that we not have any more houseguests for the next six months, that we let people know they are welcome in our home only on an invited basis, and that we agree on two nights a week that are regularly just for us, with no other people around."

Jeanine looked stricken. "Are you kidding?"

Mattie looked her straight in the eye. "No. I am dead serious."

"Are you trying to make me lose all my friends?"

"No, I'm trying to make us into the lovers we should be."

"Well, I don't see why I have to give up my dear friends in order for us to be 'lovers.' Does it have to be either/or?"

"Jeanine, I'm not proposing you give up your friends. I'm proposing that we just rearrange our social schedule so we have time to be together."

"Well, I think you are being very cruel. You are forcing me to choose between you and my friends. That's quite unfair."

"Jeanine, I am not forcing you to choose between me and your friends." Mattie hesitated. "I am asking you to give up the buffer that your friends are between you and me. I'm asking you to give our relationship a chance to become more intimate."

Mattie took Jeanine's hand. "I love you. I am your friend. You don't have to hold me off. You are precious to me, and I only want to *be* more to you so that I can *do* more for you. Now, let's talk about how we can make that happen."

Jeanine shook her head. "I don't believe this. You think we have to become hermits to be more to one another. I just can't accept that."

Mattie felt her anger rising. "You think that asking for two nights a week to be alone, not having constant houseguests, and asking people to call before they drop in amount to being hermits? Come on, Jeanine!"

"It's not my fault that you don't like people, Mattie. I am not going to hang out the 'Not Welcome' sign to my friends just because you don't like to have people around as much as I do. I'm just not going to do that."

Mattie backed off. "Okay, then let's talk about *three* months of no houseguests and *one* night a week to be alone."

"No way, it all amounts to the same thing. It means I have to hang out the 'Not Welcome' sign to my friends."

Mattie took a deep breath. "Then you tell me what you think we might do to have more time alone together. You tell me what is acceptable to you."

Jeanine shrugged her shoulders. "I don't know, Mattie. I don't know. Maybe we just have to understand each other better. I like people. You don't like people. We'll just have to accept each other as we are, I guess."

Jeanine continued to reject Mattie's proposals out of hand. Mattie continued, on subsequent occasions, to try to engage Jeanine in negotiating this issue. Jeanine continued to be unresponsive. By turning a deaf ear to Mattie's feelings, Jeanine preserved the status quo, and not, incidentally, the level of intimacy in the relationship. She did not retain Mattie's love, either.

After several more unsuccessful tries at negotiation, Mattie gave up and left Jeanine to her parties and her friends. She realized that she needed to be with someone who at least was willing to negotiate mutually satisfying conditions for a relationship.

Let's look at what was right and what was wrong in this effort at negotiation.

Mattie was correct in articulating her feelings about what was happening between her and Jeanine and in making specific proposals for change. When Jeanine did not appear to understand the issue, Mattie clarified it for her: "I am not forcing you to choose between me and your friends. I am asking you to give up the buffer that your friends are between you and me. I'm asking you to give our relationship a chance to become more intimate."

When Jeanine indicated that Mattie's first proposal was unacceptable, Mattie presented a modified proposal, "Okay, then let's talk about *three* months of no houseguests and *one* night a week to be alone."

Mattie stayed on target with the discussion as long as she could.

Jeanine, on the other hand, stymied the negotiation by putting down Mattie's feelings: "What is all this nonsense about not knowing me?"

She also locked into an adversarial position: "We have to become hermits to be more to one another. I just can't accept that."

She framed possible outcomes as losses: "Are you trying to make me lose all my friends?"

By being unresponsive to Mattie's further efforts at negotiation, Jeanine, in the end, won the battle and lost the war.

How might a productive negotiation have gone? I suggest the following.

Mattie has thought through what she wants from Jeanine, and she has presented her feelings. Rather than the response Jeanine made in the first version, this time she might say, "I didn't know you were feeling that way. I'm really surprised. Tell me more."

When Mattie has expanded her statement, Jeanine might say, "I want to be sure I understand. Is it the people you object to or is it our not spending time alone together?"

When Mattie clarifies what the issue is, Jeanine might ask what her thoughts are about changing the situation. If Jeanine doesn't like Mattie's proposal, she might make a counterproposal, such as, "You know, I really have trouble with having to tell people they're not welcome in my home in the way they have always been. How about no houseguests for *one* month, rather than three? And, well, maybe *one* night a week when we don't see anybody else?"

That might prompt Mattie to say, "No, Jeanine, that's not acceptable. It still feels as if you are holding me off and giving your friends' needs a higher priority than mine."

To which Jeanine might respond, "I don't feel that way, but apparently it seems as if I do to you. I'm just so used to having a lot of people around. It doesn't mean I love you any less. I guess I haven't thought about it from your point of view before. How about this? You and I will make our plans for the week, and on the free nights that are left we'll be open to invitations or to having people over. How would that be for you?"

Mattie might say, "That's better. It feels more as if *we* would be at the center of our life together rather than our friends. How does it feel to you?"

"Fine," Jeanine might say, "though I'm still uncomfortable about hanging out the 'Not Welcome' sign to my friends."

Mattie would say, "I understand that and I don't want you to be uncomfortable. Let's work on a way to tell people what's happening so they don't feel we're rejecting them."

Jeanine would answer, "Okay. I'm still not comfortable with it, but I'm willing to work on it. I don't want my friends to feel rejected, but I don't want you to feel rejected by me either."

In the best of all worlds, Jeanine would have been able to open up the subject of her anxiety regarding increased intimacy, if only to say something like, "Mattie, what do you have in mind for us to do with all this time alone together?"

And Mattie might take that as permission to initiate a discussion of her understanding of Jeanine's ambivalence about becoming more dependent on just one person for emotional fulfillment.

This effort to correct a condition, with which one of these partners was dissatisfied, would then have had the potential of bringing both partners into a deeper and richer involvement with one another.

JOE AND HAL

Joe and Hal have been together for five years. Joe is a businessman whose yearly income is in the six figures. Hal is a commercial artist who makes a modest salary working for an advertising agency. From the beginning of their relationship they have kept their money separate. Joe pays the mortgage on the house they live in, but he lived in the house before he met Hal. Hal makes a monthly contribution to the utilities in an amount they both agreed on when Hal moved in. Joe pays for all of their trips and the lavish accommodations he is accustomed to, which are far beyond Hal's ability to afford. Usually Joe pays for their meals out. Hal takes them out to dinner when there is a special occasion, like Joe's birthday. Hal takes care of his own car expenses though he drives a car that is ten years old and is often in disrepair. Joe buys a new car every year and it is his car they use whenever they go anywhere together. Joe buys new clothes whenever he see something that catches his eye. Hal *cannot* afford to buy much on his salary, so he has to pass up clothing items that attract him. Joe often buys Hal clothes for his birthday, and he sometimes surprises him with clothing purchases. Hal always looks well dressed, though his clothes are usually not of his own choosing.

Hal's meager salary covers his medical insurance and incidental expenses, and at the end of the month he is pretty well wiped out financially. He has no savings and no investments. Joe has a portfolio of stock investments and real estate holdings. He also has an appreciable amount of available cash at all times.

Hal is ten years younger than Joe. He is good looking, fun to be around, loving, and easy to live with. Joe values Hal and feels happy in his relationship with him. One of the things he values most is Hal's independence. He likes the fact that Hal takes care of his own personal expenses and doesn't look to him for financial support. Joe is glad to pay for the house and the trips and the meals they share. He enjoys surprising Hal with gifts. He feels a little like a benevolent parent who enjoys giving to his son and at the same time highly values his son's ability to provide for himself. The financial arrangement between them is quite satisfactory to Joe.

Hal, on the other hand, has been experiencing a growing dissatisfaction with the way finances are handled in their relationship. At first, it was not important to him that Joe's resources were so much greater than his. He didn't care that Joe had a new car every year and a closet full of new clothes. He was truly in love with Joe, and more than anything he cared about their being together and having an enjoyable life. But something has been happening to Hal during the last few months. His car broke down again, and the repair bill was staggering. He barely had enough money to get through the month. The contrast between his precarious financial state and the surroundings in which he lived began to seem bizarre. After five years of being a devoted companion Hal began to think that he had earned the right to share more equally in Joe's wealth. His financial resources gave Joe a lot of power in their relationship. Hal found himself resenting Joe's money and the inordinate amount of control Joe had over their life. He wanted to talk to him about it, but he knew how important it was to Joe that he was as financially independent as he could be. He didn't want to rock the boat. He felt trapped and didn't know what to do.

Joe sensed that something was wrong with Hal, but he figured that Hal would either work it out on his own or come to him for help. It was not Joe's style to probe for information. His values dictated that people should be left alone to work out their own dilemmas. The strength to do that was an important part of what it meant to be a man. Joe had been brought up in a very traditional family in which the women were the caretakers. The women were expected to be emotional and to be interested in what was going on in everybody's lives, and the men were the providers—strong, in control of their feelings, keeping their own counsel. The men were not to be bothered with the emotional problems of others.

Joe was very proud that he had grown into the kind of man his father had been. And, it was important to him that Hal was a lot like him, self-sustaining and not overly emotional.

The "culture" of their relationship, shaped by the unspoken expectations they had of themselves and each other, made it especially difficult for them to address any problem that might challenge the value system they seemed to share. Unable to articulate his feelings, unsure of what he even wanted from Joe, Hal suffered in silence.

One night at dinner, Hal said to Joe, "I'm thinking about taking a second job."

Joe looked surprised. "A second job? What on earth for?"

"Well, I heard they were recruiting artists to work on a daily newspaper the local fashion industry is going to put out."

Joe put his fork down. "Hal, when would you do this? You already work forty hours a week at the ad agency."

Hal pushed his food around on his plate. "Well, I'd do it at night. They're going to have a 'round the clock operation. They're looking for people to work at night. It's a good opportunity, I think."

Joe looked puzzled. "A good opportunity for what?"

Hal looked up and said, with a little shrug of his shoulders, "Oh, a good opportunity to make some extra money."

Joe hesitated a moment before he asked the next question. Hal could see that he was struggling with himself. The question came out haltingly. "What do you need extra money for? Something going on that I don't know about?"

Hal looked at Joe's face. He felt like blurting out his feelings about the inequities between them, about his frustration over money, about Joe's indifference to his financial problems and the anger that had been building up in him. Instead, he said, "No. I just thought a little extra cash might be nice to have."

Joe looked down at his plate. When he looked up there was a hurt look on his face. "What about me? What am I supposed to do in the evening with you not here?"

Hal fought back his anger. "I guess you'll just have to manage, babe. Anyway, it's only five nights a week. I'll be here on the weekends."

"Oh, great. That'll give me something to look forward to. Hal, I don't like this. I don't see why you need extra money. We have everything we need here."

Hal hesitated. "Sure, Joe, we do, but I just need a little extra cash right now. My car cost a fortune to fix last month. I'm close to being overdrawn at the bank. I'm just a little strapped right now."

Joe smiled, "Gee, honey. I can take care of that. Why don't I make you a loan? How much do you need?"

Hal shook his head. "I can't afford a loan. If I paid it back out of my present salary, I wouldn't have enough money to live on. I can't afford a loan. But thanks for the offer."

"Hal, are you really serious about this?"

"Yes, I'm dead serious. I'm going down there on Monday for an interview. I feel lucky to have heard about it."

Subsequent conversations took place about Hal's second job, none of which got any closer to the heart of the matter than this one. Hal felt frustrated by his inability to ask for what he wanted from Joe. Joe felt disappointed that Hal would want to spend evenings away from him. He thought about helping Hal out financially, but in his perception, he had offered and Hal had turned it down. He felt confused and hurt. Hal took the second job and his resentment toward Joe grew. Their relationship began to deteriorate.

This couple had an important issue to negotiate, but they never got to first base with it. Unable to clarify for himself what he wanted from Joe, Hal allowed his one-down position in the relationship to reinforce his reticence to challenge the ground rules that had evolved between them. Joe, unable to transcend his value system, and emotionally invested in his position as dominant partner, could not initiate negotiation for change since he was convinced that everything was all right as it was. He did not pick up on Hal's indirect and oblique plea for help. These two partners were bound by an unspoken contract that left them stuck in their respective positions, unable to renegotiate the rules of their relationship to meet their changing needs.

In a more productive scenario, Hal would have allowed himself the right to resent Joe's selfishness and his insensitivity to what effect his affluence, matched against Hal's limited finances, might be having on his lover. He would have articulated those feelings. He would also have formulated for himself what he would like to happen by way of changing the financial arrangement of the relationship so that it would reflect more accurately the marriage of two people that it was.

Joe would have listened to what Hal had to say about his feelings. He would have listened to Hal's proposal and been prepared to work out a change in their arrangement.

They would have needed to discuss Joe's value system and his orientation to two men living together since an important part of the culture of the relationship was predicated on that orientation. One does not change one's value system easily. This discussion would probably have been an extensive one since the changes being asked for by Hal had implications for the balance of power in the partnership. Hal would have had to be as clear as possible in his own mind as to what he wanted changed—just the financial picture, or the distribution of power in the relationship in general. They would have had to work diligently on a resolution that integrated the needs, rights, values, and feelings of both partners.

Negotiation produces change. It is meant to. Indeed, you don't usually know what change will bring. The willingness to face that challenge is the ultimate act of faith in the bond you have with your partner.

7

JEALOUSY: A NEW VIEW OF AN OLD PROBLEM

"I don't want to be his damn therapist!"

Arthur was protesting my suggestion that he make himself available to his partner in a way that could facilitate Brad's *talking* out his jealous feelings rather than *acting* them out. Arthur was fed up with Brad's repeated fits of jealousy.

"I can't look at another guy. I can't go out with my friends alone. I can't go out with a colleague for a drink. He is constantly on my back about who I'm seeing, what I'm doing when I'm not with him. It's . . . it's . . . oppressive!"

"Oppressive!" Brad shot back. "That's a good one. I'm the one who's oppressed—by your incessant Don Juanism. Can't you stop trying to seduce every gay man in town?"

"Seduce? I'm not trying to seduce anybody. I just like to talk to people. I'm a friendly guy," Arthur sputtered.

"Yeah, yeah, friendly. Is that what you were being with that guy Saturday night? You seem to be very selective in your friendliness. You're only friendly with the best-looking men in the room."

"Oh, get off it," Arthur groaned. "You're jealous of anyone I talk to for longer than two minutes, especially if I seem to be enjoying the conversation. You've got a real problem, buddy. You'd better do something about it."

Arthur was right. Brad did have a real problem. He was

wrong, however, in his assertion that it was something Brad had to take care of by himself. While the origins of someone's inordinately jealous feelings may be in their own personal development, the solution to the problem is best approached as a relationship issue. There is a great deal Arthur can do to help Brad relate differently to his jealousy.

In this instance, in the safety of the therapist's office, Brad began to talk about his family history, and soon the reasons for his profound jealousy were apparent. As Arthur listened, I could see him visibly softening toward Brad, eventually reaching out to touch him and hold him as Brad got in touch with the feelings attached to his fear of being abandoned again, as he was in childhood.

Brad's father had deserted his mother when Brad was three months old. Young, frightened, inexperienced in life, his mother went to work to support herself and her infant son. Untrained, she could only find jobs that were menial. She took Brad to a nursery run by the city where he was cared for during the day. At night, at home alone with him, she would try to be attentive to his needs, but she had a very short fuse and the least frustration would frequently result in a tirade directed at his absent father, at him, at the world, after which she would cry and take to her bed. In essence, Brad was deserted by both his parents. His father physically abandoned him. His mother emotionally abandoned him. The fear of abandonment became embedded in his thinking about close relationships. The love he got from his mother was tinged with threats of abandonment as she unthinkingly vented on him her anger at being stranded in her young life with so much responsibility. She implied she would be just as happy not to have had the responsibility of a child. Sometimes she said it directly to him. It was painful to hear, and it frightened the young Brad very much.

As Brad talked, he stared at the floor. When he looked up, his eyes were filled with tears. "Why did she do that to me? I was just a little boy."

Arthur leaned over and put his arms around Brad. He held

him while Brad cried. Those tears had been a very long time in coming.

Brad was in his late thirties. He had never spoken to anyone about this. On this and subsequent occasions he continued to open up the memories of his relationship with his mother which he had stored away for so many years. He let his anger come through and his sadness. He spoke of his long-denied feelings of resentment toward his father, wondering what he had done to warrant his father's rejection, what had been wrong with him. The child, egocentrically, always believes itself to be at fault when there is desertion by a parent. The child in Brad, for the first time, was beginning to express these feelings. At last a dialogue had begun between that child and the adult in Brad. Feelings could be given a voice. Reason could be applied to ameliorate the fears of the confused child within. And, to Brad's advantage, his partner was able to share in this experience. By so doing, Arthur began to understand why Brad had such a problem with what he perceived to be threats of imminent abandonment.

Out of this understanding Arthur became Brad's ally rather than the "enemy" Brad perceived him to be in jealousy-provoking situations. Brad became increasingly better at talking about his fears rather than acting them out. Soon he was able to sort out more quickly what belonged to the unfinished business of childhood and what belonged to his present life with Arthur. He was able to see that Arthur was indeed very devoted to him and that Arthur's natural sociability did not constitute a signal that the relationship was about to end every time he talked to another man, good-looking or not.

Arthur and Brad worked out some effective signals to indicate when Brad was feeling threatened and needed Arthur's reassurance. Thus they were able to short-circuit what before had been too often an escalating spiral of accusations and counter-accusations, leading to tension and misery for them both. Brad came to understand that the fear of abandonment he so often experienced was a product of his history. The frightened little boy would always be inside him. The trick now was to be able to ask for help when that child-within became too unruly to handle alone. The caution was not to try to ignore him, because that's when he became frightened and created problems.

With the diminishing of Brad's "jealous fits," his relationship with Arthur calmed down enough for the couple to grow closer. This closeness enabled Brad to feel more trusting of Arthur and more secure regarding Arthur's commitment to him.

I have tried to illustrate here the strong role childhood experience can play in determining how one functions in adult intimate relationships. In particular, the ability to trust in the love and good will of those on whom one is dependent is very much influenced by one's earliest experiences with the caretaking adults in one's life.

In the very beginning of its life, the baby cannot make a distinction between itself and everything else in its environment. Only gradually, in the first few months of life, does it begin to have a notion of itself as something that operates separately from everything else around it.

When the baby first relates to mother, it is as if the two were one. Little by little, baby realizes that mother is not a part of itself, that mother is not always present. Mother goes away. The baby cries to call her back. Sometimes she comes. Sometimes she doesn't. Feeling totally dependent on mother for survival, the baby experiences fear when mother is not immediately available to satisfy baby's needs. "Will she ever come back?" "Is she gone for good?" "Have I lost her?" Then mother reappears, and baby is comforted.

These early experiences with dependency and fear of loss of the person on whom one is dependent set the stage for how an individual relates to these issues throughout life. If mother (or whoever might be standing in for her) is available and consistent and a good caretaker, the individual has a good start on feeling comfortable with being dependent on another. If mother is unavailable, inconsistent, or not a good caretaker, a fear of abandonment by crucially important people will most likely develop and become a component of this individual's personality. Fear of abandonment can have a devastating effect on one's ability to allow emotional dependency on a partner, a condition necessary for true intimacy to develop.

It is sometimes a subtle business. People whose histories involve parental emotional abandonment will often deny, even to themselves, that such abandonment has really occurred. If mother was ill and unable to attend to her maternal responsibilities, it is usually pretty difficult to blame her for not being there. Nevertheless, the feelings of deprivation and resentment are often just below the surface. They can easily get displaced onto a lover who might be inattentive or somewhat negligent in his/her responsibilities to the relationship.

People who come from families in which one or both parents were alcohol or drug abusers usually come away from childhood suspicious, untrusting, and emotionally guarded. They are often very self-critical, with a strong need to control, since the unpredictability of their formative years often meant danger or violence. The threat, real or imagined, of the loss of a lover in later life reactivates fear of the chaos of childhood. Also feared is a return to the self-inflicted emotional isolation that protected against the chaos in childhood. While that isolation did protect, it is remembered as a painful experience. Fearing such consequences, this person is extremely sensitive to any threat that might disturb the status quo of a relationship.

Sometimes the abandoning parent was simply too immature and self-centered to be emotionally available to the child. This kind of parent often could not discern that the child's needs were different from his or her own needs. Everything got interpreted in terms of the parent's egocentric thinking. "Your bad grades are embarrassing *me*." "*I* would worry too much if you went on that trip." "You're just doing that to hurt *me*."

There is little or no acknowledgment that the child is a separate being with separate needs. Unable to relate to that separateness, the parent deprives the child of the guidance needed to develop a sense of being able to function independently in the world. Such children, grown up, live with a fear that the person on whom they are emotionally dependent will abandon them, leaving them unable to fend for themselves. These people usually are very threatened by even a hint that they might lose their partner. They are also very reactive to a partner's moving away from them emotionally or physically for any reason. What follows is an example of this love-as-fusion-with-the-loved-one problem.

LOVE-AS-FUSION-WITH-THE-LOVED-ONE

Elaine's mother, Hilda, had a childhood marked by benign neglect. Hilda's parents were both heavily involved in their careers, father as a journalist and mother as a concert pianist, often away on tour. Hilda was cared for by a series of housekeepers who seemed always to be selected more for their ability to discipline and teach good manners than for their compassion and warmth. As an only child Hilda was often lonely. She was not allowed to go far from home after school. Not surprisingly, she had difficulty making friends. Both her parents appeared more interested in their careers than in her, and she grew up feeling that there must be something terribly wrong with her for them to abandon her that way.

Hilda was finally liberated from her lonely environment when she went away to college. She felt ill-prepared, however, to cope with life in a dormitory. She got out as quickly as possible by marrying the first young man with whom she became involved. When Elaine was born, Hilda felt that at last there was someone who really needed her. Becoming a mother made her feel worthwhile. With this little baby, she could be completely in control of the relationship. She would be loved and not abandoned. Hilda's husband marveled at what a wonderfully devoted mother she was. She took Elaine with her everywhere and kept her close at all times. When it was time for Elaine to go to school, both she and her mother went through a wrenching, painful experience as they parted. Elaine trundled off to kindergarten, tearful and frightened. Throughout her childhood and adolescence, Elaine continued to be at the center of her mother's existence. By the time she was eighteen, she was beginning to feel her mother's closeness as oppressive.

After much discussion, pleas, tears, and arguments against it from Hilda, Elaine left home to attend college. When Elaine finished college she did not return to her mother's home but took an apartment a few blocks away.

When Elaine was about twenty-two, she realized she was a lesbian. She had fought the idea in college, but living alone, without the constant activity of campus life, she came face to face with herself. She found it harder and harder to turn off her erotic fantasies about women. She longed for contact with a woman, but she didn't know what to do to make that happen. Also, she was terrified that her mother would be devastated if she knew. It would mean that she couldn't fulfill her mother's dreams for her. She didn't know what to do, so she did nothing. After five or so years of inhibiting herself in this way, Elaine found herself feeling lonely and desperate. Through a feminist group she belonged to, she learned about the organized gay and lesbian community and where she could go to meet other women.

Elaine enjoyed the activities of the groups she joined. She did, however, continue to avoid developing a relationship with another woman. It felt more important to her to protect her mother from the truth of her sexual orientation.

When Elaine was about thirty, she met Giselle. By then she was able to understand the ways in which she was contributing to the deep loneliness she felt inside. A relationship was now more important than protecting her mother. Giselle pursued Elaine. After a brief period of resistance, Elaine allowed herself to become involved with Giselle. Following several months of courtship, they declared themselves lovers and moved in together.

At first things went smoothly. They were very absorbed in one another and saw few other people. Toward the end of the first year of their relationship, Giselle said she would like to resume the work she had begun before she met Elaine, on a poetry project at the local women's center. Elaine said she thought that was a fine idea, and Giselle began attending meetings of the workshop group to which she had formerly belonged.

Giselle felt quite elated with her reinvolvement in the poetry project, but as she talked to Elaine about what was happening in the group, Elaine became more and more agitated. She said she didn't want to hear about it and furthermore, she wished Giselle had never rejoined the group.

In an effort to deal with Elaine's feelings, Giselle insisted that she come with her to some of the project meetings and the occasional social events of the group. What Giselle had hoped would help Elaine to feel included and more secure actually had the opposite effect. Elaine began accusing Giselle of being attracted to several of the women in the group. Giselle acknowledged these women were indeed attractive, but she said she had no personal interest in them. Elaine didn't believe her. She became convinced that Giselle was seeing one of the women behind her back. Giselle protested that she wasn't.

Elaine persisted in her accusations. Their relationship became more and more tense until Giselle felt she had to drop out of the poetry project to protect it. She resented this, but she loved Elaine and she didn't want to make her unhappy.

In the following year a series of incidents occurred which convinced Elaine that Giselle was pursuing a sexual interest in other women. Giselle swore that this was not true. Elaine could not seem to leave it alone. The relationship became even more tense. Finally, in despair, Giselle announced that she was leaving because Elaine's unfounded jealousy had become intolerable to her. Elaine was distraught and begged her not to go. They tried again, but Elaine seemed incapable of rising above her jealous feelings. They broke up.

Elaine felt abandoned. She vowed that she would not become involved with anyone else because breaking up was too painful ever to go through again.

Elaine entered therapy, where, after a long period of self-exploration, she was able to understand what had happened with

Giselle. She saw that the model for closeness and love that her mother had provided was about fusion-with-the-loved-one. Elaine had never learned the lesson that one could move away from the loved one to pursue independent interests and return to find love still intact. Elaine's mother, Hilda, did not understand that and therefore she could not teach that lesson to her daughter. Hilda had been too busy replacing the love-means-abandonment model of her childhood with the love-means-fusion-with-the-loved-one model in her relationship with her daughter. Elaine had incorporated the love-means-fusion model into her own thinking. When Giselle began to pursue independent interests Elaine could only interpret that as abandonment. Since love-means-fusion-with-the-loved-one was the only model she knew, a threat of abandonment stirred up very primitive feelings left over from childhood. These feelings amounted to a threat to her survival. The expression of Elaine's "jealousy" feelings was a plea not to be abandoned and left helpless, as she felt she would be if she was not attached to someone.

Since it was romantic love that bound Giselle to Elaine, anyone who was potentially of romantic interest to Giselle posed a threat to their bond, in Elaine's mind. Thus, the presence of "attractive" women in Giselle's life was enough to activate Elaine's fears of abandonment. Her jealous fits were, of course, maladaptive. They did not get her the devotion she wanted. That would have been impossible, actually, since what she wanted was for Giselle to behave like her mother, devoted beyond all doubt or distraction to her little girl, to the exclusion of any other interest. Once Elaine understood the problems that had been created by her mother's clinging to her in order to feel loved and validated, she could begin to relate to her memories of her relationship with her mother with a new perspective. After a time, she was able to deal with the feelings of deprivation and anger toward her mother that this new perspective produced.

In therapy, Elaine was able to free herself from the model of love her mother had imposed on her. She was able, finally, to separate herself in her mind from her mother so that she could experience and express her own individuality. In so doing, she learned to understand and accept a lover's need to be separate and independent, as well as attached.

Elaine progressed in therapy until she was able to enter a relationship with another woman. This time, when she felt threatened by her partner's independent development, she understood what was happening to her. She could sort out what was left over from her relationship with her mother and what truly belonged to the relationship with her lover. She learned also to deal with her old fears of abandonment by treating them as just that and not as real threats to her contemporary relationship. She learned to take her partner into her confidence and use her support to combat those fears.

One might say that Elaine was one of the more fortunate persons with her kind of history. Many avoid intimacy altogether because they associate love with abandonment. Still others become involved with a partner whose personality resembles that of the parent who did not meet their needs in the first place. In this reproduction of the original situation, they unconsciously strive for a more favorable outcome than they had the first time around, with their parent. But, alas, the person they choose all too often is also unable to love in a nourishing way. Alcohol, drugs, illness, immaturity, self-centeredness, whatever the reason, this partner cannot offer the needed emotional security. The threat of abandonment is reinforced by the tenuousness of the bond. Jealousy is easily triggered. The model of intimate relating here is love-always-means-abandonment.

People who are inordinately jealous because their earliest developmental experiences with being emotionally dependent on another human being were flawed have a special task in their adult lives. It is to bring the aggrieved child-within out of hiding and to enable that child to experience consciously and talk about the feelings attached to the unfinished business of childhood. That is not an easy thing to accomplish after years of denying such feelings. It might be necessary to seek professional help to liberate the child.

Possibly it can be done with a trusted friend if he/she is a person who can tolerate the expression of anger toward parents, who is empathic, and who will not judge and criticize but will understand the need that is being served by the expression of these feelings.

It is crucial to remember that the most important outcome of successfully exploring early experience is the newfound ability to separate what belongs to the present from that which belongs to the unfinished business of the past. The payoff is in the ability to be fully functioning in the kind of adult, contemporary relationship that can heal the emotional wounds of the past and offer increased enjoyment of life in the present.

THE CONFUSION OF JEALOUSY AND ENVY

My good friend Dr. Martin Rochlin was reminding me of the complication that sexual envy sometimes brings to same-sex relationships.

"If you and I were husband and wife, and another man was flirting with you, as a heterosexual man I might be *jealous,* but I wouldn't be *envious.* I wouldn't want him to be flirting with *me.*"

"But, as a gay man, when another man flirts with my partner, I might be jealous, and I might also be *envious* because I'd want him to be flirting with me. I am not only threatened by the potential loss of my lover, but I am also envious because my lover is more sexually attractive to this man than I am. These are separate and distinct experiences, but they may appear to be the same feeling. That can be misleading when one is seeking to remedy a jealousy-provoking situation. My partner may be perfectly willing to amend his behavior in response to my jealousy, but he cannot control the behavior of other people. When I can distinguish between jealousy and envy I have a better chance of finding remedies that are appropriate to each one."

As he talked, a series of pictures flashed through my mind. They were scenes in which women were showing obvious interest in my lover. Was she doing something to invite that interest? Was she dissatisfied with me? Was my partnership in jeopardy? Or, was my pride hurt because these women were not showing the same interest in me? I found all too often that I could berate her for what I imagined to be her "wrongdoing," but I could not admit that my real resentment was for being ignored while she was being responded to.

No. No. You don't understand, I would think to myself. I want them to find *me* attractive.

Had I been able to say that out loud, she would most certainly have said soothing and reassuring things to me. Instead, I could only glare at her in silence, isolating myself from her because I didn't want to admit that I was envious. How important being able to make the distinction between jealousy and envy could have been. What a missed opportunity to be understood and supported.

SEXUAL EXCLUSIVITY AGREEMENTS AND JEALOUSY

How often I have heard couples corroborating each other's assertions that their "open" relationship is what they both want, only to hear later that one of the partners feels hurt and resentful when the other actually strays from the marital bed. What was once acceptable between them no longer is. Perhaps it never was in the first place.

Poorly conceived contractual agreements regarding sexual exclusivity can produce painful consequences. Sometimes these agreements have simply evolved over time. Nothing systematic about it, just an implicit understanding that the agreement is more or less whatever it is. Such an arrangement, or the lack of it, often invites jealousy since the boundaries of what is acceptable are vague and open to individual interpretation by the partners. Much more desirable is the explicit agreement carefully thought through and discussed by the partners, integrating the needs of each into the "contract." Unfortunately, this direct dealing with the issue seems not as common as the casual approach.

The couple has a half-serious discussion, hurrying toward (premature) closure because it is an uncomfortable topic, especially if there is any significant difference in the way the two people feel about the subject. Too often, under these conditions, the standard arrived at in the agreement represents the values of a particular reference group rather than reflecting what the people involved actually want to happen.

For male couples the primary reference group is the gay male subculture. Before AIDS, belonging to this reference group meant incorporating standards of sexual conduct that were most often non-monogamous. Many gay men took pride in their openmindedness regarding sexual practices and their lack of jealousy.

In the idealized male couple of the pre-AIDS era, the partners enjoyed sex with one another. Separately and together, they enjoyed sex with people outside the relationship. No jealousy. No recriminations. No proprietary attitudes about one's lover owing sexual allegiance only to his partner. That was the prevailing ethos. But there were those who privately wished their relationship could be otherwise. They felt co-opted by the guiding beliefs of their peers and the traditions of their reference group. When it came to making the agreement about exclusivity in their partnerships they were hard put to go against the current. They didn't want to spoil the sport.

Most gay people grow up with a strong sense of feeling different, of being outsiders in their own peer group. Having found a "home," as it were, many gay men were reticent to once again be different from their peers. They went along. That willing suspension of the wish to be sexually exclusive with one partner, when that was the case, took its toll on the people who experienced it. Sometimes it meant using alcohol and drugs to excess to get "up" for social/sexual activities these men didn't want to be involved in at the time. It was the thing to do, and they did it. Deep down it was not what they wanted to be doing.

Gay men, like everyone else, are sometimes insecure and fear abandonment. If such a person found it socially unacceptable in his peer group to express feelings of jealousy, the tension attached to those feelings would often build in his relationship until dissolution seemed the only way to resolve the problem.

Now, in the age of AIDS, standards of sexual conduct are much more conservative, and there is a new emphasis on monogamous partnerships. The dilemma is still there, however, for many who have not decided on sexual exclusivity as the model of choice for their life as a couple. For those people, I strongly urge a thorough talking through of what each really wants for himself, no matter how different it may be from what others around him are doing.

Lesbians more frequently agree on monogamy in their relationships. This is no doubt due to social conditioning that directs women to be relationship-oriented, faithful to their mates, and sexually conservative. Yet not all lesbians follow their social programming. Some are drawn to sexual adventure and a variety of partners. To these venturesome souls I urge the same care taken in developing agreements with partners that I emphasize for gay men. While the guiding beliefs in the lesbian subculture regarding sex have not been the same as those that have prevailed with gay men, the lure of an openly sexual life with a variety of people can be great. If both partners in a relationship are equally lured, there will be fewer problems. If one, however, is committed to monogamy while the other is committed to adventure, the partners had better also be committed to working out a mutually agreeable contract regarding this issue.

Another important aspect of sexual exclusivity agreements, as with practically every other kind of agreement in an intimate relationship, is the flexibility it has to accommodate to changing needs. What was all right at one point in the relationship may no longer be all right with one, or both, partners. Sometimes people deny to themselves that they have changed and want something different. They fear that they'll be rejected if they "rock the boat" or that they won't be understood. The nonjealous partner suddenly feels jealousy. "I don't know what's come over me," he/she says. The feelings are described as "uncharacteristic."

I have learned to pay a lot of attention to that word when it comes up in a couple's discussion. Since the expression of jealousy is a way of defining the limits of what is tolerable for each partner, "uncharacteristic" jealousy means that some serious renegotiating of boundaries is probably in order.

THE CONSTRUCTIVE USES OF JEALOUSY

Jealousy is a self-protective emotion. It serves to alert the person experiencing it to the possibility of the loss of love. Just as it is normal for one to protect anything that is precious in one's life, it is normal to feel jealousy.

Jealousy has had a very narrowly defined, disparaging reputation. It has been variously seen as a sign of immaturity, flawed emotional development, weakness of character, or a quirk of the individual's nature ("she/he's just a jealous type"). In none of these instances is jealousy seen as something that might *enhance* a relationship. Recently, a new view of the role of jealousy in intimate relationships has been espoused by those who study and write about such things. I like the ideas on this subject offered by Gordon Clanton and Lynn G. Smith in their book, *Jealousy.**

> One very basic and quite legitimate function of jealousy is to alert us to threats to our personal security and to the well-being of an important relationship. The jealous flash is the cognitive and psychological equivalent of the physiological system of skin receptors and nerves which protects us from bodily harm. Physical pain warns us that the security of the organism is being threatened by some physical object or force. Psychological pain (such as jealousy) warns us that our psychic security is being threatened, that a relationship upon which we depend requires attention. We ignore physical pain at our own peril; the

* Gordon Clanton and Lynn G. Smith, *Jealousy* (Englewood Cliffs, N.J.: Prentice-Hall, 1977).

same is true of psychological pain. The pain of jealousy is a herald; it comes to warn us that greater pain may be in store unless we attend to the relationship.

. . . The language and gestures of jealousy can be employed in a variety of ways. A jealous outburst may simply be a cry for attention, a way of saying, "I am hurting! Notice me!"

Jealousy can also mark the beginning of constructive dialogue. The expression of jealousy can trigger communication which leads to clarification of needs, meanings, beliefs, and values. Such talking-through may lead to negotiations whereby the pain of jealousy is reduced and the relationship strengthened.

To make the best use of jealousy as an early warning signal that something in the relationship needs more attention, it is important to make the distinction between feeling excluded, or left out, and feeling that you are about to lose something precious to you. According to Clanton and Smith:

When your partner "attends" (in whatever way) to another, his/her attention is elsewhere. When you notice that, before you process the implications or possible consequences, your first reaction is to note that they are "in," and you are "out."

. . . This kind of experience is commonplace in our society. . . . Such experiences trigger the jealous flash, but, typically, they do not fan it into a flame. The jealous feelings usually fade when the precipitating event is over. . . .

If you find yourself troubled or upset by the "sharing" of your partner that is considered appropriate in your circle of friends, perhaps your "feeling excluded" is a symptom of an underlying fear of loss, the more serious "strain" of jealousy. If you literally cannot stand to let your partner out of your sight . . . your Jealousy is probably rooted in a persistent *fear* rather than in a temporary irritation. . . . Exactly what is it you are afraid you might lose? . . . Perhaps it is a *loss* of "face" that frightens you. . . . If your mate is too friendly with a person . . . perhaps others will assume that they are sexually involved. If you don't *like* the third party, if she/he seems "unworthy" of your mate's attention, the fear of loss of reputation can be especially powerful. . . .

So, what can we do to deal with our jealousy so that it does not spoil our loving experiences but rather helps us to maintain a high quality of relationship with our partner?

As always, it seems, the admonition to *talk about it* is in order.

Can you identify what it is in your partner's behavior that tends to trigger jealous feelings in you? If you can it might be very helpful to talk to your partner about what this is, and to work out, together, ways in which each of you might do something different to lessen the effects of jealousy-provoking situations.

To summarize the main points in this chapter:

• The roots of one's jealousy are in childhood experiences with the caretaking adults on whom one was dependent.

• If, in childhood, a person was physically or emotionally abandoned by a major caretaker, a fear of such abandonment occurring again is likely to plague that person's intimate relationships as an adult.

• The fear of abandonment, of the loss of love, often gets played out in terms of jealous feelings.

• Jealous feelings can be constructively used in a relationship to convey the limits of each partner's tolerance for independent involvement on the part of the other partner.

• Partnership agreements regarding sexual exclusivity should not just evolve. They should be carefully talked through so that the evolving agreement reflects what each person truly wants to happen.

• Sexual exclusivity agreements should be reviewed at regular intervals so they can be updated, if necessary, in accordance with the changing needs of one or both partners.

• Jealousy should not be viewed only as a sign of a person's immaturity, or flawed development, or weakness of character. It should be heeded as a warning that something in the person, or in the relationship, needs attention.

• Paying attention to a partner's jealous feelings, rather than dismissing them, can deepen understanding of that person's emotional needs. The more each partner understands the other's needs, the more likely it is that the relationship will be fulfilling and will endure over time.

8

FIGHTING THE GOOD FIGHT

Bob looked down at his hands. His voice was barely audible. "I don't understand what happened. I thought we were getting along so well. We never fought. Then one day he just announced that he was leaving. He said he couldn't stand it anymore. Couldn't stand what? I didn't understand. I still don't. We got along so well. We never fought."

Such has been the epitaph of many a partnership done in by the misguided notion that relationships are going well because there is an absence of fighting.

Every intimate relationship has its tensions. It is difficult to live with another person, to open one's life to such close scrutiny, to compromise one's needs and desires, to trust another with one's fragility, to risk rejection without tension developing on some level. Tension is the underlying condition of conflict. Once it develops, and it is inevitable that it will, it does not just go away. Learning how to reduce the tensions that exist in a relationship means learning how to deal with conflict constructively. Undealt with, relationship tensions often tend to evolve into behavior destructive to self or to the partnership. If tensions are not directly dealt with, they accumulate, building toward an explosion that can seem all out of proportion to whatever is happening at the time. Dealing with tension means dealing with conflict, which translates into what most people call fighting.

It is the purpose of this chapter to focus on constructive fighting. "Fighting" is a very loaded word, unlike "conflict resolution" which seems so much more rational and civilized. "We resolved our conflict" sounds a good deal better than "We had a fight." Conflict resolution is a good deal better, as a matter of fact, since fighting does not always resolve conflict, especially if it is unfair, destructive fighting.

Constructive fighting in the context of intimate partnerships can not only resolve conflict but also conveys information that can be used to strengthen and enrich the relationship. I believe it is particularly important for gay and lesbian partners to learn to fight constructively. All too often, I find, same-sex couples are reticent to fight. The bond is felt to be too tenuous because it is not legally sanctioned. There is that tradition of failure to contend with as well as the absence of an expectation of permanence, the lack of validation by society, no children (usually) for whom to hold it all together. Many gay and lesbian couples will go to great lengths to avoid fighting because they fear that true feelings of anger, directly expressed, will drive their partner away from them. The more likely scenario is that true feelings of anger unexpressed will find expression in underground ways, sabotaging the foundation of the relationship, making dissolution of the partnership more, rather than less, likely in the long run.

Often when I speak publicly about constructive fighting as a mechanism of growth in intimate relationships, I hear protests from people who regard fighting as unpleasant at best and destructive at worst. Why would I promote the very thing they see as most damaging to their relationship? Many people see fighting as the signal that the relationship isn't working anymore.

In reality, fighting constructively is a sign that the relationship is alive and well, and is of sufficient value to the partners to risk increased vulnerability to one another.

EXPRESSING ANGER

For many people, the mere anticipation of expressing anger fosters a feeling of anxiety. Anger is associated with loss of control. They are convinced that if they let go at all, they will let go all the way and be out of control. They so fear that possibility that they avoid confrontation at all costs. For such people, expressing their anger might mean hurting someone and having to bear the guilt or hurting someone and being retaliated against, or punished for it.

Usually these feelings have their roots in childhood experience. If anger had been expressed violently in one's family, the fear produced by that violent expression may be forever linked with feelings of anger. The child was powerless and overwhelmed. The child-within-the-adult anticipates being powerless and overwhelmed and avoids conflict in order to avoid having that experience again.

If your childhood experience included violent emotions, if anger frightens you because it triggers those feelings of powerlessness and fear that you felt as a child, you can bring yourself more into the present by talking to your partner about what the childhood experience was like for you. Being able to articulate the feelings of fear that have been stirred up helps to remind us that we are grown up now, able to speak up, able to have some influence over what is happening to us.

Unfortunately, some people are embarrassed to talk about their families in what seems like a critical way. This reticence is especially true if there was excessive use of alcohol or drugs, with the usual unspoken ground rule that everyone protect the substance-abusing family member by never speaking of what was happening at home. It is difficult to go against one's early training even if one realizes that that training is counterproductive to one's own adult relationships. It is difficult but necessary to confront one's own history in order to work through the need to avoid conflict. It is necessary so that one does not have to cheat a partner of the opportunity to ventilate feelings that might otherwise go underground and do real damage to the relationship. One should not have to cheat one's self of such opportunities either.

There are other ways in which early experience in the family influences your ability to deal with anger in relationships. Some people come from families in which *everyone* avoided anger. "Count to ten before you say anything!" was the familiar admonition. The children in these families grow up believing that people who love one another don't fight. These people don't know how to fight, even badly. They might look upon a partner who tries to deal directly with conflict as someone who is unusually combative or hostile. Once again, as with others who avoid conflict, when these people experience the tensions that develop in relationships they will probably not attend to them. The tensions will then accumulate to the point of periodic eruptions, or, of burdening the ability of the partners to be spontaneous with one another.

In the following two instances, individuals whose family "fight training" made them conflict-avoidant were helped to overcome this drawback by partners with very different backgrounds.

JENNY AND ESTHER

Esther came from a family that never fought. Everyone was extremely polite to everyone else. Esther was taught to repress her anger by counting to ten, taking a walk, or refocusing on kindnesses done her by the person she felt angry at. Esther grew up believing that people who expressed their anger openly were crude, out of control, and/or emotionally unstable.

Esther fell in love with Jenny, who came from a very different kind of background. Jenny's family was rather scrappy, but in a loving way. They gently teased one another, and not infrequently these teasing sessions erupted into all-out fights. Few concerns went unaddressed, and rarely did issues simmer under the surface of the relationships. Conflict was dealt with quickly and effectively. Family life was, generally, warm and enjoyable. Jenny's brothers and sisters were very interested in each other's lives and gave each other permission to inquire into every aspect of their individual existences.

The differences between Esther and Jenny were not immediately apparent to them. In the beginning of their relationship, Jenny hardly noticed that Esther was inordinately polite about everything. Esther hardly noticed that Jenny tended to inquire persistently into everything she was feeling, thinking, and experiencing. They were excited by each other's presence, by being in love, and that was all that mattered to them.

Jenny and Esther had been living together about eight months when their relationship seemed to take a turn. Esther began to feel that Jenny was constantly picking on her, and she didn't understand why. Jenny began to feel that Esther was shutting her out, and she didn't understand why. Jenny tried to get Esther to talk about what was happening, but Esther avoided these discussions. Jenny became more and more frustrated. One day she erupted at Esther.

"Where are you? I can't seem to make contact with you anymore. You've closed off to me. I can't stand it!"

Esther said, "I don't know what you're talking about. Why have you become so angry all of a sudden? I suggest you cool off before we talk anymore."

"You see," Jenny exploded, "this is an example. I'm trying to tell you how I feel about something that is happening between us and what do I get from you—stiff armed. That is exactly what I am talking about."

"Jenny," Esther said in a deliberately calm voice. "I believe you are nearly out of control. I am going out to the market, and when I get back I hope you will have settled down."

"Oh, no, you don't," Jenny persisted. "I am not going to let you go off and leave me here with a head of steam. I'm talking about *us*. This is our relationship that's on the line here. I'm not going to just let you walk away from it."

Esther spoke in a calm and deliberate voice. "Jenny, you are becoming irrational. I'm going to try to ignore what you're saying. I'm going to think about the good times we have had together. I'm going to think about how much I love you."

After a long sequence of encounters such as this one, Jenny felt very discouraged. She briefly thought about leaving Esther, but she didn't really want to do that. She thought about the ways in which conflict was dealt with in her own family. She wished Esther could be like her parents and her brothers and sisters.

Then she thought through a plan to help Esther learn to *deal with* rather than *avoid* the tensions between them. Very slowly, Jenny initiated a "fight training" program with Esther. When she wanted to express dissatisfaction with something Esther had done, she did so gently. In graduated steps she demonstrated to Esther that one could express negative feelings in a sane and civilized manner. She conveyed to Esther that she wanted to hear about any dissatisfaction she might have with what was going on between them. She coaxed out of Esther her thoughts and feelings about their partnership. Esther didn't realize she was doing something very different for her until she had been doing it for a while and feeling relatively comfortable with it. Little by little, Esther learned not to run away from conflict. She felt secure with Jenny. She felt loved by her. The discussions soon didn't seem as irrational as they had before. Jenny's patience with Esther paid off, allowing for a richer mix of messages in their communication.

RAOUL AND CHARLES

Raoul and Charles had been together for a little over two years. Charles came from a family that dealt with conflict in an open and direct way. When his parents were displeased with him or his brothers, they said so. When Charles or his brothers were displeased with something the parents had done, *they* said so. Sometimes these confrontations became heated, with the parents and/or their children raising their voices to assure being heard or to express the strong emotions they were feeling. Charles's parents never scolded their children for showing their anger. They did let it be known that gratuitous insults were not permitted in these arguments. They also encouraged their children to keep at their discourse until the issues were resolved and the air was cleared. Charles grew up feeling that it was just fine to express anger, as long as it was in the service of improving relationships.

Raoul came from a large Hungarian family. His predominant memories of childhood were of people in his house constantly yelling at one another. His mother and father argued. His brothers and sisters argued. The children argued with the parents. The parents argued with the children.

As the youngest child, Raoul often felt lost in this war of words. To get any attention at all, he often had to raise his voice and demand it. Even then, he did not always get what he needed. He felt very frustrated by all of this and he swore to himelf that when he got away from his family he would never argue with another living soul.

For the first year of their relationship, Raoul and Charles were two lovebirds. Nothing about either one bothered the other. Their life together was loving and harmonious. In the second year, Charles began to express annoyance at some of Raoul's living habits—small things, minor but irritating.

Raoul stoically accepted all of Charles's comments. He had no retorts. By the halfway mark in the year Charles had stepped up his complaints. Raoul began to feel somewhat persecuted by his lover's criticisms, but he remained stoic and did not argue when Charles confronted him.

By the end of the second year both Raoul and Charles felt dissatisfied with their relationship. When Charles tried to talk to Raoul about his dissatisfaction, Raoul changed the subject, or he suddenly found something he just had to do. Charles began to resent these aborted attempts to work out their differences. Eventually things got so bad that they decided to seek professional help.

In my office it very soon became clear that the problem they were having had its origins in their differing orientations to dealing with conflict. For Charles, it was natural and comfortable to fight. His memories of the family fights were that they always cleared the air and that everyone felt better afterward. For Raoul, discord brought back memories of being lost in his family's acrimonious confrontations with one another. He was determined not to behave like that himself, even at the cost of his partner's unhappiness with him.

Because Raoul had never talked to Charles about his intolerance of fighting and the reasons for it, Charles was mystified by his behavior. He assumed that Raoul didn't care enough about the relationship to deal with him. That was not true, of course. As Raoul talked about his family and his recollections of the pain he had suffered because of it, both came to understand better his resistance to dealing openly with conflict.

Raoul was soon able to see that the kind of constructive fighting that Charles wanted to do with him was different from what had gone on in his own family, where there had been sufficient rivalries and unworked-through anger mixed in with the usual family disputes to turn arguments into go-for-the-jugular encounters.

Because his own "fight training" had been so positively handled by his parents, Charles was able to help Raoul reshape his attitudes about fighting in their relationship. Raoul came to see that dealing with conflict need not be the acrimonious, never-get-anywhere agony it was in his family. He learned from Charles the productive results a fight fairly fought could bring. They were soon able to deal with the problems between them as they arose. Their relationship resumed its earlier enjoyable quality for them both.

If you are a person who has trouble with the expression of anger, try this experiment. The next time your partner expresses anger toward you, let your mind "run free." See what associations you have with this experience. Think about whom your partner might sound like in anger. Whom does he/she remind you of in this state?

Try to conjure up past experiences when anger expressed toward you was overwhelming. Try to make a connection with something in your past that might be causing a fear of anger beyond what there is to be feared from your partner, as the adult you are now. If you are able to identify any sources of your discomfort, talk to your partner about what you have discovered.

WHAT IS CONSTRUCTIVE FIGHTING?

We've looked at some of the reasons why constructive fighting is necessary to a growing partnership and why some people have the need to avoid fighting at all in their relationship.

Now let's look at what constructive fighting is.

What is the difference between a fight that produces growth and one that either increases tension or goes nowhere at all?

A good fight is one in which specific information is conveyed regarding the behaviors being objected to so that one knows exactly what change is desired by the partner. In a good fight, tension is reduced, and intimacy is enhanced. One comes away from a good fight having learned something that, potentially, will improve the relationship.

Following is a list of Do's and Don'ts for constructive fighting (for those of you who have read *Positively Gay,** these ideas will be familiar as they appear in the chapter "Achieving Success As A Gay Couple"). These guidelines for fighting constructively are based on the very creative work of the late Dr. George Bach** who has taught thousands of people in relationships how to "fight fair."

---

* Betty Berzon, ed., *Positively Gay* (Berkeley, Ca., Celestial Arts, 2001).

** George R. Bach and Peter Wyden, *The Intimate Enemy* (New York: William Morrow, 1969).

THE "DO'S" AND "DON'TS" OF
CONSTRUCTIVE FIGHTING

"Do's"

1. Do be willing to risk fighting.
2. Do be specific about your complaints.
3. Do be specific about the changes you'd like to see in relation to your complaints.
4. Do send "I" messages, not "You" messages.
5. Do try to get to underlying issues and concerns.
6. Do express the feelings attached to the issues you are angry about.

Don'ts

1. Don't get stuck in the past.
2. Don't "kitchen sink" your partner.
3. Don't deliver sweeping condemnations.
4. Don't threaten abandonment.
5. Don't give your partner the "silent treatment."
6. Don't abort the fight.

1. Do Be Willing to Risk Fighting.

Sometimes people in relationships fight with their partner in their head. They play all the parts, usually assigning to the partner the role of the villain who doesn't listen, therefore can't understand, and won't change. The person then decides that actually fighting with the partner would be a no-win game. They are off the hook and are free to nurse their grievances privately and nonproductively. The risk of confrontation is avoided, and that gives comfort in the short run. However, it is the long run that counts in relationships. The confrontation avoided today easily becomes the stored resentment that erupts a week from now. The willingness to take the risk of fighting, especially when the outcome is unsure, is an act of faith in one's partner. It is also an investment in the future of the relationship.

2. Do Be Specific About Your Complaints.

"I don't like the way you've been with me lately."

"You're always more interested in your own needs than in mine."

"I'm tired of your wanting to control me all the time."

"You're inconsiderate and insensitive."

"You're too possessive."

"You expect too much of me."

In each of the above statements there is not enough *specificity* for the person being so characterized to know what is being objected to by the partner. These statements are vague, global, unfocused. They make me want to say, "What do you mean? Give me examples! Be specific! If I don't know what you are objecting to about what I do, I cannot change it. It is, after all, *behavior* that is being objected to. You may go beyond the behavior to describe what you think is my motivation. You may speculate on what aspects of my character are being expressed in what you object to. You may analyze, correctly or incorrectly, what personal dynamic I am playing out with you, but, in the end, it is behavior that occurs and it is behavior that we have to start with in making desired changes in what happens between us. The question is, what am I *doing* that upsets you?"

The more you can tell me about what I am doing that bothers you, the better chance there will be that I can change it. For instance, you might say something like:

"Your habit of turning on the television during dinner every night makes conversation impossible. I want to talk to you. I feel as if you are more interested in what's on television than you are in me. I'd like you to stop turning on the television at dinnertime so that we can talk to each other."

Or, "When you don't give me a chance to say what I want to do but just make plans and then tell me about them, I feel as if I have very little control of my life. I want you to discuss your ideas with me about what we are going to do together. I want to have some input. I want to share in these decisions. I want you to ask me what I would like to do."

Or, "When we go to parties together, especially if we don't know most of the people there, I'd like you not to go off on your own and leave me to fend for myself all evening. You don't have to sit by my side, but I'd like you to check back from time to time, to make contact. I want to feel that I am there with my partner and not just on my own."

The more specific the better. Of course, accomplishing this specificity may take some thinking through on your part to be truly in touch with what you do want. It will be time well spent. Clarify for yourself what you want, and communicate it to your partner. Each time you do this, you will be shaping the alliance between you to be the most satisfying one possible.

If you don't like the way I've been with you lately, tell me what I have been *doing* that causes you to feel that way.

If you think I'm more interested in my own needs than in yours, tell me what I am *doing* to cause you to feel that way.

If you think I am controlling, inconsiderate, insensitive, possessive, and expect too much, tell me what I am *doing* that causes you to feel that way.

3. Do Be Specific About the Changes You'd Like to See in Relation to Your Complaints.

Again, if I am going to change whatever upsets you, I have to know specifically what you want changed. If I ask you what you want me to do about whatever is upsetting you, I need specifics in response. It is not helpful if you tell me:

"I want you to be a better partner."
"Care more about me."
"Don't be so controlling."

4. Do Send "I" Messages, Not "You" Messages.

Of all the "Do's" and "Don'ts," this is one of the most subtle but most powerful aids to making fights constructive rather than destructive.

When we are irritated or angry with our partner, when we feel wronged or cheated or punished, it is easy to go on the offensive, to attack. For instance: "You don't care about anything. You borrow clothes and ruin them for me. You are irresponsible and destructive!"

Those are all "you" messages. *You* don't care. *You* are irresponsible. *You* are destructive. If I am the *you* being spoken to, it is likely that I will focus my attention on the attack under way against me. I will pull in, become defensive, fight back. Whatever message there is about something I am doing that you don't like will be lost. My first priority becomes to protect myself against you, just the opposite of opening myself up to you and the information you have to give to me.

If, on the other hand, I can send you an "I" message, rather than a "you" message, I have a much better chance of getting your attention. I might say, "I feel so frustrated when you borrow my clothes and wear them out. It makes me feel as if you had no respect for me and what is mine. I feel devalued and uncared for. When that happens, I feel just terrible."

Quite a difference, isn't there? Now there is a much greater chance that you will hear what is bothering me since you don't have to defend yourself against attack at the same time.

5. Do Try to Get to Underlying Issues and Concerns.

"What are we fighting about? This isn't worth getting so upset over! What are we doing?"

How often have you thought or said those words? The kinds of things most couples fight about often do seem trivial and hardly worth all the *sturm und drang* they create. So what if your partner gets toothpaste all over the bathroom mirror and doesn't ever wipe it off? So what if she doesn't put her clothes away right after she takes them off? So what if the kitchen looks like a cyclone hit it after he has cooked even the simplest meal? So what if she likes staying indoors watching football games on Sunday afternoon when you want to get outside in the fresh air. So what if he falls asleep at the opera while you are being transported to a higher plane.

Hardly issues to get heated up over, yet people do, all the time. Sometimes these disagreements take on huge proportions. It feels as if your very identity is being assaulted when your partner takes an opposing view or, worse still, ignores your protestations altogether. It becomes critical to be the one who is right. Yet, all the time, the combatants might be thinking or even saying, "Why are we getting so excited about this? It isn't that important." Well, "it" may not be, but *something* is. When two people become heavily invested in differing points of view, arguing, fighting, perhaps even threatening abandonment of the relationship over what is happening, you may be sure that important underlying issues are involved.

The most common issues can be stated as questions that all of us at one time or another have had of our partner:

"Do you understand me?"

"Do you care about me?"

"Am I still attractive to you?"

"Can I trust you not to hurt me?"

"Can I rely on you?"

"Will you stay with me?"

Or, they may be questions that we have of ourselves:

"Am I still important to others as an individual, outside of this relationship?"

"Am I giving up too much control over my life?"

"Am I being as good a lover (companion, sexual partner, friend) as I can be in my relationship?"

These are the kinds of issues that underlie the conflict that every couple experiences. The more quickly the partners can uncover these concerns and deal with them directly, the more solid the relationship will be.

In constructive fighting the partners make every effort to get underlying issues to the surface so they can be dealt with directly. The clue that this is the task to be attended to is in the feeling that there is more of an emotional investment in whatever is being fought about than would seem to be warranted. This awareness should be the signal to the partners to stop and try to talk about what might be going on beneath the surface that needs airing. For instance, consider the following:

Janet and Rae, who were lovers, had a close friend who lived in another city. Actually, he had been Janet's friend first, before she had met Rae, but over the years the three of them had formed a close bond. Janet and Bill, who was a gay man, were in the same profession and had worked together in the past. They usually had a lot to talk to each other about. Janet considered Bill her best friend.

Bill came for a weekend visit along with another mutual friend. On Saturday morning, Rae, who was more athletic than Janet, invited Bill to accompany her on a hill climb that she knew Janet would not want to do. On Sunday, Rae and Bill went off on another hill climb. By the end of the weekend, Janet found herself feeling deprived because she hadn't had any time alone with Bill and was resentful because Rae had.

Later in the week, she called Bill at home. He wasn't there so she left a message on his answering machine. When he called back, both Janet and Rae picked up the phone. It was not unusual for both of them to talk to Bill when he called, but on this occasion Janet felt very frustrated. Once again she was not able to be alone with Bill. Janet proceeded to tell Bill her feelings about not being able to spend time alone with him during his visit.

"Well, at least *Rae* got to be alone with you," she said pointedly. When they got off the phone with Bill, Rae confronted Janet.

"What is this 'at least Rae got to be alone with you' business? You sound so deprived."

"I felt deprived," Janet answered. "You went off with Bill two days in a row, and I didn't get to be alone with him at all."

"We went for a walk. What's the big deal?"

"It's no big deal. I just felt frustrated. And, here you were doing it again. I couldn't even be alone with him on the telephone."

"Well, pardon me," Rae said in a mock apology. "I didn't know you were so unable to speak up for what you wanted. You know, I'm really hurt by your implication that I spirited Bill away to have him all to myself. It wasn't that way at all."

"You're hurt? I don't see what you have to be hurt about. I'm the one who was on the losing end."

Rae said, "I'm really getting angry now. Leave me alone."

Janet said, "No, I won't leave you alone. I think you're just competing with me, as usual. I feel bad, so you have to feel worse."

Rae said, "This is ridiculous. What are we fighting over?"

Janet said, "I can't seem to ever express my feelings without your getting bent out of shape. Now, *I'm* angry."

And it went on from there, escalating, but going nowhere. Had they stopped there, Janet and Rae would have learned nothing from this fight. By going on, to ferret out the underlying issues, they defined for one another ways in which each could change to make things better between them. Going on might have sounded like this:

RAE: What do you think all this resentment is about, surely not just what happened with Bill last weekend?

JANET: I don't know. I guess it's about me. I'm not feeling too good about myself. Not much is happening in my career these days. I feel bored, stuck. I need some outside stimulation. Bill has always been so good for me in that way. I guess I depend on him for that, and when you went off with him, twice, it felt as if you were stealing something from me.

RAE: Honey, please try to stop seeing me as your competitor. I'm not. I have needs, too. Sometimes they may clash with yours, but I don't mean for that to happen. If I'm doing something that hurts you, please tell me.

JANET: I will try to do that. I just get frustrated when things seem to be out of my hands.

RAE: But you don't have to control me to get what you want. I'm on your side. Try to trust me.

JANET: I have a hard time . . . I get so caught up in my own feelings.

RAE: I know, but when you do that, and you ignore *my* feelings, I feel invalidated, as if my own lover doesn't know or care about what I'm feeling. It's a very lonely experience.

JANET: I don't want it to be that way.

RAE: Then, please, if you're feeling angry or deprived or hurt by something I'm doing, tell me.

JANET: I will. I will really try to do that. I'll try to trust you more. I guess I need to deal with my own self-doubts differently.

RAE: I'd like to help.

JANET: I'd like that, too.

So Janet and Rae uncovered the issues underlying their argument about what happened with Bill. Janet was not feeling good about herself as an individual, and she was placing the blame for that on Rae. Rae, in turn, felt invalidated when Janet interpreted her actions only in terms of her (Janet's) own needs. The issue of trust was an important one for Janet, who was trying to work out her own dependence versus independence dilemma. Trusting Rae meant giving up even more control, and she was having a hard time with that in the relationship. These particular issues—trust, control, dependence versus independence, sensitivity to a partner's needs, the importance of communicating feelings—are all common to the struggle any couple has in trying to build a workable relationship.

Think about the concerns that typically underlie the relationships you have been in. Is there a pattern? If so, does this tell you something about what you might need to feel safe and satisfied in an intimate partnership? Next time you have a fight with your partner, try to determine what the underlying concerns are that are getting played out through the surface issues. Try to bring these concerns out in the open. Doing so can save much wear and tear on your relationship. It can provide the basis for a more honest and fulfilling partnership experience.

6. Do Express the Feelings Attached to the Issues You Are Angry About.

Coolly calculated presentations, carefully thought through, and sanitized of feelings that might get out of control are not productive ways to deal with conflict in a relationship. Every point of conflict is not rife with emotion, of course. But when there is strong emotion attached to whatever is at issue, it is important to get these feelings out. I know that doing this while being specific about complaints and the changes desired, sending "I" messages, and uncovering underlying issues, must feel like being asked to juggle half a dozen balls in the air at once, but these are the very things that can make a difference between a partnership that grows in importance to the people involved and one that stagnates and disappoints.

So, if you are furious about your lover's carelessness, dereliction of duty to you, or serious infraction of the ground rules of the relationship, don't hold it in or disguise it as something else, let the feelings out and deal with them so that you can move on.

1. Don't Get Stuck in the Past.

It is amazing how good we are sometimes at sabotaging ourselves. For instance, in the middle of a fight, just when your partner says something such as, "All right, I'll change. I won't do that anymore," you feel the need to say, "Well, you've said you would change in the past, and you haven't, so you probably won't now." And you are back at square one.

Getting stuck in the past is very easy to do.

One might say of himself, "I've *always* been this way," as an explanation for some unacceptable behavior. In a growing relationship, such a statement should never be accepted as a justification for undesirable behavior.

"You've always been this way? Well, now is a good time to change," would be an appropriate response to that declaration.

Berating one's partner for past misbehavior and refusing to

let go of the indictment, no matter what the miscreant promises for the future, is one of the ways in which fighting can become destructive to the potential of a relationship.

Present conflicts do not get resolved when parties to the conflict insist on being victims of their own history. Partners should be wary of the pitfall that getting stuck in the past can be.

2. Don't "Kitchen Sink" Your Partner.

You are feeling resentful about something your partner has done. You address the issue directly, but, somehow, once you get started, you keep right on rolling:

"And not only that, but I didn't care much for the way you behaved at the party Saturday night. And, while I'm at it, I really resent the way you spoke to my mother on the phone last week. As a matter of fact you've been less than courteous to my friends on a number of occasions recently. Come to think of it, you haven't been very nice to me lately, and, oh yes . . . I'm sick and tired of picking up after you. . . ."

That's "kitchen sinking" (as in throwing in everything, including the kitchen sink.)

Thus inundated, the person being addressed shuts down completely or strikes back at his/her "attacker." The original issue is lost in the barrage. The opportunity to convey information that might be useful in effecting change in the relationship is gone. Rather than reducing tension, "kitchen sinking" is more likely to increase it.

If you are angry about something your partner has done, focus on that piece of behavior. Don't drag in everything you have been building resentment about for the last six months. Your best chance to improve the relationship through constructive fighting is through clean confrontation on single issues. Don't bury your point in a barrage of criticism.

3. Don't Deliver Sweeping Condemnations.

"You are a thoughtless, self-centered, immature child!"

"You are absolutely incapable of understanding me."

"You are hopelessly naive."

"You are a very hostile person."

"You are impossible to talk to."

After you have swept over me with that kind of wipe-out wave, I am certainly not in the mood to hear anything else you have to say about me. I am either mobilized for battle, or I'm finished with the conversation altogether.

It is so easy to make these sweeping condemnations, gratuitous insults that do not convey information that could be put to work in the service of the relationship. They simply put the other person on the defensive. Be wary of doing this to your partner and to yourself.

4. Don't Threaten Abandonment.

I believe this threat is one of the most destructive things gay and lesbian partners can do to one another. It reinforces the homophobic notion that same-sex relationships are bound to fail. It undermines trust, and thereby weakens the bond between partners.

It is unfair and unwise to keep the threat of dissolution of the relationship uppermost in your partner's mind by repeatedly talking about leaving. It is a surefire way to ensure that a solid basis for being together will never develop. I know how tempting it is in the heat of an argument to let fly with "Maybe we should just split up?" or "I don't need this, why don't I just leave?" or any one of the multitudinous versions of the abandonment anthem. The next time you find yourself thinking in those terms, please remind yourself of how damaging these threats can be to your partner's sense of security, and, eventually, to her/his love for you. Don't threaten abandonment as a way of getting your partner's attention. There are better ways to do that which don't have the potential of sabotaging your relationship in the bargain.

5. Don't Give Your Partner the "Silent Treatment."

A young woman client told me, "When I was a little girl and I did something my mother didn't like, she often gave me the silent treatment. She would not speak to me for hours, sometimes a whole day. I felt very isolated. I felt very frightened. I would then do everything I could think of to get back in her good graces. I'd follow her around. I'd offer to do something for her. And, finally, I'd cry and plead with her, 'Please talk to me.' Her silent treatment worked great as punishment. I felt very chastised. The trouble is, since she wouldn't talk to me, I could only guess what she was displeased about. I was often at a loss to know what I should do differently. I came away from these episodes feeling mostly her displeasure and disapproval. That, in turn, convinced me that there was something terribly wrong with me. I couldn't do anything right. I was fated to displease and be disapproved of. Eventually I came to resent my mother for this way of handling discipline. I didn't feel informed about life. I didn't feel I'd been taught the difference between right and wrong. I just felt hopelessly flawed. I have carried this feeling into my adult life. I have become a super pleaser in my important relationships. I will go to any length to avoid disapproval and the silent treatment that I'm afraid will follow. I can't tolerate my partner telling me what she is unhappy about in our relationship, I just want to hear from her that she loves me. I know that is wrong. I know it's important for us to be able to talk with each other about our problems, but I just can't cope with it."

That story illustrates the kind of damage that is done to significant relationships when one person gives the other the "silent treatment" as a way of dealing with conflict. It punishes. It isolates. It doesn't reveal. It engenders resentment. It is inimical to growth. If you find yourself inclined to giving the "silent treatment," perhaps because it is what you learned in your own family as a way of dealing with conflict, resist. Try to *talk* to your partner, no matter how difficult it is for you. Being silent is no way to treat a person you love, and it certainly is no way to build a trusting and supportive relationship.

6. Don't Abort the Fight.

How many times, in the midst of an altercation with your partner, have you quit, saying to yourself, "I've had enough of this." It may have felt good to be out of the combat zone, but the tensions that did not get worked through in this aborted fight do not just go away. They persist, accumulating to demand attention another day.

If you have had a fight with your partner and then walk around for hours or days continuing the dialogue in your head, the fight is not over. While you still feel anger or resentment toward your partner the fight should be allowed to continue.

If a fight started on the way to an evening out with friends, resume it when you get home. Resolution may be minutes away and save days of tension between the two of you. Continue the dialogue until the tension you felt is gone, or sufficiently reduced, so that you can relate to your lover in a comfortable and caring way again.

Don't run away from fights. Don't stop in the middle. Don't abort your chance to achieve clarity of communication with your partner in those areas where there is a tendency for conflict.

Following are four descriptions of couples fighting. Keeping in mind the "Do's" and "Don'ts," try to identify what is happening in each fight that is productive or counterproductive.

Eric and John

They are seated at dinner.

ERIC: *(Throwing down his fork)* You know, just for once you could stop thinking only of yourself. You really are the world's most selfish person!

JOHN: What the hell are you talking about?

ERIC: Thanks! Thanks for listening to me and paying attention to what I have to say, as usual.

JOHN: What did you have to say? What did you say except to tell me that I'm selfish, for the four thousandth time? You know,

I think you're crazy. I don't think you even know what you're talking about.

ERIC: I know exactly what I'm talking about.

JOHN: Well, then, how about letting me in on it?

ERIC: Sure, and I know exactly what will happen. You'll do what you've always done. You'll pretend you're interested in what I'm saying when you're really not listening at all. You have no respect for me, just as you have no respect for my things. You rummage through my drawers messing everything up, looking for god-knows-what. I've really had enough of your meddling. Actually, I think I've probably had enough of this relationship.

JOHN: Great, get into your big, farewell scene now. You really are ridiculous. I'm getting out of here.

ERIC: Good. Go. As usual you aren't interested in what I have to say.

JOHN: I might be if you said something besides telling me what a lousy partner I am.

ERIC: You've never been interested in what I have to say since the day we started this relationship. You don't respect my ideas or my needs any more than you respect my belongings.

JOHN: That's not true. I'm always interested in what you have to say when you tell me what's going on rather than just criticizing me. You know, you stopped really talking to me about the time you started hanging around with your friend Stewart. I'm still furious about your telling Stewart that you were considering changing jobs before you told me. Why did I have to hear it from him? I was really quite embarrassed that I didn't know what he was talking about because you hadn't bothered to tell me. How could you do that to me?

ERIC: Oh God, that was two years ago. Are you still stuck on that?

JOHN: You bet I am. When your lover doesn't think enough of you to tell you about something as important as that? Yes, I'm still furious about it. Why *did* you tell him before me?

ERIC: I've had enough of this. I'll see you later.

Now that's an unproductive fight.

Both Eric and John made sweeping condemnations of one another: "You are the world's most selfish person!" "I think you're crazy."

Eric "kitchen sinked" John. Eric threatened abandonment: "I think I've probably had enough of this relationship."

Both got stuck in the past: "You'll do what you've always done . . ." "I'm still furious about your telling Stewart. . . ."

To make this a productive fight, Eric might have talked about his feelings more, using "I" messages rather than so many "you" messages. He might have been specific about his complaints and the changes he wanted. Eric and John should have continued the fight until they could get down to whatever more difficult-to-deal-with issues were underlying their conflict. Finally, Eric should not have aborted the fight when he did. One certainly would not expect anything positive to have come from this encounter.

Jean and Delia

Jean walks into the living room holding Delia's underpants with the tips of her fingers. She holds them up as though they were a prize specimen of something.

JEAN: What do you want me to do with these?
DELIA: I don't care what you do with them.
JEAN: They're yours.
DELIA: I know they're mine.
(Jean walks over to the wastebasket and throws the panties into it.)
DELIA: What are you doing?
JEAN: You said you didn't care what I did with them.
DELIA: Why are you doing anything with them at all?
JEAN: Because they were on the floor and in my way.
DELIA: You couldn't walk around them?
JEAN: No, because they were the crowning glory of a rather size-able pile of similar articles.
(Delia feigns a yawn and goes back to her book.)

JEAN: Excuse me. I am trying to tell you something, to wit—you are an unspeakable slob. You are disorganized and disorderly. You don't care how our home looks. You have never cared, and you probably never will.

DELIA: What do you want me to do?

JEAN: You won't do it, so what's the use of telling you? You are not only slovenly, you make promises and don't keep them. You are really ungrateful. I work my tail off trying to keep this house looking nice, and you treat it as if it were a garbage dump. Not only that but when you left here last night you took my car without asking me, and this morning I had to spend half an hour cleaning out the backseat, as usual.

(Delia ignores Jean, sticking her nose further into her book.)

JEAN: Talk to me, dammit! It's about time you paid some attention to what I say. I'm sick and tired of picking up after you.

(Delia continues reading her book.)

JEAN: C'mon, Delia. We need to talk about this. It's driving me crazy.

(Delia does not respond.)

JEAN: All right. I have to tell you that I can't stand it anymore. This is not working for me. I'm just too unappreciated, and I resent it. I think this relationship has had it. I'm ready to call it quits.

(Delia continues reading.)

JEAN: Fine. Have it your way. You withdraw from me. I withdraw from you. That's it. I'm leaving . . . now . . . *(Pauses in the doorway, stamps her foot in exasperation. Delia does not look up.)* I'm not even going to try to talk to you anymore. I give up.

(Jean storms out of the room.)

Unproductive fight Number Two. What did they do wrong? Jean made sweeping condemnations: "You are an unspeakable slob." Jean "kitchen sinked" Delia, and she got stuck in recriminations regarding past behavior: "You have never cared and you probably never will." She also threatened abandonment: "I think this relationship has had it. I'm ready to call it quits."

One might say she aborted the fight because she gave up trying to talk to Delia, but it wasn't much of a fight to abort. Delia's "silent treatment" made any further discourse impossible.

Jean *was* specific about her complaints (but she didn't follow up with specific changes she'd like to see made). She didn't talk about her feelings, though they were readily apparent. There was no attempt and no opportunity to uncover the issues underlying their conflict. Nothing is likely to change as a result of this little skirmish.

Kerry and Nancy

Kerry plants herself in the middle of the doorway, arms akimbo, and glares at Nancy, who is talking on the telephone. Nancy tries to ignore Kerry but under Kerry's continuing stare Nancy puts her hand over the mouthpiece.

NANCY: What *is* it?

KERRY: I thought you were going to take care of the puppies today. You said you were going to take care of them so I could get this paperwork done. It's one o'clock in the afternoon, and they haven't been fed. They are screaming at the top of their lungs. Can't you hear them?

NANCY: *(Rolls her eyes skyward, then speaks into the phone.)* Sandy, I'm going to have to call you back. I have a little problem here. Just give me a few minutes. *(She hangs up and faces Kerry.)* Now, what do you want from me?

KERRY: I just want you to do what you said you were going to do. The dogs are hungry. Their poop from this morning hasn't been cleaned up. Their water dish isn't filled. These are neglected dogs. You said you would take care of them today.

NANCY: *(Takes a deep breath.)* Now, look. They have been fed once today and it was only a few hours ago. I filled their water dish, and, as dogs will do, they drank the water. As for the poop, I haven't gotten around to that yet. *(She pushes past Kerry on her way into the kitchen.)*

KERRY: *(Following Nancy.)* Don't you ever look around? Can't you see what needs to be done? I mean excrement is lying there picking up bacteria. It's really quite disgusting. How can you stand it?

NANCY: *(Eyes the two tiny turds lying in the puppies' pen and shakes her head in mock disgust.)* It really is pretty awful.

KERRY: You haven't made the bed either.

NANCY: What bed?

KERRY: What do you mean, "what bed?" The bed we sleep in. It isn't made.

NANCY: It's only one o'clock in the afternoon. I'll make it some time this afternoon. What's the big deal? Is the Inspector General on the way?

KERRY: Very funny. You said you would take care of the house this morning while I get this work done. You have spent most of the morning on the telephone, as usual. *(Begins opening cans and spooning food into the dogs' dishes.)*

NANCY: What are you doing?

KERRY: I'm feeding these poor dogs.

NANCY: *(Takes the spoon out of Kerry's hand.)* Now *I'm* beginning to get angry. Why don't you just go down to your office and do your paperwork. I don't think you want to do your paperwork. That's why you're out here bugging me.

KERRY: I am out here trying to take care of these things you said you would take care of.

NANCY: *(Leaning into Kerry, speaks in a cold, flat voice.)* I am getting pretty tired of your criticism.

KERRY: I'm getting pretty tired of your irresponsibility.

NANCY: I am not irresponsible, goddammit. You prowl around looking for things I've done wrong so that you'll have something to criticize. Well, I'm sick of it. Take care of your own damn house. Leave me alone!

KERRY: *(Whirling around to face Nancy.)* Oh, great. Now you're abdicating responsibility altogether.

(Nancy starts to walk away from Kerry.)

KERRY: Come back here. I'm talking to you.

(Nancy keeps on walking. Kerry runs after her.)

KERRY: Listen to me.

NANCY: What for? I've had enough criticism for one day.

KERRY: I'm not criticizing you. I have to tell you how it makes me feel when I see the dogs uncared for.

NANCY: Kerry, the dogs are not uncared for. You asked me to do something. I was doing it in my own way. It's not the same as your way, but I care about the dogs just as much as you do. And, I happen to care about the house, too. I just don't do it the way you would do it. We are different people. But, when you criticize me over and over, I feel terrible. I feel angry. I feel misunderstood. I feel devalued. My needs and my feelings don't seem to count. You know you could have just said, "I think the puppies are hungry." That's all. I would have fed them, and we could have avoided all of this.

KERRY: I know. *(Sighs.)* I think I resent it when you talk on the phone so much. I hate to talk on the phone, and I can't understand how you enjoy it so much.

NANCY: We're *different*.

KERRY: I guess also that I feel neglected. Why are you having such a good time with someone on the phone when I'm here to talk to. It's as if I have to get your attention.

NANCY: When you do it by attacking me, you get more than my attention. I feel put down. I want to strike back at you. If you're feeling left out and neglected, just tell me about it. It's natural for me to talk on the phone a lot. I'm not aware that I am doing that. But I'll be aware if it bothers you. You just have to tell me.

KERRY: It's hard, you know. I'm not always in touch with what I'm feeling at the moment. Even when I realize what I'm feeling I hesitate because . . . I mean, I don't really think there's anything wrong with talking on the phone, as long as it doesn't take too much away from our time together. And . . . I guess it doesn't really. You don't do it that much. I guess I'm just sort of envious of your ability to keep up your friendships with so many people. I can't seem to do that.

NANCY: Honey, we're just two different people. You can do things I can't do. I can do things you can't do. There's nothing wrong with that. We just have to learn to respect our differences and not see them as *faults* in the other person.

KERRY: You're right. I will try to tell you what's going on inside me, rather than clobbering you over the head.

(Kerry and Nancy embrace. The puppies watch quietly.)

Definitely a more productive fight than the first two. Both Kerry and Nancy were willing to risk fighting. Nancy's "I" messages gave Kerry the information she needed to understand what effect her behavior was having: "When you criticize me over and over, I feel terrible. I feel angry. I feel misunderstood. I feel devalued."

In turn, Kerry's "I" messages did the same: "When you talk on the phone so much . . . I feel neglected." Nancy was specific in her complaints and about the changes she wanted: "When you do it by attacking me you get more than my attention. I feel put down. I want to strike back at you. If you're feeling left out and neglected, just tell me about it."

Both Kerry and Nancy talked about their feelings, and they did a good job of identifying some of the underlying issues that were being played out in their encounter: "I think I resent it when you talk on the phone so much. I hate to talk on the phone and I can't understand how you enjoy it so much." "We're two different people . . . We just have to learn to respect our differences and not see them as *faults* in the other person."

These two people used their point of conflict to clarify an aspect of their relationship, thereby enhancing its potential for enduring and meeting their needs.

Frank and John

John comes into the room, slams a book down on the table, and fixes his lover with a "death look."

JOHN: You know, you really have a nerve! I can't believe the nerve you have. For three weeks now you have heard me talking about how important this presentation I have tomorrow is, and then you invite a whole gang of people over here for drinks tonight. How could you do that to me?

FRANK: *(Holding up both hands as if to ward off John.)* Wait a minute. First of all, you told me yesterday that you were as ready as you were going to be for your presentation, so I assumed that you had completed your preparation. Second, this "gang" is six people I work with who are going, as I am, to an event a few blocks from here, and I just invited them over afterward for a nightcap. You don't have to join us. You don't even have to appear. This "gang" should not get in your way at all. What is the big deal?

JOHN: The "big deal," my friend, is that I would like to get a good night's sleep tonight so I can be fresh in the morning. This is not Hearst Castle. This is a one-bedroom apartment, and I cannot go to sleep with a raucous party going on in the living room.

FRANK: Raucous party? Who said anything about a raucous party? Six people having a nightcap a raucous party doth not make. C'mon now.

JOHN: *(Walks toward the bedroom but stops at the door and pounds his fist against it.)* Dammit, you just don't care, do you? You just don't care!

FRANK: *(Surprised, leaves his chair and moves quickly toward John.)* Hey. What is this? You're really upset. C'mon, what is this all about? *(Guides John to the couch and sits with him. John takes a deep breath before he speaks.)*

JOHN: You just don't care about me.

FRANK: That's not true. I care a lot about you. This must be about something more than a few people coming over tonight. Let's have it. What is it?

JOHN: *(Looks at Frank for a long time before he answers.)* It's the way I feel when you do something that seems as if you don't care about what's happening to *me*. I feel as if I don't count. I feel deserted. I feel as if I can't trust you.

FRANK: John, I don't want you to feel that way. I really didn't think inviting a few people over tonight would interfere with what you're doing tomorrow.

JOHN: Whenever you make plans without consulting me, I feel terrible. I feel as if you don't care about my opinion. I don't feel like an equal partner in this relationship. I resent that, and it hurts.

FRANK: Look, I know what you like and what you don't like. I just make plans accordingly. I always take into account what you would want.

JOHN: But it's not the same. I want to be consulted. I want you to ask me before you make plans that involve me or affect me.

FRANK: *(Frowning)* You mean ask your permission?

JOHN: No. Of course not. It's not about asking my permission. It's about my sharing in decisions. I want to have just as much say in what we do in our life together as you do. I don't want to be surprised.

FRANK: You know that kind of cuts me off. I thought I was doing a good thing, bearing the burden of decisions, making plans you'd like.

JOHN: I know you are well-intentioned, but please see it from my point of view. I need to participate in decisions more.

FRANK: Okay, I didn't realize I was taking over so much. I'll try not to do that. I really will.

(John kisses his lover and begins moving around the room picking up newspapers and ashtrays.)

FRANK: What are you doing?

JOHN: *(Smiling)* Just getting the joint ready. We're having a raucous party tonight.

In this encounter John was specific about his complaints: "Whenever you make plans without consulting me, I feel terrible." He was specific about what he wanted to change: "I want to be consulted. I want you to ask me before you make plans that involve me or would affect me." He told Frank, through his "I" messages how he was affected by Frank's behavior: "I feel as if you don't care about my opinion, I don't feel like an equal partner in this relationship. I resent that and it hurts."

John talked about his feelings, and he dealt with issues underlying the conflict they were having: "I don't feel like an equal partner in this relationship . . . It's about my sharing in decisions. I want to have just as much say in what we do in our life together as you do."

As with Nancy and Kerry, John and Frank, in their encounter, clarified something that had been creating tension between them. The air was cleared, and they each had more information to use in building their future together.

How about your relationship? When there is conflict between you and your partner, are you both able to:

- risk fighting
- be specific about your complaints
- be specific about the changes you want
- get to underlying issues and concerns
- express angry feelings

Do either of you have an inclination to:

- get stuck in the past
- "kitchen sink" your partner
- deliver sweeping condemnations
- threaten abandonment
- give your partner the "silent treatment"
- abort the fight

Using the above checklist, think about what you and/or your partner might do to improve the productivity of your fights.

Remember, no relationship is without tension, and the best way to dispel tension is to deal directly with the issues causing it. Anger is a natural emotion that everyone feels. When it occurs in the course of conflict, pay attention to it. Your relationship will be enlivened and will grow if you learn to use conflict and the feelings that go with it to increase your understanding of who your partner is and what he/she needs from you.

9

THE SEXUAL AGENDA

GENDER-ROLE CONDITIONING AND
SEXUAL ISSUES

It begins at a very early age.

Little girls are subtly (and not so subtly) nudged toward the playthings of domesticity. They are taught the tasks of home-making and encouraged early to begin thinking about the most important decision of their life, whom they will marry. In enlightened families, other concerns are also dealt with, of course, such as education, personal development, career, but nearly always it is against a backdrop of anticipated marriage and family. The expectation is clear and present from very early in a little girl's life. She will be a wife and mother. She will make herself attractive to men. She will not be too aggressive. She will learn to be a good caretaker and a supportive, pleasing partner. She will learn to value her ability to be vulnerable and needy because these qualities appeal to a man's "natural" inclination to protect and provide. The message is driven home in many and varied ways. It is constant. It is inescapable.

Little boys, on the other hand, are directed toward the playthings of power and achievement. Competition is a cornerstone of their programming. Excellence of performance is emphasized, and it becomes a major criterion against which one's worth is assessed. Little boys are taught to control their feelings, be self-sufficient, not show their vulnerability, and aggressively go after whatever they want.

The entire system of male-female relationships is based on this trained-in complementarity. It is a flawed system, but it does go a long way toward shaping the expectations of men and women as to what their lives will be about.

When these men and women turn out to be gay and lesbian, their complementary programming no longer provides the foundation on which an intimate partnership can be built. On the contrary, partnerships in which both parties have been conditioned to the same role face a special kind of challenge. Nowhere is that challenge greater than in the sex life of gay and lesbian partners.

For instance, males in our society are taught that they need sex more than women do, that they have a right to it, that they should aggressively seek it out. Females are taught that they don't need sex in the same way men do, that they are not particularly expected to enjoy it, that they owe it to their male partners to provide them with it, and that it is undesirable for a woman to be sexually aggressive. When we have two males together in a relationship, we have two people conditioned to believe that they need sex, have a right to it, and should aggressively seek it out.

Or, we have two females together who have both been conditioned to believe that they don't need sex as men do, aren't particularly expected to enjoy it, and should not be aggressive in seeking it out.

As one would expect typical dilemmas arise with two males, as with two females. For instance, in a gay male relationship one partner may desire sex much less than the other partner. The high desire partner is functioning on the belief that he needs sex regularly, that he has a right to it, and that he should pursue it. The low desire partner does not believe that he must provide his partner with sex even if he doesn't feel like it, as a woman might. The high desire partner agitates for more sex. The low desire partner ignores this, or ridicules it ("He's a sex maniac; he wants to do it *all* the time"), or freezes up in the clinches or avoids any physical contact that might end up in a sexual encounter. The high desire partner is often heard to say such things as, "Why can't you do it for me?" or, "You're just doing this to punish me." Both the question and the statement focus on the need of the high desire partner to get the sex he has a right to expect, as per his programming. As long as the high desire partner continues to operate in accordance with his social conditioning, the couple is unlikely to get down to really exploring the reasons for the discrepancy in their level of desire and doing something to solve the problem.

Another example of a problem that can occur as a result of male conditioning is that of the partner whose orientation to sex separates it from affection. Some gay men, accustomed to casual or anonymous sex with multiple partners, behave sexually with a partner as they did in their pre-relationship sex life. Sexual encounters are genital/orgasm oriented. No romantic overtures, no gentle caresses, no tender nothings whispered into the ear. Habit might be reinforced by male conditioning that teaches that sex without affection is okay because "that's the way men are." The partners of such people often feel deprived because they want a more integrated kind of love-making, including tenderness, affection, and romance.

In lesbian relationships gender-role conditioning can create problems related to who initiates sex between the partners. Here we have two people conditioned to believe that they should not be sexually aggressive. In the beginning of the relationship passion shows the way, but as passion wanes, neither partner assumes the responsibility for initiating. Sex might happen less and less frequently. Typically, female conditioning teaches that women do not really need sex, as men do. Soon, sex might stop altogether. If both women in such a relationship are satisfied with this state of affairs, there is no problem. But, if one partner is unhappy, feeling deprived and frustrated, the matter needs attention. The dissatisfied partner might not be able to break out of her programming sufficiently to initiate the sex she wants. All too often a conspiracy of silence develops around the issue. They don't talk about it. There is no opportunity to address or challenge the gender-role conditioning that makes it so difficult for women to be initiators of sex, even the sex they might feel deprived of and long for.

Another fatality of gender-role conditioning might be communication about sex. Nice girls don't talk about sex. Real men know what to do and don't *have* to talk about it. Those are the myths.

The reality is that both men and women profit by talking to their partners about what is (or isn't) happening between them sexually. Such communication informs sexual experience and improves the ability of the partners to satisfy one another. Communication about sex has the potential of opening up new areas of eroticism to be explored and of integrating sexuality more effectively into the couple's enjoyment of their life together.

MESSAGES FROM HOME

Let's begin with how one feels about being sexual at all.

Many people have been saddled in their lives with sexual attitudes, passed on from parents, that guarantee conflict when they try to enjoy their sexuality as adults. Those who come from families deeply involved with a religion that equates sexual pleasure with sin often must struggle with their own internalization of that idea. Sexual pleasure is tinged with guilt and a sense of doing something wrong. Add to that the prohibition most religions place on homosexual behavior, and the ability to enjoy or even be comfortable with sex can be seriously affected.

Those with this kind of religious conflict might be able to allow themselves sexual pleasure only under special conditions, perhaps only with nameless strangers ("This is not really me doing this"), or perhaps only when numbed by alcohol or drugs, perhaps only in degrading circumstances, as though the punishment had to be simultaneous with the sin.

Religious beliefs are not the only inhibitors to a free and easy sexual relationship. The kind of models one's parents were with regard to sexuality and the expression of affection count for a lot. Think about your own parents. Were they affectionate with one another? If so, was it only when they thought they were unobserved or was it also when the children were around? Did they touch each other? Hold hands? Caress? Exchange affectionate glances?

Did they talk about sex? If so, did they present it as something natural and nice? Or were they tense when they talked about it, as though it was wrong even to speak of it? How were your parents with you? Did they hug and kiss and caress you? Was affection freely expressed, or did it happen only when one was arriving, leaving, or saying good night or good morning? Or, did it not happen at all? What were the messages you received with regard to the physical expression of affection? Was it enjoyed? Was it taboo? Was it just tolerated by a parent who was obviously uncomfortable with it?

Whether you are following the model provided by your parents or trying to be anything *but* like them, you will do well to examine the ways in which their influence might be showing up in your present partnership.

EARLY TRAUMA

Some people enter adulthood with a sexual self-image marred by childhood experience with an adult who used them sexually. A parent. An older sibling. A relative outside the immediate family. A neighbor. A friend of the family. Usually the person is too embarrassed to talk about what happened, even decades later.

This person's ability to function freely in a sexual relationship might be seriously affected by that early experience. What makes the difference is being able to talk about it, as many women for whom incest has come out of the closet have found out. I hope this will happen more and more for men also.

If you have experienced sexual trauma early in life, and have found it difficult to talk to anyone about it, think seriously of getting professional help to break through the silence. You don't have to live with your secret. With help you can move beyond it.

THE POSITIVE SIDE

It is an occupational hazard, when you are a clinician, to focus on the *problems* life yields up more than the joys and delights. Of course, I recognize that the majority of people do learn to love from their parents, having experienced early in life two people who cherished one another and showed it freely. Most parents feel great affection for their offspring and let them know it in all kinds of ways, including spontaneous hugs and kisses. Such people grow up feeling comfortable with the physical expression of affection and usually have sex lives that are enjoyable and free of tension.

SEX EDUCATION

In one of the most memorable celebrations of ingenuousness in cinematic history, Ingrid Bergman, as the unworldly mountain girl in Ernest Hemingway's *For Whom the Bell Tolls,* about to receive her first kiss, whispers breathlessly to Gary Cooper, "Where do the noses go?"

Watching that film as a child, I leaned forward in my seat, fixated on the screen, to see where, indeed, the noses did go. For most people, learning "where the noses go," as well as where everything else in sexual activity goes, means struggling through a kind of timid discovery process.

Some people are fortunate enough to have parents who were comfortable with their own sexuality and able to provide reasonable preparation for explorations into eroticism. Precious few, however, had parents who could give guidance in the matter of gay or lesbian sex. We were really out there on our own to find out what we needed to know.

For gay men, their same-gender sex education came mainly in the form of early exposure to the idealized sexual fantasies found in erotic films and publications. While this may have provided the information necessary to know what to do, it also presented standards of personal attractiveness and sexual conduct that were, for most people, impossible to live up to.

Many gay men adopted as their sexual models the handsome, brawny, athletic, ever-tumescent gay porno stars whose performances were never wanting. The effort to live up to that standard has been one of the most dispiriting factors in the lives of whole generations of gay men. Life as a porno flick doesn't work, they've found, particularly if they did not look like Adonis, were shy, chose not to spend hours working out at the gym, weren't "hung like a horse," couldn't always get or maintain an erection, or ejaculated too early or late. So, easy access to these data of sexual activity was a mixed blessing. It informed, but it also imposed, for many, standards that in the long run were often *inhibiting* to the development of a full and satisfying sex life.

Lesbians, on the other hand, have had relatively little outside help in learning the intricacies of making love to another woman. Only recently have we seen the advent of true lesbian erotica, that is, films, videos, and publications written by women for women, as opposed to those exploitative "lesbian" frolics put out by men for men, in which female actresses nervously groped and kissed each other and undulated on cue.

In the mid to late 1970s lesbian sex began to come out of the closet with the publication of such books as *Loving Women** in 1975, and *The Joy of Lesbian Sex*** in 1977. The publication of JoAnn Loulan's *Lesbian Sex**** in 1984 provided a comprehensive manual complete with an illustrated guide to the physiology of

* Nomadic Sisters, *Loving Women.* (Sonora, Ca., 1974).

** Emily Sisley and Bertha Harris, *The Joy of Lesbian Sex:* (New York: Crown Publishers, 1977).

*** JoAnn Loulan, *Lesbian.Sex.* (San Francisco: Spinsters Ink/aunt lute, 1984).

lesbian sex. No lesbian need suffer any longer from a lack of information on the mechanics of lovemaking. The resources are now there for the using.

So, things are better, at least insofar as learning "where the noses go." One hopes the availability of publications that deal explicitly with gay and lesbian sex will enable people to be better informed and, therefore, better able to develop a satisfying sex life. A partial list of such publications appears at the end of this chapter.

In the gay and lesbian couples' groups I have conducted over the years, I have been particularly impressed with the value that discussions about sexual issues have had for the participants.

"Are you monogamous?"

"How often do you have sex?"

"Who usually initiates it?"

"What do you do in bed?"

"Do you talk during sex?"

There is a hunger for information about what other people do in their sexual relationships. There is also a reticence to talk about the subject with others. Generalizing from the experience I have had in my couples' groups, I would encourage a greater effort on the part of gay men and lesbians to push through their reticence and begin talking more openly with friends about these sexual issues.

One of the important ways in which we educate one another about sexuality is through the sharing of our own experiences with sex. Following are some questions you might want to use to structure a discussion with your partner about your sexual histories. Such a discussion can be particularly helpful if you have never talked with one another about these experiences before.

• What do you remember of your first awareness of sexual feelings?

• What do you remember of your early masturbating experience? Where did you do it? How? When? What were your thoughts about it? How did you usually feel about yourself afterward?

- What do you remember of your first sexual experience with another person? Who was it? Where was it? When was it? What was it?
- What other significant early sexual experiences did you have?
- What do you remember of your first homosexual thoughts?
- What do you remember of your first homosexual experience?
- What other early (or later) homosexual experiences were significant for you?
- What is the worst thing that ever happened to you sexually?
- What is the best thing that ever happened to you sexually?

COMMUNICATION AND SEX

Some people believe that sex and talk don't go together.

Some people approach sex as though it was a religious experience, not to be profaned by talking during the ceremony.

Some people have so compartmentalized their sexuality that they can only perform in silence, in the dark, as though they were doing it with the "not me" part of themselves.

Some people are embarrassed by talk about sex, during or after, as though God, or mother, or both, had their ear to the door.

Some people have never talked about sex and are at a loss when asked to do so. "What's to *say?*" they query.

I have watched the most mature, verbal, articulate, sophisticated people trying to tell one another what they liked and didn't like about their sex together, and they sounded like embarrassed adolescents. Experiencing their discomfort, one needed no further proof of how "sexophobic" our society is. In educating our young people we try to open them up to so many aspects of the world. When it comes to this most universal of experiences, we conceal information and impart an attitude toward sexuality that creates guilt and embarrassment even in the most worldly among us. It is no wonder that people, even in the most intimate of relationships, don't talk comfortably with one another about sex.

The truth is that couples who are able to talk about their sexual repertoire are more likely to have a good one.

A lot of people don't talk. They slip into routines that make their sex life predictable and remove the need for discussion. Everyone knows what to expect, so, once again, "What's to say?" But, often, there is quite a bit to say. It just isn't being said. Routines grow old and tiresome. Spontaneity wanes. It becomes easier to do it in the same old way and not have to talk about it. Sex loses its appeal and often then happens less and less frequently.

The key is communication. For instance, answer the following questions:

- Do you have sex with your partner less frequently or more frequently than you'd like?
- Do you have sex with your partner only on the weekends?
- Do the two of you have sex only at night?
- Do you have sex only in the morning?
- Do you have sex only in the dark?
- Do you have sex only when you've used drugs or alcohol?
- Do you have sex only when the two of you are out of town together?
- Do you have sex only if there is no one else in the house?
- Do you have sex only using toys or vibrators?
- Do you have sex in the same way all the time?

If you answered "yes" to any of these questions, think about whether or not you are satisfied with what you answered "yes" to. If you find you are dissatisfied, think about what change you'd like to see regarding that particular arrangement.

Being able to ask for what you want or what you no longer want is an act of faith in the relationship. Being unwilling to ask for change is a vote of no confidence in the potential of your partnership.

USING FANTASY

Another route to increasing awareness and enhancing communication about sex in a couple's life is through the use of fantasy. In fantasy we can make anything we want happen. If there is something we are embarrassed about or afraid to try in real life, we can make it happen easily in fantasy. Our fantasies inform us of needs and wishes that we sometimes are not completely conscious of or do not want to take responsibility for. Many people have such rich sexual fantasies that their real-life sexual experience cannot compete.

Fantasy can be used constructively by a gay or lesbian couple to open dialogue about sexual topics the partners feel are too difficult to talk about directly. Sometimes the use of erotic publications or audiovisual materials can facilitate the building of collaborative fantasies by the partners, leading to more varied and interesting sexual activity than had been possible before.

If you are up for adventure, try the following experiment:

First, you and your partner should do the following, independently. Write out a sexual fantasy involving the two of you. In this fantasy you can make anything happen, sexually, that you want. You are not constrained by any rules or expectations or limitations. You might want to include in your fantasy something that you have thought about but never spoken to your partner about, or something that you haven't done together, but would like to do.

When each of you has finished writing your fantasy, which can be as long as you like, have a session together in which you read each other what you have written. *In this session it is very important that neither of you is judgmental about the other's fantasy.* Be as open to hearing what your partner has to say as you can. Encourage elaboration and as much detail as you would like to hear from your partner.

Second, when you have finished with your individual fantasies, spend time with your partner developing a mutual fantasy. You may want to write it out or just talk about it. You might want to work in elements from each of your separate fantasies.

Do what you can to make this experience as much fun as possible. If this kind of fantasizing is not something you tend to do with your partner, do it again in the near future. Perhaps you will want to make it a regular part of your sexual relationship? Above all, use your fantasy experiences to learn from and to make your sex life with your lover a richer and more adventuresome one.

MONOGAMY VS. NON-MONOGAMY

For some couples, determining how sexually exclusive to be is no issue at all. They both agree at the outset that monogamy is for them. They mean it. They stick to it, and that's that.

Other couples agree that they want to have a non-monogamous relationship. Sometimes they actually conduct their lives this way. Sometimes the non-monogamy agreement merely acts as a kind of "escape hatch." It's comforting to know it's there, but it goes unused as long as there isn't anything to escape from.

Some couples start out agreeing on sexual exclusivity with one another, and then change the agreement later in their relationship as their needs change, or as they get more in touch with what they really wanted all along. Sometimes it's the other way around: the agreement is to be non-monogamous, and the partners come to realize that they really do want to be sexually exclusive with each other.

What goes into the decision that a given couple makes? It is often a more complex matter than it appears to be on the surface. Each partner brings to the relationship an ideological stance on the monogamy issue, which is the combined product of the pattern in their family, their moral training, their gender-role conditioning, the current standards of whatever part of the gay or lesbian subculture they identify with, and their personal sexual history. Each partner also brings her/his own particular level of tolerance for uncertainty that influences how much he or she can put up with potentially threatening non-monogamous activity by a partner. It all goes into the mix of beliefs that determine how one approaches the topic.

In 1983, sociologists Philip Blumstein and Pepper Schwartz published the findings of their extensive research on intimate partnerships in *American Couples.** Comparing heterosexually married, heterosexual cohabiting, lesbian and gay couples, they drew the following conclusions regarding the monogamy issue:

Relationships in which there is at least one woman (heterosexual marriages and cohabitors, lesbian couples) tend to be more monogamous because, in the main, women usually want sex with their partners to be as exclusive as possible.

Heterosexual men have the implicit permission of society to pursue sex outside the primary relationship, particularly if it's done discreetly. Because men are programmed to separate their libidinal experience from emotions, sexual adventures are presumed not to threaten the primary relationship. The "double standard" further protects the primary relationship since it prohibits non-monogamy on the part of the female partner, who might very well become emotionally involved in the course of an affair in a way that would threaten the partnership.

Just as men are programmed to be able to separate sex from love when it serves them to do so, women are programmed to prefer a loving context for their sexual expression. In a relationship between two women, sex outside the primary relationship can be a very serious matter. It is likely that the sex will not be casual and that there will be emotional involvement because that's the way women usually function. The non-monogamous act more often threatens the bond of the lesbian couple than that of other kinds of couples.

The least troubling effect of non-monogamy is on the male couple. With no female around pressing for sexual exclusivity, casual sex with outsiders can be more easily integrated into the couple's lifestyle. Furthermore, a whole subculture has supported

* Philip Blumstein and Pepper Schwartz, *American Couples* (New York: William Morrow, 1983).

open relationships between men. Because of AIDS the emphasis
has shifted now to making contact in nonsexual (or at least non-
genitally-oriented sexual) ways.

The factor of AIDS also strongly influences decisions about
sexual exclusivity. I find that most of the male couples I know and
work with are choosing to be monogamous and are demonstrating a new willingness to improve their relationship skills as a way
of making sure their partnerships will work well and endure.

THE HIDDEN AGENDA OF OUTSIDE SEX

People in officially monogamous relationships sometimes use
outside sexual experiences to express dissatisfaction with something in the partnership. Sometimes it is a bold and blatant statement made directly and angrily to a partner. Sometimes it is more
subtle, the partner not quite sure what is happening but knowing
that something is wrong.

Sometimes the non-monogamous partner leaves a trail of
breadcrumbs leading to the scene of the crime, ensuring discovery by the other partner. For what purpose? To precipitate the
confrontation that it was too difficult to effect, to force the other
partner to take the responsibility for ending the relationship? Of
course, there are always those who believe that frustrations taken
care of elsewhere will relieve tension in the partnership, which
can then continue to exist for its good parts. Sometimes they are
right. More often they are wrong.

Actually, people who look outside their relationship for relief
of partnership tension do not trust their partner's ability to understand, to care, or to change. Once convinced of that, they do
not have to face dealing with the real source of their disappointment, their anger, their boredom. Instead, they turn away from
the partnership to others for proof of personal attractiveness, for
proof of their lovableness, for validation in general, or for simple
distraction.

If you are in a monogamous relationship and find yourself

sexually involved outside the relationship, ask yourself these questions:

- Am I looking for a way out in order to avoid confrontation with my partner and the work that might make necessary?
- What is happening in my relationship that is so difficult to deal with?
- What is missing with my lover that causes me to be so available for erotic connections with others?

From what I have seen in these situations, it is a good bet that there is usually a lot more work that could be done to improve the relationship, which is, of course, the hard way. The easy way, too often taken in gay and lesbian partnerships, is to "unplug" from the present lover and "plug" into a new one, hoping it will be better this time around, but having done nothing significant to enhance that possibility.

INITIATING AND REFUSING SEX

Think about your own relationship. Who controls your sex life with your partner? Do you? Does she/he? Is control shared equally? Who does most of the initiating? Who does most of the refusing?

Blumstein and Schwartz, in *American Couples,* provide us with the following insights from their research:

In heterosexual couples initiating sex is usually left to men. Should we therefore expect lesbians to be uncomfortable with taking the lead? And find gay men ready and able? Our interviews tell us that this is the case. We feel that many lesbians are not comfortable in the role of sexual aggressor and it is a major reason why they have sex less often than other kinds of couples. . . .
Another real consideration for lesbian couples is

their disdain for conventional male and female role playing. Over and over again they tell us in the interviews that one partner resents "always being responsible" for initiating. The other partner then feels pressured because she would like sex to "evolve more spontaneously." For this to happen, however, both women would have to want to be, and learn how to become, the initiator. . . .

What happens when both partners are male? They both feel free to be the initiator. This may account, in part, for gay couples' frequent sex in their early years together. But we think having two initiators in a couple can create problems. Initiating symbolizes maleness and dominance; therefore double initiation, which goes unnoticed in the romantic beginning of the relationship, can escalate into competition—not to prove who can provide greater satisfaction but to demonstrate to the other who is running the show. In reaction to being pushed, one partner may begin to refuse, exerting his own method of control. He then places himself in the same situation as traditional heterosexual women. By using his veto, he strikes back at his male partner's attempt to define the terms of their sexual relationship. This may trigger a rapid decline in the couple's sex life, because a gay man, unlike a heterosexual woman, is not compelled out of "duty" to respond to his partner's sexual desire. Gay couples may attribute the fact that they have sex less often to a diminished sexual attraction for each other, but sometimes it may actually reflect the fact that each partner is reading the same male script.

. . . The act of refusal is one way a person may achieve power. . . . When a person refuses sex, he or she can become a force to be reckoned with.

SEXUAL DESIRE

"Not tonight, honey."

That familiar refrain resounds through relationships with the regularity of clocks ticking and the sun rising and setting. Differences in the level of desire by partners in a sexual relationship occur commonly. Sometimes it is a matter of timing, of one partner feeling disinclined to be sexual, for whatever reason, at the time her/his partner is eager to have sex. That occurs routinely in nearly all relationships.

Usually, the difference in how sexual one person feels on a given occasion versus how sexual the other feels balances out over time and is not defined as a problem by the couple. Inconvenient, annoying, perhaps, but, not a problem. Nor is it a problem if the couple agrees not to be sexual very often, as long as both partners truly do not object to that arrangement. That becomes the norm for that couple in that period of their relationship, and it is no one's business but their own how often they have sex. This is equally true for the couple who has sex twice a day. If both partners are doing what they truly want to be doing, that is the norm for their relationship, in that period of time.

The frequency with which a couple has sex becomes a problem only when one or both partners feel dissatisfaction with what is happening and that dissatisfaction continues over a significant period of time. Usually when that is the case, it is a matter of one partner consistently wanting to be sexual and the other partner consistently not wanting to. Such difference in desire comprises one of the main reasons couples seek help from therapists.

Given that being sexual with one another on a regular basis is a primary way of defining two people as lovers, the diminution of sex in the relationship is often mistakenly taken to mean that the couple is "out-of-love," and the relationship is over. Sometimes that is the case, but more often it is not. The relationship is salvageable if the partners can come to understand and appreciate that sex is not the only way to bond, that it is normal for sex to wane after a period for even the most passionate of lovers, that

consistent loss of interest in sex by one partner happens for a reason which is fathomable, that a satisfactory level of sexual activity
is possible to regain if both partners are willing to do the work
necessary to make that happen.

Before going into some of the typical reasons for loss of interest in being sexual, I'd like to put the issue of "sexual desire"
into perspective.

In the mid-1950s sex researchers William Masters and Virginia Johnson began what was to become a decade of observing,
recording, and analyzing the human sexual response. They studied some ten thousand orgasmic events in their laboratory and
concluded that the human sexual response occurs in two main
phases. The first they labeled "excitement." The second they labeled "orgasm."*

It was over twenty years later that another sex researcher** labeled as the "desire phase," the internal activity that leads one to
seek out, or become available for, sexual experience. That activity was thought to originate in the "sex center" of the brain and
become translated into directly genital sensations or a more
vague feeling of being "turned on." The desire phase was believed to continue until orgasm brought resolution or until some
inhibitory force caused desire to diminish and die.

Inhibitory forces might come from any of a variety of sources.
The most common source is the perception of danger. Since in the
hierarchy of motives survival takes precedence over the urge to be
erotic, the perception of danger cancels out the experiencing of
sexual desire. The high priority that survival demands over erotic
experience is an adaptive mechanism that allows the human ani-
mal to shift energy from pleasure-seeking activity to mobilization
against attack, when the danger of an attack is perceived to be present. But, remember, we are dealing with *perception* here, and per-

* William H. Masters and Virginia E. Johnson, *Human Sexual Response* (Boston:
Little, Brown & Co., 1966).

** Helen Singer Kaplan, *Disorders of Sexual Desire* (New York: Brunner/ Mazel,
1979).

ception, a complex of internal experiences, is not always accurate. For instance, the sex centers of the brain are connected to those parts of the brain that store and process *past* experience. If we have learned, to inhibit sexual desire in the past when we felt some clear and present danger, it is quite possible the link between that perceived danger and the inhibition of sexual desire will have become established and will be hard to extinguish. Many gay men and lesbians have learned to inhibit sexual desire at an early age because of a conviction, or an impression, that such feelings for someone of the same gender were wrong. While the danger of discovery may no longer be of any importance, the feelings attached to that fear may persist in association with homosexual desire and continue to act as an inhibitory force in the person's adult sex life.

In other words, while sex gives us pleasure, it can be pre-empted by the need to avoid pain, which demands a higher priority in our psychological functioning. Anything associated in our minds with pain or danger activates our pain centers, which, in turn, inhibit the sexual centers. Designed to aid in survival, this mechanism diminishes sexual desire in order to prepare the organism to deal with what it perceives to be an impending crisis. So, this is, roughly, the *process* by which sexual desire becomes inhibited. Now the question is, "Why does it occur?".

REASONS FOR INHIBITED SEXUAL DESIRE

In a given instance of the loss of sexual desire, there may be a single reason or a combination of reasons. The cause may be a function of something that is happening in the individual's life currently or has happened in the past. It may be situational, or it may be a problem of long standing. Or, the reason may be a function of the relationship the individual is in.

Let's look first at some possible reasons that are more about the individual than the relationship.

Organic Causes

It is rare that a person loses sexual desire because something is wrong physiologically. If there is a suspicion that this might be true, however, one should consult a physician to have it checked out. Usually it is a urologist who deals with such problems for men and a gynecologist for women.

Stress

It is common for people to lose their sexual desire when they are experiencing an unusual degree of stress. This stress might be caused by the person's worklife or by illness or problems with friends or family. Severe loss of any kind will often result in the temporary inhibition of sexual desire. If you think this might be happening to you, try to identify what is causing the stress so you can come to see the sexual manifestation of it in more perspective.

Sexual Identity Conflict

Sometimes this occurs in such a way that it is quite obvious just what the problem is. More often, it is a subtle matter. Sex in a given relationship may be terrific in the beginning while the person is under the spell of being in love, but then reality sets in, and with it comes the realization, at some level of consciousness, that it is, indeed, the kind of sexual relationship that it is. Whatever undealt-with discomfort there might be with one's homosexuality begins to make itself felt. It might be a short step from there to the inhibition of sexual desire.

In this time of high gay and lesbian consciousness, people are often loath to believe that their sexual difficulties in a relationship might be caused by the wish not to be in this kind of relationship in the first place. The struggle to accept ourselves fully as gay goes on for most of us, at some level, all our lives. It will as long as there is homophobia in the society we live in. Even though I have been an activist for more than thirty years,

I still surprise myself on occasion with some manifestation of the struggle to accept and integrate my homosexuality. Checking up on yourself, to see how you are currently doing with the struggle can be very helpful in correctly identifying the sexual acting out of one's ambivalence about being gay, when that is what is happening.

Performance Anxiety

It happens to men and women. It is basically a problem that occurs in the "excitement phase" of the sexual experience. A man is unable to get or maintain an erection, a woman cannot be brought to orgasm. While the result may be the same among a variety of individuals, the possible causes are many. Most commonly the individual feels anxiety about the ability to perform, before the fact. "Will it work tonight?" "Will I take too long?" The summoning up of such fears has to have an inhibiting effect on the person's ability to function sexually.

Why would one want to *prevent* the ability to give or receive sexual pleasure? Sometimes the cause is a deep psychological fear of abandonment, as a punishment for not performing perfectly. It is easier not to meet the challenge at all than to have to face the pain of rejection for a flawed performance. So, the individual "arranges" not to have to perform at all. Now the problem may well become one of inhibited desire. The person may avoid perceived pain by avoiding sexual encounters altogether.

Another common reason for preventing one's self from being able to give or receive sexual pleasure lies in a deep-seated *fear of sexual success* that probably has its roots in childhood when prohibitions against being sexual (successfully) were strong. So, one consciously fears failure while unconsciously fearing success. Again, this may result in the individual inhibiting sexual desire so as not to have to deal with whatever penalties the once-forbidden sexual pleasure might produce.

Sometimes recognizing the dynamics of a sexual problem can go a long way toward resolving it. Other times recognition may, properly, lead to the therapist's office for a more profound exploration of why one is having the trouble one is having.*

Drug and Alcohol Abuse

Inhibited sexual desire may be caused by chemical substances, which, if used excessively over time, may cloud awareness and block the ability to feel and act spontaneously. In extreme instances there may be organ failure or damage to the central nervous system.

Prolonged use of alcohol or drugs may have become so closely associated with sexual experience that the individual cannot even approach the sexual scene without, sniffing, snorting, dropping, or downing a few.

If you think you might have developed a chemical addiction problem, I strongly recommend that you involve yourself in a recovery program based on the Twelve Steps of Alcoholics Anonymous. AA is listed in the white pages of your local telephone book. From them you can obtain a directory that will indicate which meetings are gay, or for women only, should that be your preference. If your problem is with drugs rather than alcohol, you will also find Narcotics Anonymous and Cocaine Anonymous in your local white pages. If you are in a relationship with someone who has an addiction problem, you can get help from Al-Anon, also listed.

In the process of recovery from substance abuse there might be special problems regarding sex. In her book *Lesbian Sex,* Jo Ann Loulan describes them. Her description applies equally well to men:

> Most newly sober women have rarely or never had sex
> without the use of alcohol or drugs. Facing sex sober for

* For referral to a qualified sex therapist in your area, contact the American Association of Sex Educators, Counselors and Therapists (AASECT), 11 Dupont Circle, N.W., Suite 220, Washington, D.C. 20036. (202) 462-1171.

the first time raises tremendous fear and anxiety. Fears of incompetence, inadequacy, intimacy, and lack of control are common and frequently continue throughout the first year. The fear of losing your partner, losing your own sobriety, or never regaining an absent sex drive may be constant. The changing power dynamics in relationships brought about by sobriety can be confusing and anxiety producing. Experiencing genital intimacy without the use of a chemical "aid" may create so much anxiety that being sexual becomes an unpleasant or even impossible task. As a recovering addict, you may feel unable to perform sexually, unable to receive sexual attentions, or simply have no sexual desire at all.

If you are in the process of recovery and are having sexual problems, talking with others who have been through the same experience can be immensely helpful. You may have chosen to recover on your own, but it's most likely at AA or NA that you will find people with similar experiences to talk to.

Childhood Trauma

Abusive sexual experiences as a child or adolescent often plague an individual into adulthood, particularly if such experiences have not been dealt with directly. The ability to be freely and comfortably sexual can be very much affected by the memory of traumatic events associated with childhood sexual experiences. Such memories may be triggered at any time by something (often seemingly benign) happening in a sexual experience with a lover. If information about the early sexual trauma is not available, unexplained inhibitions may be taken to be expressions of disinterest or rejection of a partner, when that is really not the case.

Sometimes, the person is unable to access memories of sexual trauma, especially if it occurred in early childhood. By definition, childhood sexual trauma is about wounding, frequently devastating experiences. We tend to ameliorate our psychic pain by blotting out memories of experiences too frightening to deal with. Even if these memories are inaccessible for the individual to contemplate, much less share with a partner, they may still seriously affect the person's ability to experience their own sexual desire as such, to tolerate sexual excitement, to reach orgasm, or to enjoy pleasurable feelings related to any aspect of sex.

If you think that early sexual trauma may be affecting either you or your partner, you should seek help from a professional counselor, preferably one experienced in the subspecialty of sex therapy. You might find a qualified therapist through your local psychological or mental health associations. For a list of certified sex therapists, contact the American Association of Sex Educators, Counselors and Therapists (see footnote earlier in this chapter).

Several cautions regarding a partner exploring early sexual trauma. First, it frequently takes some time into the therapy process for a person to admit fully into consciousness memories that have been long suppressed. A partner may need to be particularly patient and supportive during this process of exploration. Second, a partner should avoid trivializing, in any way, the importance of early sexual trauma, especially if the person has been inclined to deny or downplay the significance of the experience.

Dr. Rex Reece has commented to me, in this regard, "I've found I've had to help lovers get beyond, 'That happened a long time ago, why are you hanging onto it?' and thus *contributing* to feelings of guilt and inadequacy."

Because Dr. Reece works primarily with men, we are reminded that, although the overwhelming majority of childhood sexual abuse survivors are women, this phenomenon among men is by no means uncommon and can be every bit as painful as it is for many women.

In either case, in those instances where the individual's memories of trauma are intact, talking about them to a loving and accepting partner can go a long way toward destigmatizing the feelings so often attached to these memories, like shame, guilt, and fear of reprisal. Open communication about such things in a relationship creates the opportunity for the healing effect that a good, adult, intimate partnership can have.

Basic Sexual Guilt

Fear regarding discovery of one's homosexual thoughts and feelings is very specific. For many people the fear that inhibits may be of a more global nature, involving a fear of being sexual at all. If one's parents were uncomfortable whenever sexual matters came up because of their own conditioning, it is likely that they would have passed on their discomfort to their children through punishing behavior regarding anything sexual or through avoidance of dealing with the issue at all.

Basic sexual guilt may be an important contributing factor in the inhibition of sexual desire. Restructuring of early, ingrained, negative attitudes toward sex is not an easy task. It can be greatly facilitated by a supportive and understanding lover.

Now let's look at some of the causes of inhibited sexual desire that are more a function of relationship to others than of individual development.

Fear of Intimacy

Intimacy is about the willingness to be known by and be vulnerable to another person with whom you share an emotionally close relationship. It is about trusting that other person to take you seriously, to care about what is happening to you, not to abandon you, to want to and be willing to try to please you.

While these seem like the ideal conditions that one would want in one's relationship, many people fear the intimacy these conditions define. If one's earliest experiences with intimacy were negative it is likely one will not be comfortable being intimate in adult life. If you had parents who were more interested in their version of who you were than in who you really were, you will have learned to keep to yourself any thoughts and feelings that seem as if they might not please the other person. Disclosure feels risky or even dangerous.

If you had early experience with trying to show your feelings that brought you punishment or, indifference, it is likely you will not too easily allow yourself to be vulnerable in adult life. You will be afraid that exposing your inner self will bring a repeat of the punishment or indifference of your childhood experience.

If you felt uncared for, devalued, or emotionally deserted by a parent, it is probable you will defend yourself against attempts by another person to emotionalize your relationship. You certainly won't do anything to make that happen. You don't want to want what was missing in your earlier life. It feels too painful to be unrequited, which you always expect. So, you avoid intimacy beyond a certain point. It feels safer that way.

For some people the absence of parental interest in who they were, or the lack of affection openly expressed to them early on, came to mean they were undeserving. Thus, they come into adult life feeling basically undeserving of love. If someone tries to give them the affection they need, they might well feel guilty accepting the love that their parents "taught" them not to expect. Or, perhaps they are so accustomed to not being loved that that's what feels "right" to them, and anything else seems alien. They don't know what to do with love freely offered. Too often they reject it directly or arrange conditions in their life so that it becomes impossible for anyone to love them, for very long.

The barriers to intimacy one puts up when one has a fear of intimacy can become a strong inhibitory force in maintaining sexual desire. Intimacy can be very much enhanced by good sexual experience. If one has a fear of increasing intimacy, one may be inclined to inhibit sexual desire whenever that fear is activated. This is usually not a conscious experience, nor is there consistency about it. The person who fears intimacy may have learned to tolerate or even enjoy it for periods of time. When the level of tolerance is reached, however, the person will most likely do something to push the partner away. If both partners experience the same fear of intimacy, there will likely be a discernible pattern of moving closer, then moving away from each other (precipitated by conflict, illness, or distraction from some other source). Then, after sufficient distance has been achieved, there is movement toward one another again.

One can learn to look for signs that point to intimacy fears if sexual desire seems to wane in connection with developments in a relationship that symbolize growing commitment. I have seen couples who were passionately sexual with each other until they decided to move in together, at which time sexual desire became significantly diminished for one or both of them.

Even though threatened by the possibility of increasing intimacy, an individual may well love his/her partner very much and not *consciously* want to push that partner away. The person may, nevertheless, achieve needed distance through loss of interest in sex, which then can be attributed to other causes. Unless the real, underlying intimacy issue is addressed, the couple's sex life will suffer and, very likely, the emotional spontaneity of the relationship with it.

Acknowledgment that the intimacy issue might be relevant to lack of sexual desire in one or both partners is the first step toward remedying the situation. Partners should then be able to explore together their individual reasons for anxiety about increasing intimacy. They can help each other heal the wounds of childhood and find new comfort in their adult intimacy experiences.

Disappointment with Sexual Repertoire

The disinclination of many lesbians and gay men to talk to their partners about their sexual relationships can be another cause for inhibited sexual desire. Perhaps one or both find the repertoire too limited, but do not say anything about it. Perhaps the problem is with specific acts that one partner either has an aversion to or wishes would be included in the repertoire more often. The dissatisfied partner may not have the nerve to call attention to his/her wishes, or may not want to hurt the partner's feelings, or may think that she/he should be the one to change, as in learn-to-like-it-because-it's-what gay men/lesbians do. Eventually, it may just seem easier to turn off to sex altogether rather than to deal directly with the issue. Or, barring a complete turnoff, the person may participate in sex but only in the most mechanical way—not really present in the experience, going through the motions—while resentment builds.

Obviously, this is a communication problem. Talking about what is happening, or not happening, is what will make the difference. I have found several recent books on gay or lesbian sex that can be very helpful in facilitating the kind of discussion called for here. (See the reading list presented at the end of this chapter.)

Anger

There are few things more undermining of growth in intimate relationships than unexpressed anger at a partner. The couple's sex life is often the first part of the relationship to go. Your partner wants to be sexual. You are furious, but not expressing it. Your partner presses for sex. It's the last thing in the world you want to do with him/her. Strangulation, perhaps? Shooting would be too quick and easy. Some slow and tortuous method of extermination would be preferable. But, *sex*?? Never!! Partner, of course, does not know that he/she is under indictment and has become the "enemy."

Covert warfare is always the hardest kind to deal with. Open warfare gives everybody a fighting chance or at least a chance to fight.

Even more problematic is the situation in which you are not even admitting to *yourself* that you are angry with your partner. You have no desire to be intimate with this person. You're not sure why. Everyone involved is perplexed and frustrated, and you cannot negotiate yourself out of the bind because you don't have access to the important information that you need about your own anger. Impasse.

What can be done? Let's begin with the unexpressed anger. If your partner seems to have no interest in sex over a significant period of time, and this is different from her/his usual behavior, you should begin to ask certain questions: "Are you feeling something toward me that you are not saying?" "Did I do something that made you unhappy?" "Are you angry with me?"

If you find that you have lost interest in sex with your partner and you are not sure why, you should ask yourself these same questions. "Am I feeling something toward her/him that I'm not saying?" "Did she/he do something that made me unhappy?" "Am I angry with her/him?"

Anger may not be the cause of your lack of interest in being sexual, but if it is, you will have opened an important channel of communication about it within yourself or with your partner or both.

Differing Motivations for Sex

Why do people choose to be sexual in the first place?

Those who have studied sexuality suggest the following as the most common motivators (not ranked in order of anything):

- Needing the comfort of physical contact
- Wanting to express love and warmth
- Sharing pleasure
- Relief from sexual tension
- Escape from unpleasant preoccupations
- Relief from loneliness
- Relaxation leading to sleep
- Demonstration of sexual competence
- Validation of personal attractiveness
- Reassurance of being loved

It is not unusual for partners in a sexual encounter to be there for differing reasons. If, however, partners in an intimate, ongoing relationship consistently are motivated to be sexual for different reasons, the discrepancy in motivation between them is likely, eventually, to affect the quality of their sexual experience.

Probably the most common example of differing motivations occurs when one partner is oriented to functional sex and the other to sex as lovemaking. Gay men, in particular, are at risk for this problem.

Dr. Rex Reece, a Los Angeles sex therapist who specializes in working with the sexual problems of gay men, describes it this way:*

> Many men seem to fear gender-inappropriateness and therefore avoid tender, devotional surrender which might mean passivity and femininity, for which they compensate with genital-centered, explosive sexuality. . . .
>
> . . . A particular gay man who has extensive experience with strangers in directly sexually oriented settings, internalized negative attitudes about homosexuality, and difficulties with intimacy, may be quite uncomfortable with other than genitally-oriented sex.
>
> Conversely . . . a partner whose sexual needs include reassurances of attractiveness and love . . . may not be able to enjoy a sexual relationship that is frequently genitally focused. . . .
>
> Knowing their own and appreciating the meanings of their lover's individual preferences can give a couple permission to ask for sexual activities that fit their needs or moods of the moment and motivate them to develop a wider repertoire for themselves.

Sexual transactions in which there is little or no communication about what is happening are always in danger of becoming vehicles for the acting out of personal and relationship tensions.

* Rex Reece, "Causes and Treatment of Sexual Desire Discrepancies in Male Couples," in *Integrated Identity for Gay Men and Lesbians: Psychotherapeutic Approaches for Emotional Well-Being*, ed. Eli Coleman (New York: Harrington Park Press, 1987).

Sometimes the agenda, rather than being one of simple sex, is loaded with issues extraneous to sex itself. "Do you really love me?" "Am I still attractive to you?" "Do you care about my needs?" "Do I still have power over you?" How much easier it would be if those questions could be posed directly, leaving the sexual encounter to be one of nonjudgmental pleasuring. At least it would be helpful for the individual having the experience to be able to "read" his/her own internal cues as a guide to what is really being asked of a particular sexual experience.

RELABELING INTERNAL CUES

Now we know some of the reasons a person might lose the appetite for sex with his/her partner, thus creating a "sexual desire discrepancy" between the two. One partner desires sex significantly less often than the other. The other partner is frustrated, sometimes to the point of despair. The relationship suffers. What can be done about it?

Obviously we can only deal here in generalities. I hope they will be in some measure pertinent to your situation if you are dealing with a desire discrepancy problem in your relationship.

How we interpret and label what is happening inside us usually determines what we do about it. The configuration of emotions and sensations most often associated with sexuality is so varied it is easy to see why there might be confusion about the meaning of particular internal experience. For example, perhaps what I want is to feel closeness to another person—I want to be held, comforted, caressed, reassured, calmed. If I have trouble accepting this need in myself or expressing it to another, I might "fool" myself by labeling it "sexual arousal," a more "acceptable" condition in my scheme of things. Then I can give myself permission to ask for the physical closeness I need in the context of sexual activity. If, however, I am asking for sex every time I feel the need for closeness, I might seem to have a *sex drive* that my partner finds too demanding. If I can learn to relabel my internal cues and ask for the affection I really need, what appears to be a sexual desire discrepancy might be shown not to be that at all.

I believe women know a good deal more about asking for warmth and tenderness from a partner than men do. In part it *seems* more gender appropriate for women than it does for men. Because of this, women have usually had more experience asking and can get their need to be held, comforted, and non-genitally pleasured met more easily than men can. It pains me to think about the many gay men I have worked with who long for physical closeness and warmth from their partner but hold back asking for it because they are afraid it will be interpreted as nothing more than a prelude to genitally focused sex. They dread either rejection from a partner who doesn't "feel like being sexual" or the disappointment of having their need for closeness only minimally met in the rush to achieve orgasm.

Knowing what you really want from your partner at a given time and being able to ask directly for *that* can often clear up the confusion surrounding the mixed messages of a couple's sexual/affectional transactions. Next time you want to be comforted, reassured, soothed, or just held because it feels good, try expressing this directly to your partner, rather than embedding your request in what seems to be an act of sexual initiation.

CONTROLLING THE "TURNOFF"

"I started out feeling interested in being sexual, and then, I don't know what happened. I just didn't feel like it anymore."

What happened? In this kind of inhibited sexual desire, the person, at some level of consciousness, does not want to *feel* sexual, so he/she "turns off" the sexual feelings. Just as one can turn one's self on with sexual fantasies, one can turn one's self off by thinking about a partner's negative attributes, or about past injustices perpetrated by a partner, or about feeling trapped in the situation, or about discontent with any aspect of the partner's functioning. Another way to turn off to sexual desire is to concentrate on anything that is external to the immediate sexual situation—work problems, recent conversations, social plans, what's for dinner.

Two elements are critical to reversing the inclination to block your sexual feelings. First, you must explore the reasons for the need to turn off to sex. Something about sexual surrender is producing anxiety sufficient to suppress your desire in order to avoid that surrender. What is the fear? Where does the danger seem to lie? Second, you must accept the concept that you are playing an *active* role in inhibiting sexual desire, therefore, you can learn to exert control over that inhibition.

The next step is to begin to replace the negative thoughts about your partner, the concerns about performance, or the preoccupation with business or historical injustices in the relationship with more positive thoughts about the partner and the sexual interaction that is happening or might be about to happen. When you have been evoking unpleasant thoughts about a partner, you might instead begin to think about what is attractive and arousing about this person. When you are remembering upsetting episodes from the past, you might refocus on the pleasurable interludes. When you are thinking about people and events external to the immediate sexual situation, you might refocus on the here-and-now—being as present as possible in the moment of what is happening. Only when you take such control can you begin to reverse the process of inhibited sexual desire and reopen yourself to the enjoyment of eroticism in the context of a loving relationship.

AIDS, A SPECIAL ISSUE FOR GAY MEN

Despite the current advances in the medical treatment of AIDS, and although research will undoubtedly continue to progress, the most recommended course for a gay male couple is that of safer sex practices. That is, unless either partner has never had unprotected sex with any other male and the couple is monogamous.

The safer sex course has its drawbacks, articulated well, I think, by the following:

THE CHALLENGE OF AIDS

Sex therapist Dr. Rex Reece writes of the dilemma some male couples are experiencing with regard to AIDS:

> Another potentially seriously inhibiting factor for gay couples is the anxiety about whether one has been or will be exposed to the AIDS virus. Some individuals have become so obsessed with the fear of getting the virus or giving it to their partners that sex is next to impossible, even within current educational guidelines for safer sexual practices. Even if the anxiety is not so rampant, it may still be high enough for the couple to avoid discussing what they feel comfortable doing now within those guidelines. Certain practices then begin to drop out of their repertoire or they may decrease their frequency without much understanding of the real reasons. This anxiety or lack of insight leaves much room for hurt, retaliation, and more conflict . . .

The challenge presented by the dilemma is especially well put, I think, in the following excerpt from a 1985 article by Tim Vollmer (*New York Native*, Oct. 28–Nov. 3):

> The problem with the current safe sex campaign is that it does not confront the task of restructuring the premise of gay male sexuality. Instead, it implies that all gay men can do is simply wait till the epidemic is over before resuming life as before. It is a holding pattern, a freezing of an obsolete culture at its least dysfunctional level. The danger with such a policy, if it is allowed to be more than just a transitional phase, is that it preempts any innovation of the gay experience. It is a policy of con-

finement and restriction, concentrating on what gay men
can't do, what homosexuality isn't.

No matter how valuable the safe sex campaign is, gay
men need more nowadays than a list of don'ts. In terms
of coping with an injured self-image, sexuality, and lifestyle, today's situation has an urgency that must at least
be equal to anything that existed in the 1950s and 1960s.
Indeed, gay men today need something every bit as radi-
cal and sustaining as the movement inaugurated by the
Stonewall riots, if they are to be liberated from the new
oppression ushered in by AIDS. They need, in effect, another gay liberation movement.

To avoid the twin dangers of sinking with an obsolete
culture or shifting back to an oppressive one, gay men
must respond with the same energy and creativity they
exhibited in the early days of gay liberation. They need
consciously to create a culture that once again stresses
the positive sides of being gay, the advantages and the joy.
While limitations in the present situation must be taken
into account, they must be approached with the funda-
mental consideration that gay desires are normal and
healthy and that there is still much in life that gay men
can enjoy as gay men.

Certainly the specter of AIDS has created confusion and frustration for gay men not only in terms of the comfort level of their
sexual practices, but also in their sense of who they are as sexual
beings. The process of redefining what gay male sexuality is will
go on for some time to come.

I see gay men achieving new depths of attachment with their
partners. The focus now is much more on working through problems with a partner and putting energy into building a solid foundation for trust, rather than looking outward for the validation
that *seemed* to be missing in the relationship.

I see this new order paying off in relationships that provide more long-term satisfaction, more security, and more mutual support than was often true before.

Unfortunately, younger gay men today, untouched by the wrenching experiences of living through the worst part of the AIDS crisis in the United States, too often ignore the warnings about unsafe sex. Because there have been significant advances in medicine for the management of AIDS and of HIV as a chronic condition, it has become easier for men to ignore the fact that this remains a serious and deeply affecting disease. If one ends up becoming infected, there are still the symptoms and treatments that accompany being HIV+ and having AIDS. It is not an easy condition to integrate into one's everyday life.

Education about safer sex is still very important, as is general attention to breaking developments in the treatment of AIDS and HIV, and lifestyle management with the disease. An excellent book to read in this respect is *The Ins and Outs of Gay Sex* by Dr. Stephen Goldstone. Also try magazines like *POZ, HIV Plus,* and *Art and Understanding,* each of which focuses on different aspects of preventing, living with, and managing the AIDS virus. Visit the Gay Men's Health Crisis website to remain current on the latest information.

LESBIANS AND AIDS

While gay men are at a particularly high risk for AIDS, some lesbians may also be at risk. Any lesbian who is an IV drug user can become infected through the use of contaminated needles. Any lesbian can become infected who has had sex with, or been artificially inseminated by, a man carrying the AIDS virus; therefore, caution is the best approach when having sex with an HIV positive partner. The most extensive presentation of safe sex guidelines for lesbians appears in JoAnn Loulan's book, *Lesbian Passion: Loving Ourselves and Each Other.* See the chapter on "AIDS and Safe Sex for Lesbians." The book is available for Spinsters' Ink: (303) 761-5552; www.acquisitions@spinsters-ink.com.

For anyone wanting up-to-date information on any aspect of AIDS or AIDS risk reduction, call your local AIDS hotline, or, toll-free, 1-800-342-AIDS (the Public Health Service National AIDS Hotline).

NON-GENITAL PLEASURING

For several decades now, sex therapists and sex educators have been using structured pleasuring exercises to assist couples in enhancing their sexual experience. Originating with Masters and Johnson, this "behavioral" approach to enhanced sexual functioning has been employed not just with people who have sexual dysfunction problems but also with anyone interested in learning to feel more comfortable with their own sexuality.

I offer these experiences to you now in the hope they will be enlightening and enjoyable. Used correctly, they can provide a pathway to increased intimacy. Where there are barriers to intimacy along your particular path, they provide the opportunity to identify the nature of those barriers and to develop a strategy for eliminating them.

The non-genital pleasuring exercises presented here are taken from the book *Sexual Awareness: Enhancing Sexual Pleasure* by Barry and Emily McCarthy.* With their permission I have adapted the exercises for use by partners of the same sex. The McCarthys state the purpose of the exercises as follows:

> The concept underlying non-genital touching and plea-
> suring exercises is to reorient your attitudes and feelings
> to more pleasurable and sensual feelings about your
> body and your partner's body. The emphasis will be on

* Barry McCarthy and Emily McCarthy, *Sexual Awareness: Enhancing Sexual Pleasure* (New York: Carroll & Graf, 1984).

discovering, in a relaxed, non-goal-oriented situation, the sensual pleasure you can derive from touching and being touched. Perhaps most important, it allows you to discover for yourself and with your partner what style of touching, stroking, and caressing feels most comfortable and pleasurable. Couples assume a lot, fall into ruts, and feel awkward about asking their partners for different types of stimulation. These exercises are designed to make you comfortable with touching, discovering, and sharing with as little demand toward performance or goal-orientation as possible.

A caution from the McCarthys:

You are the best judge as to whether our approach to enhancing sexual awareness and comfort might be appropriate for you. . . . We recommend that you do not proceed with the exercises unless both you and your partner have first discussed the exercises and your expectations and have then agreed they would be worthwhile for you to try.

By way of preparation for beginning the exercises:

Time and privacy are often problems. It is important that you not worry about external factors such as the phone ringing. Plan a time, at least half an hour, when you won't be disturbed. Take the phone off the hook. You are encouraged to proceed in a gradual, step-by-step fashion, enjoying one experience before moving on to the next. The most important factor is your feeling comfortable and receptive so you can explore, discover, and enjoy feelings of sensuality.

Before beginning an exercise, you might bathe or shower together. We recommend this for two reasons: First, it serves to relax you and enhance comfortable feelings about your body; second, proper care and cleanliness can be important in enhancing feelings of sensuality.

Below are four sets of exercises. I suggest they be used as follows:
Week I First Set: Exploration (done twice)
Week II Second Set: Guiding (done twice)
Week III Third Set: Mutuality (done twice)
Week IV Fourth Set: Sharing (done twice)
Each of these sessions should take thirty to ninety minutes, with time allotted for a shower (optional), the exercises, and the opportunity to talk about what happened afterwards.

First Set of Exercises: Exploration

Before beginning, sit and talk for ten or fifteen minutes, perhaps over a cup of coffee. Recall a particular experience when you felt close to and intimate with your partner. Express this feeling of tenderness. Put your hands palms-down on the table. Ask your partner to do the same, and allow your hands to be caressed. Notice the difference in size and texture between your hands. Much can be communicated by hands touching.

If you shower as a prelude to the pleasuring, you might experiment with different types of spray or temperature; if bathing, try a new type of bath oil or soap. This can increase awareness of different sensual stimuli. Start by soaping your partner's back, caressing it as you do so. Trace the muscles and contours; gently rub and massage. Ask your partner to face you. Soap the front of the neck and chest. Touch especially the hollows of the neck and the soft area below the ribs and the navel. Move downward to the hips, bypassing the genital area. Wash your own genital area. Soap the legs while telling your partner how it feels to wash him or her. Let your partner soap you in the same manner. Be sure to say what feels particularly sensuous.

When you have finished, dry each other off, except the genitals. Take your time; slowness and tenderness are also important here. Stand still for a moment and take a good look at your partner. Look at your partner as if he or she were a new person. Notice one or two things you find particularly attractive and share them. You might walk toward each other, extending your hands and then holding your partner's hand. Slide your partner's arms around your waist; stand still and enjoy the closeness of each other. Feel and share the beginning of a new intimacy, warmth, and closeness.

Proceed to your bedroom and try to feel natural being in the nude. If you don't feel comfortable walking through the house nude, you can put on a robe or towel, but drop it to the floor when you reach the bedroom. Pleasuring is best done in the nude. Later, you can feel free to vary the amount of clothing, but first learn to be comfortable with your own and your partner's nudity. The room should be at a comfortable, warm temperature; there should be a moderate amount of light. If you're more comfortable, you can partially darken the room, only be sure you can still see your partner's nude body. If you like, put your favorite music on.

One of you will be designated the pleasure-giver and the other the pleasure-recipient. Typically, you will switch roles during the middle of the exercises, though some people do one session as the giver and the next as the recipient. Be sure each partner has an opportunity to do both, since a mutually satisfying relationship requires comfort of both partners in receiving and giving. Interestingly, many people find it harder to receive than to give. Neither role carries connotations of dominance or submission, of femininity or masculinity.

The recipient has three tasks. The first is to be passive and to receive pleasure. The second is to keep his or her eyes closed throughput the exercise. This allows you to concentrate on your own feelings, though you may feel awkward doing this for the first time. The third task of the recipient is to be aware of what parts of his or her body and what types of touch are sensual. Be in touch with your body and its natural sensual and sexual feelings.

For this first exercise decide who will be the giver and who will be the receiver.

The giver should focus on viewing his/her partner in a new way and on feeling comfortable in giving a wide variety of touch and body stimulation. Rather than trying to second-guess your partner, engage in touch that you enjoy. The recipient should begin by lying on his/her stomach, feeling as receptive, relaxed, and comfortable as possible.

During this phase of the exercise, the emphasis will be on communication by touch rather than by words, so both should be as silent as possible.

Begin by massaging your partner's shoulder muscles. Gently massage the shoulders, being careful not to squeeze the upper neck muscles. Rub tenderly with the entire hand, moving slowly down the back and sides; try to avoid sudden movements. Be aware of what you see that is appealing and what you have not noticed before—freckles, tiny scars, muscle indentations, and the like. When you reach the waist, place your thumbs together, spread your fingers, and press and knead gently as you caress the sides and lower back. Then move up to the head, and either give a scalp massage or gently run your fingers through your partner's hair. Return to the back, but this time you might press down vigorously and give a back rub. Perhaps you would like to run your fingers over your partner's back in a playful, disorganized manner. You could trace special little features of your partner's back with only your fingertips.

The task of the giver is to provide the recipient with a variety of experiences so he/she can learn what produces the most sensual and sexual feelings. The giver should enjoy trying out various types of touching and should experience the partner's body in a new way. The emphasis is on exploring rather than on proving oneself sexually. Feel comfortable with it; enjoy it. These exercises are guidelines; feel free to innovate and be spontaneous.

Hold your partner's feet and caress them with your hands. Notice the length of the toes, the texture of the nails. Place your palm so it covers the arch, and curl your fingers over the top of the foot. Notice the heel as you rub the palm of your hand against it. Outline the division between the top and bottom of the foot

with your fingertips. Holding one foot in your hand, caress the
top of the foot with your fingers and trace the valleys between the
toes. Gently massage the top of the foot up to the ankle. Moving
up the same leg, hold the ankle in one hand while exploring it
with the other hand. Gently and slowly move up the calf, caressing and massaging to help your partner relax even more. Pay special attention to rubbing the soft area behind the knee. Examine
and explore the thigh; look for little places you haven't been familiar with before. Then move up to the buttocks area and massage both buttocks simultaneously. Some people feel negative
about this area because of the association with defecation. For
many people it is one of the most sensual areas of the body. The
buttock and anal area is an erogenous zone with a multitude of
nerve endings. Touch in a manner that will bring out enjoyment
and sensuousness.

When you feel you have provided a nondemand sensuous exploration, you can switch roles as giver and recipient and repeat
the same sequences. There are large individual differences in the
time spent on this exercise; they range between ten and thirty
minutes per person. The focus is on exploring, enjoying, touching, learning, being comfortable, and feeling sensuous. The key
words are slow, tender, rhythmic, and caring.

After this exercise is completed, sit over a drink or a cup of
coffee, discuss the experience, and share your feelings. Because
talking tends to isolate you from your bodily feelings, it is best to
do the exercise in silence. Afterwards, we strongly encourage discussing your feelings and reactions in a direct, open manner. We
suggest you first share the positive feelings and then say what was
negative. Rather than seeing the negative as blame or a put-down,
view it as constructive criticism with suggestions of what to try
next time.

Second Set of Exercises: Guiding

You might begin by taking a bath or shower. Make it an even
more relaxed, comfortable, and sensuous experience than it was

the first time. Dry your partner off, commenting and sharing as you do. For this set of exercises, the partner who was the recipient should now be the giver.

The recipient is lying on his/her stomach with eyes open and this time guides the partner's hands to certain areas of the body. This can be difficult from this position, so feel free to speak and offer guidance as well as touch. Try to find at least two parts of the back of your body that are particularly sensuous and let the giver know so that he/she can be more fully aware of your preferences. The giver can use kissing and licking to stimulate the partner's back. This includes kissing the back of the neck, rubbing the tongue from the top to the bottom of the spinal cord, blowing in the ear and flicking your tongue in and out, taking gentle "love bites" at various parts of the legs. Remember, different people like different things. Partners do not know what they like until they try it. This is not a test; there are no right or wrong responses. Explore and enjoy.

When the giver feels ready, help the recipient turn over on his/her back. The receiver with eyes shut, should relax, and assume a more passive and receptive attitude. Males are not used to the passive role, but it is important that they experience being passive and receptive so they can learn what sensual feelings they are responsive to. The giver should examine the front of the body visually and notice what parts look particularly attractive.

In touching, you as the giver should begin by covering your partner's hand with your own. Notice the difference in the size and texture. Gently massage the fingers down the hand and look for things you have not noticed before. Trace the knuckles and the small lines on the fingers with a fingertip. Gently kiss the soft inner palm of each hand. Caress your partner's forearms, one at a time. Notice the softness of the skin on the inner side of the arm. Trace the elbow with your fingers. Placing your thumb in the bend, grasp the forearm and slide your hand down to the waist. Then caress both arms in their entirety.

Switch focus and gently explore your partner's face. Notice the signs of relaxation and comfort on the face; be aware of the difference between these expressions and the tense expressions you have observed in other situations. To enhance the feelings of relaxation and sensuousness, very gently massage your partner's forehead, then move from the cheeks to the chin, and with the fingertips outline your favorite facial features. You might want to tenderly kiss your partner's closed eyes. In fact, you might want to kiss all the parts of your partner's face.

Explore the chest area, use smooth, tender strokes and cover not only the chest but also the sides. Move up to one armpit and run your hands over it. How does it feel to touch your partner's navel? What about running your hands sideways around the stomach area? Be aware of how the stomach muscles react to your touch. At this point, avoid the genital area, but do spend time exploring what touches are most sensuous around the inner thighs.

It may happen that at this point or elsewhere in the exercises you feel sexual arousal. The male may get an erection or the female may lubricate vaginally. Simply accept it as a natural, sensual, and sexual response. If it does not happen, that is fine, since the focus is to explore and learn. Non-genital pleasuring is not a pressured experience to begin sexual arousal.

Explore the front of your partner's legs and feet. In ending this exercise, visually reexamine the front of your partner's body and caress the two or three areas you find most attractive. Remember, there are no right or wrong areas. Perceptions of attractiveness vary; you might especially like the eyes, the neck, the chest, the inner thighs—touch whatever is appealing to you personally.

Switch roles of giver and recipient, and do the same exercise. Each person does the touching and pleasuring differently, which is as it should be since you are learning to be comfortable with *your* personal style of giving and receiving pleasure. Afterward, spend time discussing the differences between your style and your partner's in order to discover how you can utilize these differences and thus make your sexual relationship more mutually satisfying.

Third Set of Exercises: Mutuality

Sit across from your partner, separated by a table. Make sure it is narrow enough so that you can reach your partner's face easily.

Put your hands palms-down on the table. Ask your partner to do the same and to let you caress his or her hands. Cover your partner's hands with yours. Grasp them gently and lift them from the table. Slide your hands underneath so they support your partner's. Releasing one hand, cover the other so that it is enclosed within yours. Lift the hand to your face and rub the back of it on your cheeks, first one, then the other. Make eye contact as you do this. Then repeat with your eyes closed.

Pick up both hands and place them on your face so they enclose it, from your cheeks to your chin. Close your eyes and slowly move your face from side to side. Holding the wrists, bend your neck forward, inclining your face toward your chest, and move the hands to the sides of your neck. Then raise your face, bring the hands together under the chin, and separate them so that they slide up your face; stop when the fingertips reach your eyes. Gently kiss the soft inner palm of each hand. Make eye contact with your partner and communicate with your eyes how you are feeling about the closeness. . . .

You can go directly to the pleasuring exercises or if you prefer, start with a shower or bath. The emphasis during the pleasuring will be on guiding your partner and teaching him or her what feels particularly sensuous on the front part of your body. Allow this to be a more *mutual* give-and-take experience, moving away from the structured roles of giver and recipient. Keep your eyes open so you can communicate feelings by eye contact. Most of the guiding will be nonverbal, using your hand over your partner's to show what kind of touch and where on your body the feelings are particularly good. To enhance the experience, we suggest you use a lotion while massaging. People experiment with several varieties, including wild lemon lotion, hand lotion, abalone lotion, and baby oil. It might be fun to go shopping together and choose one or two lotions you would like to try. When using lotions, it is important to have them readily available so you don't have to stop caressing to get the lotion. If possible, have the lotion heated. Having cold lotion poured on bare skin can shock anyone out of a sensuous mood. If the lotion is not heated, leave one hand on your partner's body and pour the lotion onto the back of that hand. When it is warmer, rub it on your partner's body.

In ending this experience, lie with one partner facing the other's back, bodies touching. Talk and share your feelings. Then lie quietly until sleep overtakes you.

Fourth Set of Exercises: Sharing

Begin by discussing what degree of cleanliness is acceptable to you. We suggest using a different lotion so your awareness of various smells and sensuous feelings will be enhanced. The focus is on allowing yourselves increased amounts of mutuality and spontaneity. Both partners can more naturally initiate touching and caresses. Your learning about yourself and your partner can transfer into a mutually satisfying foreplay/pleasuring pattern. Let the touching and pleasuring remain non-genital.

Try not to miss an opportunity to share honestly with your partner. We hope you are more comfortable in making requests and sharing feelings. Attempt to express your thoughts in new and different words. Express your desire for each other. Let your partner know how special a person he or she truly is.

You might try a different position. This time one partner should be stomach down, the other lying on his/her side, facing the first partner, touching his/her entire body, the upper leg bent at the knee so that the leg rests across the first partner's legs. Slowly and gently caress the first partner's back, from the neck to the waist.

When you have finished the back caress, gently move your leg up and down your partner's legs, feeling his/her skin with the inside of your thigh and calf, while exploring and touching with the instep of your foot. Talk to your partner while you are touching.

Tell how you are feeling emotionally. Ask your partner how what you are doing feels, what else he/she would like and would find pleasing. Try a different position. Make the caresses more gentle, tender, and mutual. Feel comfortable in simultaneously giving and receiving pleasure. Allow this to be a mutually enjoyable, sensuous and sharing experience which can be repeated for itself or as part of a sexual intercourse experience.

Afterword

By this point, we hope you and your partner are more aware and accepting of the natural responses of your bodies to non-genital touch and to the pleasures of sensuality. Couples fall into a trap when the only touching they do is genital and leads to orgasm. We hope you have learned to appreciate new feelings of sensuousness and non-genital touch, that you now know what kinds of non-genital touch are most enjoyable to you, and what parts of your body are more responsive. You can share this with your partner, communicating in a direct, comfortable way.

With a basic foundation of acceptance of touch and your bodily reaction, with an emphasis on slowness, tenderness, warmth, sharing, and intimacy, you can move on to become a more sexual couple.

Books on Gay Male Sex Practices

Silverstein, Charles, and Felice Picano. *The Joy of Gay Sex*. New York: Harper Resource, 2003.

Berzon, Betty, ed. *Positively Gay*. Berkeley, Calif.: Celestial Arts, 2001. Chapter by Michael Shernoff. "Gay Men's Sexualities: Reflections at the Dawn of the Millennium."

Goldstone, Stephen E. *The Ins and Outs of Gay Sex: A Medical Handbook for Men*. New York: Dell Publishing, 1999.

Books on Lesbian Sex Practices

Caster, Wendy, and Rachel Kramer Bussel. *The Lesbian Sex Book.* Los Angeles: Alyson Books, 2003.

Newman, Felice. *The Whole Lesbian Sex Book: A Passionate Guide for All of Us.* San Francisco: Cleis Press, 1999.

Loulan, JoAnn. *Lesbian Passion: Loving Ourselves and Each Other.* Denver, Colo.: Spinsters Ink Books, 1987.

10

MONEY ISSUES

Is it best to commingle assets, or to keep them separate? Is it better to divide expenses evenly or to split them according to size of income? What is the best arrangement when one partner has considerably more money than the other? Should checking accounts be separate or joint? What's fair? What's right? What works?

As gay or lesbian couples we do not bring to our relationships the same preset expectations regarding the earning and management of money that heterosexual partners bring to theirs. While heterosexual couples may choose to deviate from their expectations of who will do what in the relationship, at least they have some guidelines to get them started.

Gender-role conditioning prescribes that the male partner will be the major wage earner and will work outside the home. The female partner, on the other hand, is expected to be the major caretaker of the couple's domestic needs, her ability to do that protected by the male partner's financial support for it. These gender-role prescriptions are designed to be complementary and to set up the conditions that facilitate raising a family. These days, however, both the male and female partners may be wage earners, even equal ones. Both may share in the care of home and family. Both may experience the stimulation of working in the world and the satisfaction of creating a warm and loving home environment. But if a heterosexual couple should choose to follow the more traditional path, no one is going to criticize or punish the female partner for staying home and not working, even if there are no children to care for. It's okay for her to do that. Her mother is not going to call up and say, "How can you let that man support you? Have you no self-respect? Why don't you get out and work, like a real woman?"

If, on the other hand, one male partner in a gay relationship decides to stay home and take care of the house, a great hue and cry might well be raised, often by this person's family, possibly by friends, sometimes by the partner, and even within the person himself. A man is supposed to get out and work. He is less than a man if he doesn't. Less than a man? Too often that translates to "like a woman." Who would want to occupy such an inferior place in the sun as that occupied by a woman? To many it means giving up the power and prerogatives of maleness, and is, of course, the quintessential sexist point of view born out of the feelings of male superiority drummed into the heads of little boys by parents who had the same ideas drummed into their heads.

The tragedy, all too often, is that this programming does not fit the needs and interests of a particular male who may really enjoy being domestic but does not allow himself to follow this need because it goes against gender-role prescriptions. I have watched too many gay male relationships break up over the issue of one partner's being unable to match the other's accomplishments in the outside world and suffering for it when both he and his partner really wanted him to stay home and create beauty and comfort there. One or both of them would not allow him to do that peacefully because it was not what a male was supposed to do. I have so often felt pained at the victimization these men suffer.

So, the heterosexual couple is assisted by cultural expectations as they work out the financial arrangement that best suits them, unless, of course, they do not follow tradition. Then, God help them, they are in for the same raised eyebrow treatment (or worse) than the non-working-out-in-the-world gay male experiences from those around him: "What? *He's* staying home and taking care of the house, and *she's* out working?"

For lesbians, it's a bit easier. No one looks askance at a woman who chooses homemaking as her career. Nor, alternatively, does anyone condemn the lesbian ("unmarried woman") with no husband to support her. She is expected to have to work to support herself.

We are very influenced in our decisions about our occupational life by our social programming, and, in turn, the patterns of relating to the management of money in intimate partnerships are also seriously affected by the same conditioning.

For gay and lesbian couples, our gender-related social programming does not help us design easy arrangements regarding our finances; rather, it tends to confuse the task. It prescribes the way men should relate to money—earn it, maintain control over its use—but not the way two men together should relate to *their* money. Our social conditioning prescribes the way women should relate to money but assumes, in the main, that money will be earned by a man. How should two women together relate to their finances? What is the best arrangement in male-male partnerships?

No roles. No rules. We're on our own. What do we do? We do all sorts of things.

Some couples run their financial relationship like a business. Books are kept. Running balances are carefully maintained. The end of the month brings a careful settling of accounts. Strictly adhered to is the agreed-upon split of responsibility for bills. Deviations from it are permitted only after the "financial committee" meets and approves them.

Then there are partners who treat each other as adversaries in money matters. One or the other usually has a complaint regarding their partner's delinquency. One or the other feels taken advantage of.

At the other end of the continuum, there are couples who treat their relationship like the most egalitarian of marriages. All income, whatever the source, belongs to both partners equally. Resources are pooled. Assets are commingled. Decisions on how money is spent are shared equally. The partners operate financially as a single unit.

What is likely to determine how a given couple develops the arrangement that they do? In any primary relationship the way in which a couple relates to its money, at a given time, usually reflects what is happening in terms of their trust for one another, their expectations regarding the permanence of the partnership, the balance of power between them, and the degree to which they are able to accept their dependency on one another. Gender-related attitudes round out the picture.

Sociologists Philip Blumstein and Pepper Schwartz have provided us with more data on the inner workings of cohabiting couples than we have ever had before. In *American Couples,* they tell us the following about financial arrangements:

> Gay men have the hardest time of all. . . . Because earning power is a central part of a man's identity, having more money gives a man symbolic—and therefore real—advantages over his partner. This also happens in marriage, but there, although the husband's higher income gives him power, with it comes the responsibility to support his wife and family without rancor—and, ideally without its being a reflection on his wife's adequacy as a person. Both husband and wife take pleasure in his ability to support them, whereas gay men are often uncomfortable when being the provider or being provided for. Each man thinks he should be able to pull his own weight, but if one greatly surpasses the other, he may feel entitled to be dominant, leaving the other feeling inadequate.

With lesbian couples, they found almost the direct opposite was true:

> Their power balance is not determined by either woman's income. Since women in this society are not accustomed to judging their *own* worth by how much money they make, we feel that lesbians do not fall into judging their partners by such a standard. . . . They make a conscious effort to keep their relationships free of any

form of domination, especially if it derives from something as impersonal as money.

This difference is reflective of the differing ways men and women relate to money. As Blumstein and Schwartz point out:

> To men it represents identity and power. To women it is security and autonomy. These male-female differences are most obvious among our gay male and lesbian couples. The gay men are likely to equate power and money, but this is not true for lesbians; income does not give them the same feeling of control. . . . When we look at the female couples we see that they can find autonomy and security together. Each woman earns her own living and thus provides her own security.

POOLING

One possible arrangement for the management of a couple's finances is the pooling of all resources and assets. Blumstein and Schwartz tell us that "the longer same-sex couples live together the more they want to pool their incomes."

> By looking at the cohabitors and same-sex couples, where there is no law or tradition to push them toward pooling, we are able to see that pooling begins when a couple senses that their relationship is going to last. Indeed, if we were going to use one major indicator to determine when these couples became solidified as a unit, it would be the point at which they joined their resources.

David McWhirter and Andrew Mattison concur, as reported in their book, *The Male Couple:**

---

* David McWhirter and Andrew Mattison, *The Male Couple*. (Englewood Cliffs, N.J.: Prentice-Hall, 1984).

Stage One (first year) couples infrequently consider their possessions as jointly owned, but clearly think of them as "mine" and "his." They divide household expenses and may even open a joint checking account for their shared expenses but they are apt to keep individual accounts for personal use.

. . . Although, in previous stages couples may have purchased a home or condo together, it is at the beginning of Stage Four (years six through ten) that they begin combining their money and possessions. . . . We have observed that the gradual merger of money and possessions is clearly a symbolic and actual commitment to the relationship, often unspoken and unrecognized. . . .

It is a proud accomplishment of male couples to find it possible in Stage Five (years eleven through twenty) to develop a true sense of "our" possessions. . . . This is a process, not an event. It starts when one man pays for the movie simply because the other man is engrossed in telling an event of the day. After ten years they are no longer the Stage Two (second year) couple, proud of their shared contribution in buying a new chair. They are no longer the Stage Three (years three and four) couple who pay for their vacations out of the joint household account. Over the years they have learned how to invest in the relationship and in each other. . . . This is the single most consistent finding among all couples who have been together longer than ten years. It is the single identifiable phenomenon signifying ongoing commitment.

It should be noted that McWhirter and Mattison collected their data between 1974 and 1979, well before the advent of AIDS and the new emphasis in gay male partnerships on working toward permanence of relationships. I believe today they would find that the merging of finances that is so indicative of commitment would typically be occurring much earlier than the tenth year of the partnership.

Finally, Blumstein and Schwartz, in the Epilogue to their book, reported on the reasons couples in their study subsequently broke up. With regard to the issue of finances pooled or kept separate, they found that lesbian and gay male couples were more likely to break up when they chose *not* to pool their money:

> Failure to pool often indicates that couples have not given up their independence and may never have visualized the relationship as lasting into the indefinite future.

RESISTANCE TO POOLING

The findings of Blumstein and Schwartz were consistent. The willingness to pool finances seems to be highly correlated with the degree of commitment and the potential for permanence in gay and lesbian partnerships. Given the significance of this finding, let us look more deeply into why people have such resistance to the merging of their resources.

Money is a metaphor for independence. Insofar as you have the money to do so you can live on your own, buy what you want, go where you please, be as extravagant or as frugal as suits your mood. Having one's own money enables the moving away from family, the building of a separate life and identity, the transition from the dependency of childhood to the independence of the adult.

For many people the pooling of their financial resources with those of a partner represents a loss of that independent status. It is as if they were being asked to give up the freedom of adulthood and return to the dependency of childhood. This time, however, in the place of reliable adults, there is a virtual stranger wanting to control one's financial life. While, of course, a partner is probably not asking for that kind of control, it can easily feel that way.

It certainly felt that way to me when my lover and I moved in together, and she began to suggest that we pool our incomes. I was horrified and said so. Give her my *money*?! Give up my security, my ability to support myself? I was quite certain she would squander my assets and leave me destitute. After all, she was so young and inexperienced. What did she know about managing money?

Had I not been so panicked by the imagined imminence of being thrown back into the dependency of childhood, I would have made better use of the data I had about her (and not acted like such a damn fool). For instance, when I met her she was twenty-nine years old. Completely self-supporting, she owned a lovely, fully furnished three-bedroom house, two cars, and a boat. She had investments and money in the bank. When I was twenty-nine years old I lived in a one-bedroom apartment, was still painting walls flat black for effect and hadn't yet graduated from canvas wing chairs and telephone cable spool tables to real furniture.

It took a while for my brain to clear enough to realize that she had shown herself to be a most prudent money manager who had made better use of her limited funds than I was making of my more ample income.

I came to my senses. We pooled our money. Under her care our financial picture is better than I ever imagined mine would be. When I was able to let go of my tenacious hold on my own income and assets and allow her to be the money manager, I realized what I had known but not faced before: I don't like dealing with money. I'm not good at it. I've not done much of a job of using my assets well, and it is only a matter of luck that *I* had not made *myself* destitute. She, on the other hand, loves to deal with money, is an adventuresome and talented investor, and does a terrific job of keeping us financially comfortable and secure.

I still, on occasion, have moments of panic when she makes an investment that is particularly daring. The old fears return.

She will spend all our money. I will be destitute, et cetera, but quickly the fear subsides. I understand now what the fears are really about.

The struggle is with my own fear of dependency. It is about the loss of the illusion that I could do for myself better than anyone else could do for me. It is about letting go of control and the fear that letting go conjures up of the powerless state of childhood. It is about the unfinished business of my personal development. It is anything but a realistic evaluation of her ability to manage money.

I was lucky that I had a patient and understanding partner and that I was able, finally, to explore my own motivation successfully. I believe many people experience the same kind of feelings I did. The resistance to merging resources feels so much more like giving up something than gaining something. I wish it were possible for people more often to see that their resistance is, as mine was, about fearing a kind of dependency that belonged to another era in their life. I wish it were not so difficult for some people to let go of the illusion that only *they* are capable of looking after their own best interests. As long as they cling to that notion, it is unlikely they will ever find out otherwise, that they will ever experience the depth of trust in a partner that is much more dependable a source of emotional security than any that money can ever buy.

DISPARATE INCOMES

Let us look at some of the consequences of one partner's earning (or otherwise acquiring) significantly more money than the other partner. How then are decisions made about who pays for what? Often, in this situation, problems arise because the more affluent partner may eventually come to resent picking up the tab once again for the trip, the dinner out, the fund-raising event that the less affluent partner couldn't have participated in on his or her own. Or, the less affluent partner may begin to feel frustrated because she/he can't afford to keep up with the lifestyle of the more affluent partner and feels uncomfortable being paid for so often. This discomfort may lead to feelings of inadequacy or resentment at being put in the position of having to be paid for or having to opt out of activities that are not affordable. In this situation, as long as funds are kept separate, awareness of the disparity in the partners' incomes is ever present. Some form of pooling might go a long way toward resolution of this dilemma.

Let's go one step further and look at same-sex couples in which one partner has enough money to support them both easily and the other has no income at all. This may be a temporary situation or an ongoing one. Most likely if it is ongoing, it involves an older and a younger partner. This arrangement can work well if the younger partner is doing what he/she wants to be doing, which might be taking care of the house, the pets, the logistics of the couple's everyday life, personal and/or business needs of the older partner, going to school or otherwise pursuing interests that may or may not produce income.

The arrangement doesn't work well when the younger partner is not doing what he/she wants to be doing. There's nothing wrong with tending to home and hearth, unless the person really wants to pursue a career and doesn't have the wherewithal to do so, or doesn't know what steps to take, or feels trapped in the homemaker role. There's nothing wrong with being involved outside the home unless the person is avoiding the homemaker role because it lacks sufficient prestige, all the while wishing that he/she could be doing just that. Unless the younger person is following a personally satisfying path he/she may come to feel used, deprived, or resentful of the respect and admiration the older, more accomplished partner gets. Or the younger person may just become restless and begin to act out frustrated feelings in a nonconstructive way, such as sexually with other people. This ill-defined role that non-income-producing partners often experience can too easily sow the seeds of destruction of what might otherwise be a loving relationship. I believe this outcome is avoidable if the partners can talk through what they really want for themselves and from each other.

One of the greatest difficulties in dealing with this kind of situation comes from negative gender-role stereotypes that both men and women have internalized from this society. For many people, being the "little wife" is a role so stigmatized that they will go to any lengths not to be so tagged. Lesbians eager to be egalitarian partners (or motivated by competition with an achieving partner) might resist the homemaker role even if there is no necessity for them to be out earning money. A gay man who may love everything about being a homemaker and do it superbly may, instead, get a job because as a *man* he believes he should be out there earning money. Perhaps he has a partner who, in response to the same programming, nags him about getting a job: "You'll feel better about yourself if you're out there working." The truth may be that he feels just fine about himself when he is at home taking care of the begonias, and he feels angry and resentful when he is working for money the couple doesn't need, at a job he doesn't want.

To work through this kind of dilemma, one first has to break through the inherent sexism that underlies it. Since women still occupy a lower status than men in the eyes of most of our society, many people do not want to be seen as doing "women's work." It is as if one were being demoted by devoting a major part of one's time to creating the house beautiful, the table bountiful, the environment serene as a context for the sharing of two people's lives. It does take creativity. It is work. It can impart extraordinary value and substance to an otherwise commonplace existence.

Unfortunately, sexist attitudes are so embedded in our thinking that it is often very difficult to bring them to the surface for scrutiny. My liberal gay male friends and clients will vehemently deny that they are in the least bit sexist in their thinking. They swear they do not think of women as less than them, that such notions have nothing to do with any dilemma they might have regarding roles in their relationship. But, when confronted the dialogue often goes something like this:

I say: "Well, it sounds as if you really would like to stay at home and be the wife."

They say (facial grimace): "What do you mean 'wife'? I didn't say I wanted to be a 'wife.' Why do I have to be the *wife* just because I enjoy making our home beautiful?"

I say: "Why do you object so to the term 'wife'?"

They say (death look): "Because a wife is a *woman,* and I am a man."

I say: "Seems you have some trouble with the idea of being associated with a woman-identified role. What's wrong with being a woman?"

They say: "Nothing, absolutely nothing is wrong with it, but I am a MAN."

And so on.

I have seen gay men who earned enough money to keep three wives in style badgering their want-to-stay-at-home partner into getting a job, any kind of job, because they are after all two *men,* and theirs is, after all, not a *heterosexual marriage.*

"Well, what if it were?" I often ask. "What would you do differently?" Usually turns out they would do a lot differently.

So, I ask why they deprive themselves of an arrangement they might both want because they are gay. Don't we have just as much right as heterosexuals to design our lives to be what we want them to be? Are we to be restricted only to certain arrangements because both partners happen to be of the same sex? What is wrong with one man's supporting another, if that is what both of them want? Why should a woman have the privilege of being taken care of and not a man? What is wrong with a woman's supporting another woman? Is our love for one another any the less real, need it be less enduring, because we are a woman with a woman or a man with a man? Why shouldn't we express our love for one another through the same caretaking arrangements to which non-gay people have access?

How easily we get stuck in our thinking about these things. Take the following couple:

Philip and Larry have been together for three years. In their therapy with me they talk a lot about money. There's never enough. Larry has a job from which he earns a moderately good salary. Philip has a job in which he earns very little money. Larry complains that he is tired of supporting Philip. Philip complains that he is doing the best he can and that he's tired of Larry being on his back. They go round and round on this issue.

At some point, I suggested they think about pooling their money. If they shared ownership of all their earnings they would not have to be embroiled in these endless calculations of who paid more or less and why. I asked them if they planned to stay together. They said, yes, they certainly did, that they loved each other and got along wonderfully, except for the money issue.

"So why don't you behave like a committed couple and pool your earnings?"

Larry said, "If we pooled our money I'd still be supporting him because I'd be putting in so much more than he does. I couldn't ignore that."

I asked, "Larry, what if Philip became ill and couldn't work. What would you do then?"

"Well," Larry said, "I'd take care of him, of course. But that's different."

"How is it different?"

"Because a man is supposed to be self-reliant, to pull his share. If he can't because he's sick, the rules change."

Larry could overcome his conditioned attitude toward "supporting" another man only if that man were unable to support himself. What prisoners of our programming we can become! What pleasure and what peace we deny ourselves in the service of conforming to unquestioned beliefs. How we waste our energy perpetuating values that *constrain* our ability to love and care for one another. Isn't it time to change all that?

ATTITUDES TOWARD MONEY

Sometimes a couple's conflicts over money are not only a matter of disparate financial resources but of each partner's individual attitudes about how money should be spent. The partner with greater resources may be the conservative spender while the partner with limited finances may be the extravagant one who loves to spend money. Or, it may be the other way around.

Whatever the pattern, the important task here is to try to understand your partner's behavior in terms of the total picture of who he or she is. Some relevant questions to ask are the following:

- What was this person's early experience with money?
- Was money scarce or plentiful in his/her family?
- What cultural values might be incorporated into her/his approach to money?
- What parental spending habits might have shaped this person's?
- What life experiences may have influenced a need to hang onto money, or not to have to feel constrained in using it if it's there?

In addition to answering the above questions for your partner, answer them for yourself. How does your background, with regard to money, compare with your partner's? Are there significant differences that might explain why he/she handles money one way while you handle it another?

If you can effectively fathom the underlying reasons for the difference between you, it is more likely that you will be able to work out ways to accommodate one another's idiosyncrasies regarding money. It may require repeated airings of feelings about this issue. It may take developing mutually agreeable ground rules for how money is spent, especially if finances are pooled. It may involve a lot of self-examination and a real stretch of your ability to tolerate having your own values questioned and opening up to the possibility that something very different from what you believe is also all right. If you can accomplish that stretch you will be strengthening the alliance that has so much potential for enhancing your life.

Whether you are ready to pool your finances with your partner or not, a variety of options for money management are possible. Here are a few of the most common.

FUNDS KEPT SEPARATE

• Each partner has his or her own checking account. Expenses are divided either fifty-fifty or by a percentage reflecting the size of each partner's income. Separate credit cards are maintained. Once a month there is an accounting, and one partner writes the other a check for her/his portion of expenses.

• The couple maintains an either/or–signature household account which is used for food, rent or mortgage payments, utilities, laundry and cleaning, and the expenses of running the house. Each person contributes a fixed amount to the household account each month predetermined by a budget based on what actual expenses have been in a similar month. Each person has her/his own personal checking account, and what each does with that portion of their money is their own business. Separate credit cards are maintained.

FUNDS POOLED

• The couple has an either/or–signature checking account which is used for all of their major expenses, household and personal. Both partners deposit the major portion of their income in this account. Each partner also maintains a small separate checking account for incidental personal expenses. It is a "convenience" account. The main joint account checkbook is kept in the house, and each partner carries individual checks from the account. All credit cards are jointly maintained unless one or both partners also need separate cards for business purposes.

• The couple keeps all their money in one joint checking account out of which all household and all personal expenses are paid. Credit cards are maintained jointly. All of the joint checking account arrangements, of course, require careful record keeping to insure that each partner knows how much money is in the account at any given time.

The arrangement that I believe works best is the first one in the pooled funds category. Each partner always has immediate access to funds for out-of-pocket expenses. Both partners have access to the joint checking account with decisions for spending those funds made mutually. The merging of the couple's money is an expression of their commitment to each other and to the relationship.

11

EMPOWERING YOUR RELATIONSHIP LEGALLY

LEGAL STATUS

In early 1986, the California State Supreme Court heard a case involving a heterosexual man suing for loss of "consortium" following the accidental death of his female lover. His attorneys claimed that the person who caused the accident was responsible for the loss of the love and support of their client's mate. The parties involved in this case were not married. If an unmarried heterosexual man could sue over a partner's death, would not the same rights have to be extended to homosexual partners?

The *Los Angeles Times* printed the following (February 7, 1986):

> "Marriage is the very backbone, the very fabric of society," said Patrick A. Mesisca, one of the defendant's lawyers. But two justices disputed Mesisca's argument that the public would believe the court was voicing disapproval of marriage if the justices allowed such suits.
>
> Justice Allen Broussard scoffed at the suggestion, saying, "It's a matter of whether the court is going to continue to turn its back on significant numbers of people in very meaningful relationships."
>
> [California Supreme Court Justice Rose] Bird noted

that, under Mesisca's reasoning, a couple that had been married for an hour would have greater rights than two people who lived together for 25 years.

She said it all. That is just the way the legal system has always dealt with our relationships, as if they are without substance or merit. It is for that very reason the gay and lesbian community has had to develop our own strategies for legalizing important aspects of our partnerships.

Necessity is the mother of invention, and we have certainly had to be inventive. The laws of our nation, meant to protect and to provide remedies for unfair treatment of its citizens, are sometimes used to institutionalize unfair treatment against gay men and lesbians. The refusal to officially acknowledge our partnerships, no matter how stable and long lasting, is an example of such discrimination. We are not without recourse, however. We have begun to put together innovative remedies for the legal problems of lesbians and gay men. Our lawyers have become increasingly skilled in the specialized field of sexual orientation and the law. We have financial advisers to help us with our money management, and insurance counselors to help us to obtain better coverage and proper benefits. We can own property in joint tenancy with our partners. We can write solid wills to protect our partner's future. We have begun to benefit from spousal discounts on everything from health club memberships to medical insurance. And, as always, one of our most effective secret weapons is the gay people everywhere not identified as such, who provide that little bit of undercover help that makes the difference in accomplishing what seems impossible to accomplish. We are no longer entirely at the mercy of the system.

That's the good news. The bad news is that, by and large, gay and lesbian partners are still deprived of most of the benefits accruing to husband and wife. As couples, we do not have available the advantages of preferential tax treatment or of benefits from a spouse's social security, retirement, or pension funds. We do not have the right to sue in the event of death or injury of a partner.

We are discriminated against by employers who do not extend such economic benefits as health insurance and dental plans and such noneconomic benefits as as sick leave to care for an ailing spouse, bereavement leave for a partner who has died, or use of special facilities such as a library or a gym.

A strong case that discrimination does exist may be made in terms of the economic benefits available to heterosexually married couples, but not to gay and lesbian domestic partners. To quote from the Lesbian Rights Project's treatise, *Recognizing Lesbian & Gay Families: Strategies for Extending Employment Benefit Coverage:*

> The term "fringe benefits" is a misleading one which tends to trivialize the scope of economic and emotional rewards these benefits provide. First, these employment benefits are not "fringe" or "icing on the cake" when compared to wages. They make up an ever-increasing proportion of an employee's total compensation package. The Monthly Labor Review recently reported that in a survey of various white collar occupations, fringe benefits were found to constitute nearly *forty percent* of an employer's average outlay for labor expenses!

Plain and simply this amounts to heterosexual workers being paid significantly more than gay and lesbian workers for the same job done.

Now, back to the good news. With the advent of same-sex marriage, legal empowerment of a partnership one prerogative at a time becomes unnecessary. The whole package of rights and protections comes with the marriage license. However, I assume that there are still people reading this book who have not gone, or don't choose to go, the marriage route, and who can still benefit from advice on how to arrange their partnership to be as entitled and protected as possible without marriage.

What follows are two sections. The first is on legalizing your relationship one step at a time. The second is on the legal rights that come with civil marriage.

There is ongoing activity on all four fronts of this battle: litigation in the courts; lobbying in and by labor unions; legislative proposals to change the laws; and the quiet campaigns for policy change that go on within corporations and organizations.

The question of how to establish valid eligibility criteria for domestic partnerships is an intriguing one. Simply declaring that a committed relationship exists is hardly enough to set the bureaucratic machinery in motions. Something verifiable is essential. The two conditions that are most easily verifiable are cohabitation and economic integration. A couple can demonstrate that they are financially interdependent and living together fairly easily. For concreteness there is the affidavit, a sworn statement in writing. For example, the Berkeley School Board, which provides "spouse equivalent" benefits to its employees, requires an affidavit to be filed with the board attesting, among other things, that the partners live together, share the common necessities of life, are each other's sole domestic partner, and are responsible for each other's common welfare. The City of Berkeley requires its employees who apply for spousal equivalent benefits to file an "Affidavit of Domestic Partnership," an example of which follows.

CONFIDENTIAL

CITY OF BERKELEY

AFFIDAVIT OF DOMESTIC PARTNERSHIP

I. _____, certify that:
NAME OF EMPLOYEE

1. I, _____, and _____,
EMPLOYEE   DOMESTIC PARTNER

   reside together at _____ and
   ADDRESS

   share the common necessities of life;

2. We affirm that the effective date of this partnership is _____.
   DATE

3. We are not married to anyone.

4. We are at least eighteen (18) years of age or older.

5. We are not related by blood closer than would bar marriage in the State of California and are mentally competent to consent to contract.

6. We are each other's sole domestic partner and are responsible for our common welfare.

7. We agree to notify the City if there is any change of circumstances attested to in this Affidavit within thirty (30) days of change by filing a Statement of Termination of Domestic Partnership. Such termination statement shall be on a form provided by the City and shall affirm under penalty of perjury that the partnership is terminated and that a copy of the termination statement has been mailed to the other partner.

8. After such termination I, _____
   EMPLOYEE

   understand that another Affidavit of Domestic Partnership cannot be filed until six (6) months after a statement of termination of the previous partnership has been filed with the Risk Management Office.

9. We understand that any persons/employer/company who suffers any loss because of a false statement contained in an Affidavit of Domestic Partnership may bring a civil action against us to recover their loses including reasonable attorneys' fees.

10. We provide the information in this Affidavit to be used by the City for the sole purpose of determining our eligibility for domestic partnership benefits. We understand that this information will be held confidential and will be subject to disclosure only upon our express written authorization or pursuant to a court order.

11. We affirm, under penalty of perjury, that the assertions in this affidavit are true to the best of our knowledge.

_____   _____
DATE   SIGNATURE OF EMPLOYEE

_____
DATE OF BIRTH

_____   _____
DATE   SIGNATURE OF DOMESTIC PARTNER

_____
DATE OF BIRTH

If you are interested in further exploring ways to gain benefits as a gay or lesbian couple, go to the Gay Financial Network website, www.gfn.com, where you will find listings of gay-friendly accountants, financial planners, insurance agents, lawyers, mortgage bankers, and real estate agents to work with in your part of the country.

THE POWER OF ATTORNEY

For gay and lesbian couples the situation in which the power of attorney is most likely to be needed involves medical emergencies when one partner is too incapacitated to make critical decisions regarding medical care or financial matters. The power of attorney provides the legal basis for the other partner acting on behalf of the incapacitated person.

In the early edition of their book, *A Legal Guide for Lesbian and Gay Couples,* Hayden Curry and Denis Clifford describe the power of attorney as follows:

> A *power of attorney* is a legal document in which one person, called the "principal," authorizes another person, called the "attorney in fact," to act for the principal. A conventional power of attorney must terminate upon incapacity or death of the principal, and therefore is not very useful in medical emergency. However, there is a relatively new type of power of attorney, legal in all states, called a "durable" power of attorney ("DPA"), which remains valid even if, or when, the principal becomes incompetent and does not terminate until the death of the principal. One type of durable power of attorney, called "springing durable power of attorney" in legalese, only becomes effective if you become incompetent, and does not "spring" into use until then.
>
> . . . There are often different technical requirements applicable to a durable power of attorney in different states. Because of this local variation problem we recommend that you review your durable power of attorney with a lawyer. This is an important document which potentially transfers great power and you want to be sure it will accomplish your intentions.

In the much later twelfth edition of this book, the authors describe in detail the varied forms that powers of attorney currently take for medical care and for finances. Samples of the various forms used are provided. See Hayden Curry, Denis Clifford, and Frederick Hertz. *A Legal Guide for Lesbian and Gay Couples.* Berkeley, California, Nolo Press, 2004. Available from the Nolo Press in Berkeley. (800) 728-3555; fax: (800) 645-0895; cs@nolo.com; see www.nolo.com.

I believe one is usually best served by seeking the advice of a lawyer when dealing with legal matters. Referrals to gay-friendly lawyers can be obtained from the following:

National Lawyers Guild, (212) 679-5100, or at www.nlgno@ nlg.org; Gay and Lesbian Advocates and Defenders (GLAD), 30 Winter Street, Boston, Massachusetts 02108, (617) 426-1350, or at www.GLAD.org.

CONTRACTS

There are many kinds of contracts gay or lesbian partners might make with one another, from nonlegal, philosophical agreements about how they are going to treat each other, to quite legal and binding agreements regarding ownership of property and financial assets.

I have very mixed feelings about written contracts between gay or lesbian partners.

My negative feelings stem from the essence of what such contracts imply—lack of trust, presumption of conflict, the inevitable ending of the relationship.

My positive feelings come from the belief that anything that facilitates discussion of what two people need from one another is usually helpful.

The *Legal Guide* describes living-together contracts in the following way:

> Along with economic provisions, your living together agreement can include anything and everything relevant to your living situation, except sexuality or being lovers. . . . However, you should clearly understand that living together contracts are normally enforceable in court only to the degree that they concern personal

and real property. . . . Contract provisions having to do with the personal conduct of the couple are not enforceable.

There is this caution:

If the contract states (or implies) that a promise was made in exchange for sexual services, it will not be enforced. So never include any statement as to sexual rights and responsibilities in your contract. Identify yourselves as "partners," not "lovers."

This point is made even more strongly in the excellent and comprehensive volume, *Sexual Orientation and the Law,* edited by Roberta Achtenberg and published under the auspices of the National Lawyers Guild. Advice to lawyers handling the drafting of such contracts is:

It is not unusual for clients to seek a contract which, in addition to stating rights and responsibilities regarding property, income, and expenses, also includes agreements regarding aspects of their personal relationship. These agreements may include provision for regular companionship, housekeeping schedules for the parties, and rules regarding "marital fidelity," for example . . . however, references to companionship, fidelity, etc., may render the contract unenforceable. Further, describing both personal and property rights in an agreement may confuse the consideration issue even if explicit references to sexual relations are omitted. A court accustomed and willing to award contracted-for property and financial benefits may seek an excuse not to make an award where otherwise clear monetary arrangements are muddied by agreements for personal contact. Finally, the parties may not wish that their personal relations be an open record; but when rights to real property are concerned, legal recordation of the documents may be required, and if one party should have to sue on the contract, the document will become part of the court file.

CONTRACTS CONCERNING REAL PROPERTY

If your contract involves real property, the signatures should be notarized so that the documents can be filed with the County Recorder's office and that their legitimacy can be proven if a question is ever raised.

Should you and your partner feel the need for a contract that you can be certain is legally binding, you would be best served by consulting an attorney accustomed to dealing with same-sex relationship issues. To find such a lawyer you might seek a referral from a local gay/lesbian organization.

Also, most local chapters of the American Civil Liberties Union will be able to make a referral to an attorney experienced in these matters.

If you cannot gain access to attorneys who are familiar with same-sex relationship issues, you might ask your lawyer to refer to the very thorough compilation of advice on such matters, *Sexual Orientation and the Law*. This collection of practice materials was developed under the auspices of the San Francisco Bay Area Chapter of the National Lawyers Guild. As the introduction to this volume states:

In many respects, this book deals with the everyday problems of being lesbian and gay in a culture, and under a legal establishment, which often stigmatizes that status. Sometimes, major lawsuits must be mounted in order to address those problems. In other instances, simply planning for contingencies and making the choice of the right legal instrument will be enough to take care of the situation. Meeting the legal needs and overcoming the legal problems faced by lesbian and gay clients, however, will nearly always entail novel or creative applications of the law. It is unfortunately still the case that without imaginative solutions, there are no solutions possible, given the status of lesbians and gay males with the legal system. The book will help to suggest to the practitioner some of the imaginative solutions.

Mostly, I would hope that a couple's planning for the future would not revolve around the relationship's eventual demise but around the long life and success they expect it to have.

OWNING REAL PROPERTY

For many lesbian and gay male couples, buying the first house or condo together is the ritual of commitment that comes closest to heterosexual marriage vows. This is it. The couple is now joined in "holy real estate."

If you are buying or contemplating buying real estate with your lover, and it is a first for you, there are a few basics you should know. There are two main ways to own property together as described in *The Legal Guide.*

Joint Tenancy

If both of you take title to a piece of real property "as joint tenants," it means that legally you share property equally and that each of you has the right to use the entire property. Joint tenancy also has a right of survivorship. This means that if one joint tenant dies, the other (or others) automatically takes the deceased person's share, even if there is a will to the contrary. Another attractive attribute of joint tenancy is that when property is passed to the other tenant(s) at death, there is no necessity of any probate proceedings.

Warning! Joint tenancy is not appropriate in a situation in which a house is owned in unequal shares. It is appropriate only to those situations in which each joint tenant owns the same undivided portion as does the others(s). This means that you and your lover could put a house you own 50-50 in joint tenancy or that three people could have a joint tenancy with each owning one-third of a property. However, if you own 60 percent of a house and your lover owns 40 percent, joint tenancy will not work.

Tenants-in-Common

Taking title as "tenants-in-common" means that there is no "right of survivorship." When a "tenant-in-common" dies, her or his interest in the property is transferred to whomever she or he specified in the will, or if there is no will, by the process of "intestate succession." The big difference between joint tenancy and tenancy-in-common is that in the former you have an automatic right of survivorship, and in the latter you don't. Also, and of particular importance in many lesbian or gay real estate ventures, tenants-in-common can own property in unequal shares—one person can own 80 percent of the property, one 15 percent, and a third 5 percent.

WILLS AND ESTATE PLANNING

The following are excerpts reprinted from the pamphlet "Wills Give You Power," published by National Gay Rights Advocates.

Q: Can I make my own will?

A: In some states you can draft a will in your own handwriting. This is called a "holographic" will and it must meet certain statutory requirements to be valid. While this may be all right for some people, we recommend seeing a lawyer for most gay men and women. You want your will to be "air tight" so it can withstand a challenge after your death.

Q: What information do I need for the lawyer?

A: You need to decide which people and organizations you want to leave your estate to (these are called the beneficiaries). Next, you need to decide who you want to appoint to make sure your final wishes are carried out (this person is called the *executor* or *executrix*). You should also think about the type of funeral service, if any, and the disposition of your remains. For example, do you want a burial or cremation?

Q: What if I think there is a possibility that someone may challenge my will?

A: You can ask your lawyer to include a couple of extra paragraphs that will give you added protection. One is called a "disinheritance clause" and the other is known as an "anti-contest" clause. Both are desirable if you suspect there is *any* chance of somebody contesting your will.

Q: Must my estate go through "probate"?

A: "Probate" is a court procedure that provides for the change of legal ownership of your property when you die. Whether your estate will have to go through probate will depend on the size of your estate and which state you live in.

Q: Are there ways of avoiding taxes or probate?

A: Sometimes through "estate planning" you can minimize the amount of taxes to be paid. Estate planning can be done through various devices, such as insurance policies, joint ownership of property, or setting up a trust.

Q: What about joint ownership?

A: Many people buy a house, for example, together. They can own this property as "tenants-in-common" or as "joint tenants." If you own property as joint tenants, when you die the property automatically passes to the other tenant.

When you own property as tenants-in-common, the disposition of your portion of the property is governed by the terms of your will. If you don't have a will, it will go to your relatives or to the state. It *cannot* go to your lover, friends, or a charitable organization without a valid will.

Perhaps your "estate" may not seem to you to be extensive enough to bother about, but whatever possessions you share with your lover may be very precious to her or him. Without a will, everything you own may be claimed by your family. If they do not understand or appreciate the nature of your relationship with your lover, or if they choose to ignore it, that person has no legal claim whatsoever to anything you possess. You can make a simple will using either of the following:

- Clifford, Denis, and Cora Jordan. *Plan Your Estate: Absolutely Everything You Need to Know to Protect Your Loved Ones.* Berkeley: Nolo Press, 2000.

- *Quicken WillMaker Plus 2004/*Software for Windows CD-ROM. (Both available from the Nolo Press; see above.)

One way to establish clearly that the terms of your will accurately reflect your wishes for handling your estate is to videotape yourself describing what you want to happen to your estate, and to you, upon your death. Have a copy made of the videotape. Store one in your lawyer's office and one in your safe deposit box. Attach a note to your copy of the will advising where these tapes are located.

If your estate is substantial or if you anticipate that your famliy might be particularly difficult to deal with in such a matter, you should seek help from a lawyer who is experienced in handling the legal problems of lesbian and gay men.

LIFE INSURANCE

From *Sexual Orientation and the Law:*

> A good estate planning device for any lesbian or gay couple is life insurance in which one partner is named beneficiary on the policy. The proceeds are free from probate so long as the estate is not designated beneficiary or the owner of the policy. . . .
>
> To avoid inclusion in the insured's estate, the insured could irrevocably assign the life insurance policy to the beneficiary. This triggers gift tax liability when assigned, but if the value of the policy is less than the $10,000 annual exclusion, the gift should be exempt from gift tax.
>
> If the couple has not yet purchased life insurance, it may be advisable for the beneficiary to purchase the insurance on the life of the other, presumably wealthier, partner, so that the policy would be owned by the beneficiary and not included in the insured's estate. The insured could make a gift of the premiums to the owner of the policy, and if the premium were under $10,000 a year, there would be no gift tax liability.

HEALTH INSURANCE

Another area that shows signs of opening up to the needs of gay and lesbian couples is that of "spouse equivalent" health insurance.

Typically, what is required is that the spousal equivalent be eighteen years of age or older, unmarried, living in the same residence (for some set period of time), the sole spousal equivalent figure, and not related by blood.

As California has led in so many other areas, the passage of Assembly Bill 205 puts it ahead of the other states (Vermont excluded) in the rights and privileges accorded gay and lesbian couples. As of January 2005, those couples registered as domestic

partners in California enjoy the same entitlements and responsibilities as legally married couples in the state. The exceptions are
those rights and privileges that involve the federal government.

We hope that the trend in this direction will continue as
more and more communities pass domestic partnership, civil
union, and civil marriage laws, giving the lovers of lesbians and
gay men the legal status that will make such coverage much easier to come by.

INSURANCE COUNSELING

Up-to-date information on insurance strategies benefiting same-
sex relationships can be obtained from insurance agents in your
community who are lesbian or gay, or knowledgeable about and
supportive of our issues. Often such people advertise themselves
in local gay/lesbian publications, and/or they are listed in national or regional gay resource directories. Other good referral
sources are local gay business and professional associations or gay
physicians and attorneys groups.

OBTAINING LEGAL STATUS WITH CIVIL MARRIAGE

It's a package deal. With the license come all the privileges and
protections of legal marriage. By most counts that amounts to
well over a thousand ways in which the civilly married enjoy benefits that domestic partners and those in civil unions do not. That
means that millions of gay or lesbian American citizens do not actually have constitutional protection equal to that of their fellow
citizens. Thus the foundation is laid for the civil rights battle that
is same-sex marriage.

What are these privileges and protections? Why are they necessary? What do they establish?

Primarily, civil marriage rights are about two things: they set
the stage for kinship and caregiving. Kinship establishes family;

caregiving protects those one loves. Civil marriage is portable—it goes where you go. Domestic partnership and civil unions travel to only those states where such laws are in force already.

The financial benefits that come automatically with a marriage license support the institution of marriage, which in turn supports the practical aspects of the couple's life, financially and socially. Gay and lesbian couples want the same things in life as people who are not gay. We want stability, a home life, loving attachment, continuity of relationship, the choice to raise and protect children, the recognition of society, and the protection of the law in our daily lives. That's it. No more complicated than that. No less fair than that. The time has come for same-sex civil marriage.

Here is a sampling of the rights and protections that come automatically, and many *only*, with the civil marriage license.

In Everyday Life, the Right to:

- own property in joint tenancy
- have joint leases for rental property with automatic renewal rights if spouse leaves or dies
- have joint insurance policies for home, auto, health
- have access to spouse's life and health insurance from spouse's workplace
- be able to file joint income tax returns
- be relocated by the company with spouse in a job change
- receive medical care, education, home loans if spouse is in the military or a veteran
- have access to tax breaks for married couples
- invoke spousal privilege in a court of law
- sponsor U.S. citizenship if spouse is from another country

With Children, the Right to:

- have joint parenting rights such as access to children's school records

- have ready access to joint adoption of children
- have custody of children after divorce
- have custody of children after death of a spouse
- have your relationship, with all its entitlements, legally recognized in other states

Upon a Spouse's Illness, the Right to:

- visit in the hospital
- make medical decisions for the person, if necessary
- get sick leave from a workplace to care for the person

Upon a Spouse's Death, the Right to:

- receive the spouse's social security benefits
- make decisions about the manner of a spouse's burial
- get bereavement leave from a workplace
- have automatic inheritance of shared assets
- inherit retirement savings tax-free
- assume a spouse's pension
- inherit automatically if spouse dies without a will
- file a wrongful death claim

In Civil Unions Without Legal Marriage:

- No right to social security and federal pension inheritence rights
- No right to sponsor citizenship for a foreign-born spouse
- No right to have your relationship, with all its entitlements, legally recognized in states that do not have civil unions

RESOURCES—LEGAL MARRIAGE

How do I keep up-to-date on what is going on with the marriage issue? Where do I get information or assistance if I want to marry my partner? Who is actually working to make same-sex marriage a reality everywhere?

These are the main organizations that are spearheading the drive for marriage equality. You will find up-to-date information on what is happening at their websites.

ACLU Lesbian and Gay Rights Project
125 Broad Street, 18th Floor
New York, NY 10004
(888) 567-ACLU; (212) 344-3005
www.aclu.org

Freedom to Marry Project
116 West 23rd Street, Suite 500
New York, NY 10011
(212) 851-8418
www.freedomtomarry.org

GLAD—Gay and Lesbian Advocates and Defenders
Referral service to gay-friendly lawyers.
30 Winter Street, Suite 800
Boston, MA 02108
(617) 462-1350
www.gladlaw@glad.org

HRC—Human Rights Campaign
1640 Rhode Island, N.W.
Washington, DC 20036-3278
(202) 628-4160
www.hrc@hrc.org

Lambda Legal Defense and Education Fund
120 Wall Street, Suite 500
New York, NY 10005
(212) 809-8585
www.lamdalegal.org

Marriage Equality
P.O. Box 121
Old Chelsea Station
New York, NY 10113-0121
(877) 571-5729
www.marriageequality.org

NCLR—National Center for Lesbian Rights
870 Market Street, Suite 570
San Francisco, CA 94102
(415) 392-6257
info@nclrights.org
www.nclrights.org

NGLTF—National Gay and Lesbian Task Force
1325 Massachusetts Avenue, N.W., Suite 600
Washington, DC 20005-4164
(202) 393-5177
www.TheTaskForce.org

National Lawyers Guild
143 Madison Avenue, 4th Floor
New York, NY 10016
(212) 679-5100
www.nlgno@nlg.org

12

THE FAMILY, GOD BLESS 'EM

I stared down the narrow corridor of faces gathered in an ellipse around my aunt Rose's dining table. These were elderly aunts and uncles I hadn't seen in a decade, cousins I'd never met, old friends of the family who hadn't seen me since I was a little girl in Shirley Temple curls and black patent leather shoes.

They talked among themselves, and some of them talked to me, asking questions about my parents, my sister, my life in California. It was pleasant, benign, comfortable, this brief sojourn into a setting I had left so many years ago as a child.

The conversation buzzed along. Aunt Rose moved back and forth between dining room and kitchen supplying the table with one platter after another of warm delicious offerings. She was the undisputed matriarch of the family. Everyone wanted her approval. Some in the family chafed under the domination they felt she exercised over their lives, but they were always the first to run to her when they were in trouble. She ruled the roost alongside Uncle Leon; sweet, gentle, steady, he provided the financial foundation that supported Aunt Rose's charitable good works and her stewardship of the family.

She was my father's older sister, the mother of two sons. I'd always suspected she had desperately wanted a daughter. She was very nice to me and took a special interest in whatever I was doing, wherever I was. We left St. Louis when I was still a child, and though I had not seen her often we'd kept in touch by telephone.

Mine was a rare trip to the Midwest, for a speaking engagement at Washington University during their Gay Awareness Week. The family gathering was occurring early in the evening before I was to go off to the university to give my speech.

When I arrived in the afternoon, Aunt Rose and I settled down for a long talk. I told her that I was in St. Louis to give a speech to a gay group, that I was gay myself, and that I'd edited, and written part of, a book called *Positively Gay*. She said she was glad I was telling her because she'd always known it somehow, and she recounted the various clues to that effect she'd picked up over the years.

The conversation was an easy one. I felt grateful for that and good about having the chance to talk to her in this way.

Now, somewhere toward the end of the family dinner, in the midst of the conversational din, a voice at the other end of the table was struggling to be heard.

"Betty, why are you here on this trip?"

And, then, more insistently, and much louder, "Betty, are you here for some special reason?"

I heard the question. I opened my mouth to answer.

Nothing came out.

By now, the other aunts and uncles and cousins had stopped talking to one another. They were looking expectantly at me. I had been asked a question they all heard. I looked as if I were going to answer. The table grew quiet.

I searched those attentive faces; it was as if we were all trapped in this deadly silence. I couldn't believe that I was not answering the question. I didn't understand what was blocking me. I felt immobilized. So many eyes looking at me.

In the seeming eternity of that moment their faces were beginning to look distorted to me, as they would in a fun house mirror. The room seemed filled with the question, "Why are you here?" The faces demanded an answer.

I answered with a silent stare.

And then, the moment was over.

From beside me I heard Aunt Rose's calm, even voice saying, "Betty is here to give a talk tonight at Washington University. She is going to talk about her book, *Positively Gay,* which she wrote because *she's* gay. And, we're very proud of her." The eyes moved from Aunt Rose's face to my face and back to Aunt Rose's face. She was smiling and, indeed, looking at me proudly. As though cued, all the faces smiled, the heads nodded. There were a few "Umms" and they all looked at me, proudly.

I had a mixture of emotions. I felt grateful for the intervention. I felt embarrassed at not being able to respond to the question on my own. I couldn't believe I had given in to this disclosure anxiety. I felt angry at myself. I felt appreciative of Aunt Rose for her straightforwardness and for her affection. I felt embraced by her and by these relatives with their smiling faces. Even if they didn't really understand what it was all about, their willingness to hear and their amiability warmed me.

That experience brought home to me, once again, the dread still felt by so many of us as we present ourselves to our family-of-origin, wanting their acceptance for something we may not have even accepted yet ourselves. We lull ourselves into thinking it doesn't matter, or it will work itself out, or it's already worked out. Then, we are taken by surprise when suddenly it matters so much, or we are overwhelmed by a feeling of isolation from people we love, or we realize that it isn't worked out at all, that we've just begun what we thought we were almost finished with.

How we relate to our families, and more important, how they relate to us, can make the difference between a gay or lesbian identity spoiled by guilt and self-denial or one enhanced by love and understanding. Similarly, how our families behave toward our gay or lesbian lover can make the difference between a partnership enriched by family ties and the continuity of shared lives and one that suffers tension and strain when anything concerning family comes up.

Our family can influence our lives, but we can usually determine what that influence will be, often much more than we think

we can. That is the theme of this chapter. I believe that self-
determination is especially important when it comes to the role
we allow our families to play in our same-sex relationships.

Some of us are lucky enough to have families who are able to
accept and support us as lesbians and gay men. When that is the
case, they are usually also able to integrate our gay/lesbian partnerships into their lives. These I call the "All-Embracing" families.

A continuum of acceptance and support might look like this:

THE ALL-EMBRACING FAMILY	THE ARM'S-LENGTH FAMILY	THE PRETEND-YOU-DON'T-EXIST FAMILY

These, of course, are the families to whom it has been disclosed that they have a lesbian or gay member. For families who
have not been disclosed to, the continuum might look like this:

THE TOTALLY-IN-THE-DARK FAMILY	THE WE-SUSPECT-BUT-WE-REALLY-DON'T-WANT-TO-KNOW FAMILY

THE ALL-EMBRACING FAMILY

The All-Embracing Family accepts their relative's lover as a bona
fide member of the family. Mother, father, sister, brothers, some
or all might develop their own relationship with the lover, as
often happens with a heterosexual spouse.

In the best of cases, they introduce their gay relative and
her/his partner in a way that accurately depicts the relationship.
My own father says, "This is my daughter, and this is my daughter-
in-law."

In the All-Embracing Family, gay/lesbian-related topics are
freely discussed. If someone in the family reads a gay-related story
in the newspaper or sees such a program on television, that person will call the couple to be sure they don't miss it. If the couple

and the family live in a large metropolitan area with an organized gay community, family members might attend gay community events. In Los Angeles the parents of some activist leaders are as well known to the gay community as their children. My family attends gay/lesbian fundraising dinners or parties if either my lover or I happen to be involved in the event or the organization. Many parents in All-Embracing families are active in their local chapter of "Parents and Friends of Lesbians and Gays."

My own family has totally embraced my lover. My mother treats her like another daughter. She is a major confidante to my stepmother. My father frequently expresses his affection for her and his gratitude at having her in our lives.

My sister and her grown children live in another state and, therefore, do not have a lot of contact with our relationship, but when they do, they treat it with all the respect one could ask for. I am particularly proud of my sister, who, as a clinical psychologist, has made a special outreach to gay people in need. Once, at a training workshop I was conducting in the college town where she then lived, a number of gay and lesbian students came to me during the breaks to say that they didn't know what they would have done without her counsel, that she was a major resource for the gay students on that campus.

Assorted cousins have played a part, at one time or another, in easing my transition from the closet to an open and positive gay identity. Cousin Sidney heard a tearful confession on the beach in the midst of the first (tumultuous) lesbian affair of my second coming out in 1968. He put his arms around me and reassured me that he didn't feel at all differently about me and would I please hurry up and tell him everything about this person I was so upset about. Cousins Jerry and Sandy have been delightful companions in the introduction of my lover into the fold of the extended family in St. Louis.

Needless to say, this kind of support can be very reinforcing to a couple's effort to maintain a stable and secure relationship. It can only help to have the partnership treated as the valid and legitimate family unit that it is.

THE ARM'S-LENGTH FAMILY

Now let's look at the less felicitous situation of the family who holds their gay/lesbian relative at arm's length. You've told them you're gay. The initial fireworks are over. Everyone has settled into an attitude of acknowledgment, if not acceptance. You have established that the person you live with is your mate and that you expect her/him to be included on family occasions. Your family is anywhere from grudgingly polite to pleasant and civilized to your lover. It's not entirely comfortable, but it works. Well, most often it works better on *their* turf than on yours. They might go so far as to welcome your partner into their home, but, often, they won't come to yours. When that is the case, there's always a proper excuse, but the fact is they don't want to get that close to the scene of the crime. You go along with this because you are grateful that things are going as well as they are. You don't want to rock the boat.

Actually, if this is your situation, you are conspiring with your family to keep hidden an important part of your life. It is a conspiracy that inevitably reinforces their aversive feelings about your sexual orientation. It can't do a lot for your own feelings of pride in yourself and your way of life, that is, when you think about it, which you try *not* to do as much as possible.

What is the alternative?

I suggest a process of *normalization.* Your home embraces most of the normal activities of your couple life just as your family's home embraces their normal activities. If your family has homophobic attitudes toward your home, your task is to decondition them. They need to know that you do something else in your home besides having sex. You must talk about what happens at home in a way that *normalizes* for them the environment in which you live.

If there is a conspiracy of silence about your home life, you must break it. Talk about the everyday aspects of life at home. Keep talking about it whether they seem responsive or not. Hopefully, they will eventually hear you.

The next step is to get your family physically into your domain. If you live in the same city, it's easier. You can do it in graduated steps. You might start with invitations for short visits for some specific purpose, such as seeing a new piece of furniture or a new pet. Longer visits might include dinner or coffee and dessert after dinner out. You may have to insist. If their resistance is strong, your insistence must be strong. Your home, whether it's one room or a mansion, is just as important a part of your life as theirs is to them.

Another way in which the Arm's-Length Family protects itself from the "terrible truth" about you is by invoking a cloak of secrecy around the fact of your gayness and the true nature of your relationship with your lover.

They extract promises that you will never tell Aunt Bessie or Uncle Harry or Cousin Penelope or *any* of the neighbors. Even worse, they sometimes plead, "Please don't ever tell your sister or your brother." Sometimes the plea is not to tell a tyrannical father who will take his anger out on everyone else, or an ailing mother who will worsen and die, and it will all be your fault.

Entering into agreements to cloak your sexual orientation and your primary relationship in secrecy is to reinforce the notion that being gay or lesbian is something to hide. Now you've got the whole family in the closet and your lover is in there with them. I have known people who've capitulated to this kind of muzzling for years, without ever questioning that it was necessary. And, I have known people who have decided that they would disclose to the relative or neighbor or family friend in spite of admonition not to do so and have found acceptance and understanding. Support was there that they would have missed out on if they had continued to honor the vow of silence imposed upon them.

Sometimes the discouragement from the family takes on a more subtle form. Yes, they know you're gay. Yes, they've accepted it, but they let it be known that they would rather not have to deal with a person with whom you are sexually involved. They don't want to be asked to invite your partner into their house or into their hearts. That's the script. Be gay if you must, but don't ask us to relate to the people you are gay with. Don't expect us to include them on family occasions. We don't want to have to experience firsthand what your being gay is about.

The person who "dutifully" cooperates with this script often has difficulty forming a primary relationship. The cause-and-effect relationship here is one that is subtle and often not readily apparent. The task is to come to understand the pattern and the way in which it works to protect the objecting parent and nullify the person's efforts toward a relationship.

It is quite possible to stop cooperating with this family script and move on from it.

My favorite story about this happening involves a young man I will call Joey. When he came to see me, he was in his mid-thirties. He was a successful professional, living alone, popular in a circle of similar young men, all on the rise in their careers. He was handsome, well spoken, mild mannered. He said that he dated men often, had close friends with whom he went out when he wasn't dating, and that his life was in good order, with the exception that he had been unable to establish a relationship with a lover. He was worried about his ability to do this since he never had.

I worked with him for a few months, hearing about various men to whom he was attracted and who were attracted to him but with whom he could not sustain an interest in building a partnership. One day, I asked him to talk to me about his family and how they felt about his being gay. His family lived in another part of the state. He said that he had told his parents together, that his father didn't talk about it but continued to treat him in the same way as before. His mother, on the other hand, did talk about it, saying that if he were gay it was okay with her. When he asked her to meet some of his friends while she was visiting him, she said no, she would rather not. He tried again on another visit, and she again declined. Then he asked her what she would do if he had a lover; would she not want to meet him? She said that she would rather not have to do that also. He told her he was bothered by this. She just repeated that she accepted his being gay, but she just couldn't cope with having to relate to people with whom he was having sex. He said he didn't only have sex with people he went out with, that they did other things as well, just like everybody else.

She said she didn't want to hear about any more of it right now. The next time he talked to her he tried to talk casually about a man he was seeing. She changed the subject. It went on like that for several years. When he told me these stories, I said to him, "Your mother does not want you to have a lover, and you are cooperating with her."

He thought about it and said, "What you say sounds kind of right." He tested out this hypothesis a few times, trying to talk to his mother about men he was seeing, having her reject the topic, and feeling inside himself that he didn't want to upset her with more talk about it. He came to realize that if he didn't have a relationship he wouldn't have to deal with the matter at all, and there would be no question of upsetting her.

Gradually he was able to free himself of his unspoken commitment to her. Within several months, he met someone and began to establish a relationship. They moved in together, and after a year, they decided to get married, to have a public ceremony in which they pledged their love and their lives to one another. I was invited to the wedding. I was intrigued to see his mother there. She was a rather large woman, and she sat up very straight, hands folded in her lap. Pinned to her bosom was a very large corsage. She sat beside the mother of the other groom, who had an equally large corsage pinned to her bosom. The women talked to one another in a rather tentative way, often interrupted by well-wishers who approached them to offer congratulations. As I watched the two women, I thought back to the sessions when Joey first began to get the idea that he was avoiding a relationship because his mother didn't want him to have one. I thought about the sessions in which it was apparent he was freeing himself of the inhibition her script for him had created.

He had won quite a victory.

I looked carefully at the face of Joey's mother. I saw a good person there. She had done what she needed to do, what felt right to her, at the time. Now, here she was, perhaps not doing what she wanted to do, but doing what felt right to her at this time. Here she was being the mother of the groom. A little confused. A little bewildered. But, she was there. I smile at the memory.

Unfortunately, it is all too often true that parents' wishes for their daughter or son not to be actively gay get manifested in an effort to sabotage their offspring's relationship. Usually, this happens in subtle ways. There may be critical comments from a parent about the way your partner behaves around you or the way he/she relates to the family or the quality of his/her life as an individual. This parent may be very concerned about your being taken advantage of or about your wasting yourself on someone who doesn't measure up to the person you are.

Persistently pursued, a parent's efforts may begin to color your own feelings about your lover. The seeds of doubt have been sown and nurtured, and it is, so often, in the heat of conflict (inevitable in even the best of partnerships) that you find out to your surprise that the seeds have taken root. You find yourself thinking, if not saying, those very things that your parent has been saying to you about your lover. At that point, I would hope, your danger signals would be activated. You would realize that you are playing out a drama that is of your parent's making, that is expressing a need for you to be different from what you are. The agenda here, conscious or unconscious, is for you to be dissatisfied with your partner and your relationship and quit them both. It is amazing how many people cooperate with such an agenda without realizing that they are doing so. I say again, it is a subtle business usually. Its playing out takes many different forms.

Once you are aware that something like this might be happening in your own life, what do you do?

In the best instance, you sit down with the offending parent and explain the facts of life, your life. You set limits. You make it clear that you are no longer willing to listen to critical remarks about your lover or your relationship, that such comments are unacceptable. You tell your parent that to be welcome in your life, he/she has to do whatever is necessary to work through the negativity that has been expressed regarding your partner. You must tell your parent what you expect in the future by way of acceptable behavior toward your lover, and toward you, regarding your relationship.

I remind you. Your parents need you now more than you need them. Allowing them to participate in your adult life is your gift to them. It does come with a price tag, however. Their participation has to be respectful of who and what you are. They shouldn't be allowed to ignore that or to undermine that or to try to destroy it.

You wouldn't let a destructive child run rampant and unchecked through your home, I'm sure. Why then would you let a parent, bent on destruction, run rampant through your relationship? Hopefully, you would honor yourself and your partner enough to provide protection from such incursions. As the destructive child is better off for being controlled, so a destructive (even unconsciously) parent is better off for knowing what the limits are for involvement in your life. Certainly your relationship will be better off for being treated with the respect it deserves.

THE PRETEND-YOU-DON'T-EXIST FAMILY

The family has been told you're gay. You've tried to make it all right with them and it just hasn't worked. They've turned their back on you. They pretend you don't exist.

By now you may have given up. Or, you may still be trying to reconnect with them. In either case you may find that you spend more time than you'd like thinking about them.

If this has happened to you, you've suffered a serious loss. How do you deal with that loss?

First, you must allow yourself to grieve. Grief openly expressed is an antidote to the psychic pain of loss. Grief denied can create a dangerous undertow to whatever currents of emotion are happening in your life. To be rejected by the people who raised you, the people you have looked to for love and nurturance, surely has an effect on one's ability to trust, to be close, to accept affection, to function effectively in an intimate partnership.

What is crucial here is that you not internalize your family's negative attitude toward you and come to think of yourself as an emotional castaway, undeserving of love. Their rejection of you is about their inability to think beyond their own beliefs. It is not about your worth as a person or your lovableness. Don't confuse their failure to accommodate to your needs as a commentary on the validity of those needs or the right to have them met by someone else. You can nurture yourself to fill the void left by their dereliction as parents. You can achieve attachment to a loving partner. You can move beyond grief to wholeness if you remain centered in your own life. Your potential for loving experience need not be limited by what has happened between you and them.

If you are from a Pretend-You-Don't-Exist Family, you will do well to make a special effort to talk to your partner about the effect your family's behavior is having on you. You might explore together what effect it might be having on your relationship. Whatever that effect might be, it will then be out in the open, so that both of you can deal with it, together.

THE TOTALLY-IN-THE-DARK FAMILY

They don't know you're gay. Your lover is a friend, or a roommate, as far as they are concerned. Since they don't know this person is your beloved and your spouse, they need not feel any obligation to include her or him on family occasions. They have no reason to relate to this person except on the most casual basis.

Depending on your level of consciousness and the delicacy of your nervous system, you may do any or all of the following when the family comes to visit:

- sleep apart from your lover
- avoid touching or gazing affectionately at her/him
- avoid discussion of anything that is about being gay
- make sure your more exuberantly gay or lesbian friends stay away
- cleanse your living quarters of any reading material, pictures, videos, or symbols of any kind that are about being gay

In essence, you pretend you are not who you are when the family is around. You censor yourself. You monitor your lover's behavior. (Thank God the dog can't talk!) And, when they leave, it is usually with a sense of relief that you watch them go.

Visits of this kind with your family cannot help being a strain on you, on your lover, and on your relationship. There is no opportunity for them to support you, your lifestyle, or your relationship, which they very well might if they were not kept so totally-in-the-dark.

THE WE-SUSPECT-BUT-WE-DON'T-REALLY-WANT-TO-KNOW FAMILY

You've never told them you're gay, but by now they know. You know they know. They know you know they know—but no one speaks of it. At least they've stopped bugging you about getting married. They no longer ask if you're going out with anyone. They don't ask you much about your personal life. Conversation with them is about work (or school), the weather, world events, family gossip, *their* lives, all "safe" subjects. It does get a bit unreal, hearing about everyone else's life and never talking about, or being asked about, your own, as though you had no personal life.

In the worst scenario, you pretend you don't have a lover. You go to family occasions, alone. Your lover is invisible to your family and loses you to them at times (such as holidays) when the two of you should be having close, warm experiences together. Your lover resents your family and resents your unwillingness to bring the truth out in the open with them. Your family wins, and they are reinforced in their inclination to deny that you are really gay because they never have to experience you in a relationship.

In the next-worst scenario, your family knows you share your living quarters with someone, but they don't know (or don't want to know) the true nature of your relationship with this person. They politely agree if you ask to bring your "roommate" to family occasions. They don't go out of their way to encourage it. It is an issue that comes up in your relationship over and over and over. It is never settled. There is always tension about "the family" with your partner.

An improvement on the above scenario is one in which your lover is accepted into the family as "your friend," but the status of spouse is not accorded. However, it is expected by all parties concerned that you will always come to family occasions with "your friend." No one ever speaks of gay, or lover, as though such things didn't exist. Large areas of your life are never touched upon. On those occasions when you or your lover "slip" and refer to something gay-related, or speak of one another in a way that goes beyond friendship, or touch each other in a loving manner, everyone looks the other way. Not the kind of warm, supportive atmosphere one would like to conduct one's loving relationship in, but that's the way it is. The conspiracy wins out again.

What is the alternative to these scenarios?

Well, the alternative to fantasy is reality. The alternative to denial is truth. The alternative to silence is disclosure. It is my belief that fantasy, denial, and silence about who we really are represent the enemies of growth in the development of every gay or lesbian person.

On the other hand, reality, the truth, and disclosure about who we really are supports individual growth and validates the bond of gay and lesbian partnerships. Therefore, my vote goes for relationships with your family that are based on the truth of your reality as a person and as a partner in a loving relationship with a person who happens to be of the same gender you are. Only that truth will free you from the games and the subterfuge that take up so much energy, that are typical of all the kinds of families involved in denying your right to be who you really are. The only way to bring that truth out in the open is through disclosure.

DISCLOSING TO YOUR FAMILY

The following guidelines on disclosing to your family are reprinted from my previous book, *Positively Gay.**

Before You Disclose

It is important to spend some time with yourself doing two things. Examine your own attitudes about being gay. If you have mixed feelings, they will be conveyed and the disclosure will probably be a bad experience. Read some of the excellent gay-affirming books now on the market. Try to get straight about being gay before you talk about it to family.

Clarify why you are disclosing at this particular time. If, for instance, you are angry with your parents, try to deal with that anger somewhere else before you talk to them. If you bring anger into the disclosure you are likely to obscure the main message you are there to deliver, and the occasion will be remembered as a negative one for everyone. Try to get in touch with the positive reasons for your disclosure and keep those in focus.

When to Disclose

The time to disclose is as soon as you are ready, taking into account whatever else is going on in the family situation. If possible, don't make your disclosure when other events are likely to co-opt the attention and emotions of the people you are disclosing to: your brother's wedding (tempting though it may be), your grand-

---

* Betty Berzon, ed., *Positively Gay* (Berkeley, Ca., Celestial Arts, 2001).

mother's funeral (you wish you'd been able to tell her because she had more sense and sensitivity than anyone else in the family), your parent's wedding anniversary (you want to thank them for teaching you to love as beautifully as they do). Your disclosure is an important occasion for you and it deserves all the attention it can get.

Where to Disclose

I suggest that gayness be disclosed in a quiet, private place where you are unlikely to be disturbed or distracted, so that plenty of time is available to deal adequately with questions, discussions and reactions.

How to Disclose

Prepare the person you are disclosing to by stating beforehand that you want to have a serious conversation about something that is very important to you both. Present your information in the most positive light possible. For instance, you would not want to begin by saying, "I have something terrible I want to tell you," or "You're not going to like this, but . . ." A better beginning would be, "There is something about me I want to tell you because I care about you, and I want to be able to share more of myself with you."

What to Say

You've said you're gay and you've survived the moment. Now what? You might tell how you feel about being gay and how you hope they will feel about it and about you. And be prepared for the many questions parents usually ask, though they may not ask them directly at this time. You may want to bring them up yourself:

- How long have you been gay?
- Are you sure you are gay?

- When did you first know you were gay?
- Have you tried to change?
- Have you tried being involved with a person of the opposite sex? What happened?
- Does this mean you hate men/women?
- Don't you want children of your own?
- Are you happy?
- Do you think you'll always be gay?
- What is your gay life like?
- Have you told anyone else?
- Who else do you plan to tell?

At this time or later you may want to get into more abstract explanations regarding such questions as the following, which parents usually think about.

What does being homosexual mean? It means being predisposed to seek out same-gender persons as love and sex partners.

What causes homosexuality? It happens through the same complex process that causes heterosexuality. It isn't known yet what goes into that process or how it operates to result in one person being gay while another isn't. Most experts agree that people's basic sexual orientation, as well as their sense of being a female or a male, is not a matter of choice.

Can homosexuality be cured? According to research studies and to the official positions of the American Psychiatric Association and the American Psychological Association, homosexuality is not an illness; therefore it is not meaningful to talk about curing it.

Can a person who is a homosexual become heterosexual? Most experts agree that basic sexual orientation is unchangeable. A person may choose to suppress behavior that is expressive of a homosexual orientation. Sometimes that can be done successfully, sometimes it can't. Nearly always suppression seriously inhibits a person's ability to be emotionally spontaneous, since there must be constant watchfulness over homosexual feelings being experienced too strongly.

Why do you use the word "gay"? About fifty years ago "gay" was a code word to disguise references to being homosexual. Gay people have long since adopted the word "gay" as a self-descriptive term replacing the more clinical "homosexual."

Special Issues

Following are some special issues to think about in relation to disclosure. These are generalizations and do not apply to everyone. You know your own family and you are the best judge of how to use these suggestions for yourself.

Is It Better to Tell Parents Together or Separately? Use what you know of your parents, the way each relates to you and how they relate to each other, to decide on this issue. If they tend to support and comfort each other, it might be best to enable them to share this experience. If you have reason to believe that one will be more supportive of you, tell that parent alone first and have that good experience behind you when you tell the parent of whom you are more doubtful. If your parents tend to compete with one another, you may create a problem by telling one before the other. Try not to get into playing one parent against the other in any way. Tapping into your parents' anger at each other might seriously distract from the very important message you have to deliver. This is especially important if your parents are divorced and you have no choice but to tell them separately.

Don't Make the Other Person Say It for You. "There's something I have to tell you. You know what it is, don't you? It's . . . you know, don't you . . . ?" Ashamed to say the words? If so, you are not ready to make this disclosure. What counts here is the *affirming experience* of saying with your own voice, in your own words, to the face of someone important to you, that you are gay. If you have to force someone else to say the words for you, the impression you give might well be, "I can't say these awful words myself," which certainly is not the kind of tone you want to give to the disclosure of your gayness.

Should Your Lover Accompany You? The presence of a nonfamily member could make it more difficult for those to whom you are disclosing to be as free to ask questions and comment as they might be with you alone. If you feel you need your lover present for support, weigh the advantages of that against the difficulty it might pose for your family. It may be easier, particularly for parents, to deal with your gayness in the abstract before confronting them with your real-life lover. This might be true even if the family already knows and likes your "friend," who has now been significantly redefined for them.

"You're Gay Because of Your Lover"

Sometimes, in an effort to comprehend something that feels alien and disturbing at the outset, parents will attempt to explain their child's gayness by blaming it on a lover. "It's ____. If it weren't for her/him, this would never have happened to you." It's important to establish that your gayness is not something someone *did* to you but something that expresses your basic nature, that you would be gay even if you were not in this relationship.

Parental Guilt

"Where did I (we) go wrong?" This question is often heard from parents struggling to understand the news of a child's gayness. You are, of course, much of what you are because your parents directly or indirectly created the circumstances in which you grew up. Therefore, it is not surprising that they would be concerned about what they did to make you gay. No matter how good a job you do in presenting your gayness in a positive context, they might initially relate to it in terms of their own homophobic conditioning. In response to this question, first reassure your parents that there is no wrong involved, that it is unnecessarily self-punishing to think of your being gay as a failure in their parenting. It is also inaccurate since the determinants of one kind of sexual orientation versus another are as yet unknown. What is important is that good parenting does produce the ability to love others, and if you have that capacity you should be grateful to your parents for making it possible. Let them know.

Counterpersonal Family Culture

In some families it is the custom to avoid dealing with anything of an intimate nature, especially if it is sexual. To introduce information about yourself that tells family members more than they want to know about your personal life is going against family "culture." As much as anything it is often this counter-cultural behavior that brings a negative reaction. If this is the case with your family, recognize this and take it into account when you are making your disclosure. The fear that they are going to hear something sexual about their children is very strong with some parents. In the face of this kind of obstacle to communication it is best to reassure in some way that you are not going to expose them to the graphic details of your sex life in discussing your gayness with them. Not doing this effectively could make it impossible for them to listen to you at all.

Disclosure to Children

Sometimes the family members you want to disclose to are children, your own nieces or nephews with whom you want to have as honest a relationship as possible. Many would disagree with me, but I advocate open discussion with young people about being gay. With the coverage homosexuality is being given in the media, it is unlikely that any youngster who can see, hear, and read is going to escape knowing that gay people exist and that a lot of attention is being paid to them these days. In the absence of accurate information, the young person may well get inaccurate information from homophobic sources and develop the same anti-gay attitudes that prevail in much of the rest of society. If that young person is in your own family, it is in your best interests to make sure, if possible, that his/her attitudes toward gay people are enlightened ones. Listening to your twelve-year-old nephew tell queer jokes and mince around in parody of effeminate men is not likely to brighten up the family occasion you've been looking forward to. It is likely to create tension between you and him, and he won't even know why. In the meantime he goes right on thinking of gay people as strange creatures out there somewhere who have nothing to do with him or his family. It does not serve you, him, the family, other gay people or society to perpetuate his antagonistic and punishing attitudes by remaining silent about them.

How do you talk to children about being gay? First, the youngster's age should determine the level at which you talk. Obviously you aren't going to talk about sexual behavior to a child. If you talk about it at all to a teenager, do so with sensitivity to the struggles that a young person may be having to understand and feel comfortable about his/her own budding sexuality. In the latter instance, ask questions as you go to determine how much the young person knows already and how comfortable he/she is with what you are saying. The best approach, I believe, is to talk about being gay as loving and caring for and having a close, important relationship, like marriage, with a person of the same sex. Talk about familiar concepts such as marriage, and personalize what you are saying as much as possible. Bring the idea of being gay closer in so that it can be associated with that which is already known and related to as part of a familiar emotional landscape.

Sometimes adults are reticent to discuss homosexuality with youngsters because they don't want to influence unduly the sexual orientation of the young person. While we don't know exactly what determines sexual orientation, we do know that one does not become gay by hearing about it or by being in the same family or by talking about it with someone who is gay. On the other hand, young people do become honest, courageous, open, and direct in their relationship with others by seeing it happening around them.

Seeking Professional Help

Sometimes the family will try to push you to seek professional help in order not to be gay. You, of course, will gently let them know that you do not need or want such help. However, if they are having particular difficulty accepting your gayness, you might think about referring *them* for help. If you should decide to do this, take time to find gay-oriented professionals who are understanding and supportive of gay people. For referrals in your area, contact any of the following to begin such a search: PFLAG, national office: (202) 467-8180; the American Association of Sex Educators, Counselors and Therapists: (804) 644-3288; American Psychological Association, Division 44: (202) 366-6013; Association of Gay and Lesbian Psychiatrists: (215) 222-2800; Gay and Lesbian Medical Association: (415) 225-4547; National Association of Social Workers, Committee on LGB Issues: (202) 408-8600; and Metropolitan Community Churches: (310) 360-8640.

After the Initial Disclosure

If your family did not know you were gay, you have told them something that is probably very unsettling. If they did know but weren't facing it, you have broken the contract of silence and changed the rules for the way you all relate to this important fact. In either case they'll probably need some time to adjust. And different people adjust in different ways. Some do it silently, some noisily. Some do it in a thoughtful and reasoned way, some go crazy. Some will blame you excessively, some will blame themselves excessively. Some will be sad, some angry, some punishing. Some badger, some will withdraw. Some will be hungry for more information, some will not want to hear another word.

Give them time and understanding. Be available but not pushy. Keep your perspective. You have done this to improve family relations. Disclosure is a courageous act, and it is an expression of your willingness for your family to be an important part of your life. You are offering them an opportunity to deal with you as the person you are, not the person they imagine you to be. Don't lose that focus.

When the opportunity comes, begin to normalize the topic of your gayness. Don't harp, but talk about it naturally, as a part of your life. For those involved in gay community activities, that subject is often an easy vehicle for talking about being gay. Invite your family to meet your friends. Recommend reading (see the reading list at the end of this chapter), and try to bring them the books yourself. Let them know when there is going to be a gay-affirmative film or TV show or magazine story. Encourage them to talk to other relatives and to friends about your gayness. You'll probably meet with a lot of resistance to this initially. It is important that they have someone to talk to. The more they keep their feelings to themselves, the less chance there is of the normalizing process happening.

Remember, this might be a hot potato you've handed them. The gay family member often hears, "It's okay that you've told me (us) but don't tell your sister/brother/father/mother/Uncle Joe/Aunt Ida." Be prepared for this reaction. It may anger you at first because it seems to be saying, "Don't tell anybody else this terrible thing." In a sense it is saying that, but it is saying more about the person speaking than about you. Very often the notion that father/mother/Uncle Joe/Aunt Ida won't be able to handle your news is inaccurate. The real issue is usually a fear of guilt by association. "What will they think of *me*?" Your disclosure has not had time yet to work through, or even work on, this issue. Be understanding. Don't argue the point, but don't make promises for the future either.

Helping your relative (especially a parent) learn to handle the disclosure comfortably and gracefully is one of the most important things you can do as a part of your coming out. The disclosure for you probably has been the culmination of a lengthy process of preparation. It's a relief to have it over with. The people you are disclosing to are just beginning the process. Help them. Keep communications open. Don't let a mood of secrecy develop around your gayness. Use your creativity to find ways to introduce discussion of it in ways that will inform and enlighten.

Another way to help your family adjust to having a gay member involves participation in a peer support group, if one is available. If your family lives in or near a large city, there might be a Parents and Friends of Lesbians and Gays (PFLAG) organization they can participate in. Or they might be willing to talk on the phone to a PFLAG member nearby. Typically, these groups have "hot lines" which a parent can call anonymously.

Remember, both you and your family are common victims of anti-gay prejudice. You can help one another.

AMOUNT OF TIME SPENT WITH FAMILY

Usually there are three things that determine how much time a given person spends with her/his family-of-origin. First, there is the distance that has to be traveled to get to where they are. Second, there is the quality of the relationship with them. Third, there is the tradition of the family with regard to how much contact family members tend to have with one another.

If the family is close by, the relationship is good, and family members usually have a lot of contact with each other, the person most likely will be spending a fair amount of time with family. Hopefully, this fits with what the person's partner likes to do also. If the partner likes being around family, there is no problem, but if for any reason that is not the case, this can be a source of conflict.

Playing bridge with the folks may be fine once in a while but as a steady routine on Saturday night it could rank right up there with having a weekly root canal.

Perhaps one partner comes from a family that has a lot of contact and the other comes from a family that rarely gets together. Then the non-family-oriented person may resent what seems like inordinate demands on the part of his/her partner's family.

Say you have just spent a week of your vacation at your partner's mother's house. Now she's talking about coming to visit next month with Cousin Caroline who has been inconsolable since she lost her life savings playing the slots in Atlantic City. A week with your partner's mother was all right, more or less, but now you have more of mother, plus a cheerless Cousin Caroline to cope with, and you are beginning to feel oppressed by your partner's family's presence in your life.

Some families are so close that family members tend not to establish many friendships outside the family. A non-family-oriented person in a relationship with someone from this kind of family might very well come to feel deprived of the company of peers. I have often seen people in this situation who were particularly unhappy about not being able to spend more time as a couple in gay or lesbian settings. Sometimes it is not even so much a matter of the person wanting to spend time with family but of feeling an *obligation* to do so.

In the past, I saw a lot of gay and lesbian people whose families related to them as if they were not adults with lives of their own because they were not married with children. It was as if—and still is for many childless couples—one remained a child until one got heterosexually married and became a parent.

Today, an increasing number of gay and lesbian couples have children, whether through adoption, insemination, surrogacy, or other approaches. This puts them on a more equal footing with their straight married siblings, so it is less likely that the respective families will make unreasonable or excessive demands on their time.

Unfortunately, for those gays and lesbians who have not brought children into their relationships, it is still, too often, open season for demands on their time and energy. Parents make demands of their childless offspring that they would not think of making on any of their children who have a family of their own. The unmarried, childless gay or lesbian person buys into this thinking and feels as if he/she has to be there for the parents to a much greater degree than heterosexually married siblings do. The partner of such a person might have a very hard time competing with that commitment. After all, this is their parent. That particular connection is, for some people, one loaded with guilt and possibly unresolved struggles with parental influence. This is an area best approached with sensitivity to the tangled web that adult child-parent relationships can become. Approach with caution, but do approach, because a successful partnership depends on the honest airing out of conflicted feelings. When such feelings go underground, they can cause upheavals that are much harder to deal with.

Perhaps too much time must be spent getting partner's old, ailing Mom and Pop out of the house. Partner's two brothers and three sisters can't be expected to devote time to this because, you know, there's Little League, taking the kids to the orthodontist, taking the kids on trips, taking the kids to all those important activities that parents have so much responsibility for. If you have not joined the growing numbers of gay and lesbian couples who have added children to their families, complete with orthodontia and Little League, you are considered to have no responsibilities of equal importance.

I think it is unwise to buy into the notion that the absence of a biological family should obligate a gay or lesbian adult child to become the major caretaker of aging parents' needs when there are other siblings to share the load. Though more and more of us now share with our straight siblings the set of responsibilities that comes with being parents, there are still many of us who do not have children at home to care for. Nonetheless, we do have demands and obligations that are important to our lives. For instance, having someone to share social and recreational time with is one of the major reasons people enter into intimate partnerships. One reasonably expects one's partner to have the same expectations and to be available to make that companionship possible. Whatever is allowed to interfere with this high priority should happen only after thorough discussion and negotiation have taken place.

I encourage a careful exploration of feelings on this matter and continuous updating on how each partner is feeling about it. It is a very large mistake not to give your relationship the highest priority in your life. When we don't do that, we are in danger of reinforcing our own and others' perceptions of our partnerships as commitments that are transient and not to be taken seriously.

VISITING, AND VISITS FROM, OUT-OF-TOWN FAMILIES

Visiting or being visited by an out-of-town-family is likely to be a good or bad experience depending on what the family understands about your relationship with your lover, and, if they understand, how accepting they are. If yours is a Totally-in-the-Dark Family, visiting them will probably involve graciously accepting the separate beds they so generously provide you. With the Arm's-Length Family, or the We-Suspect-But-We-Really-Don't-Want-to-Know Family all kinds of possibilities exist for dealing with that which no one wants to deal with. Accept what's offered? Hope for the best? Or make known what you want in terms of sleeping arrangements because it's about time everybody started dealing with reality?

It's easier when *they* come to visit *you* because there's always the good old, "We'll share a bed so you and Dad can have your own room," unless you live in a house so large that that story doesn't fly. Or, wouldn't it make more sense, while you are welcoming these people into your home, to also welcome them into your life? As that great philosopher John Lennon said, "Give peace a chance."

Visits from out-of-town families can be a burden or a delight. Whether they are one or the other depends largely on how adequate the discussion between partners has been on the frequency and/or conditions of the visits.

One pitfall I see occurring too often is that of using a visit to an out-of-town family as a way of "testing" them to see if their attitude toward the relationship and their behavior toward your lover have improved at all. For instance, the following happened to a couple I'd been working with for about a year:

Alan and Ian lived in California. They were planning a trip to the East Coast and were discussing whether or not they would stop and visit Alan's parents who lived in Boston. They'd been together about five years and in the second year of their relationship they had visited Alan's parents during a summer trip. The visit had been strained and awkward. Alan's parents had known for a long time that he was gay, but he and they had never really discussed it, after the initial disclosure. On their summer trip, Alan's mother had set them up in separate bedrooms. No one said anything about it, though neither Alan nor Ian liked that arrangement and Ian was eager to get out of there when the short visit was over.

In the ensuing years, Alan's mother called their home in California often. Her voice always turned rather cold when Ian answered, though she did make brief attempts at polite conversation with him. She rarely remembered to ask about Ian when talking to her son. However, Alan usually created an opportunity to say something to her about Ian.

In the conversation about their impending trip, Alan said, "I really want to visit my parents again with Ian to see if they behave any better this time than they did the last time."

Ian looked miserable. "I don't," he said.

"Well, I think I should give them another chance."

"I don't."

"But, will you go?" Alan asked.

"I will if I have to," Ian answered.

It sounded like a thoroughly dreary prospect. I observed that it seemed as if Alan wanted to take Ian to his parents' home primarily to put them through a test.

"Right!" Alan said.

I suggested that might not be the best basis on which to make such a visit, if what he had in mind was to improve the relationship. Ian said he wouldn't mind going, that Alan's parents were nice and interesting people, but that the tension created by his being there made it very uncomfortable.

I asked Alan if he was willing to give up his "test" of his parents to do something that would increase the probability of the visit's being a pleasant one.

"Of course," he said.

I then suggested that Alan phone his mother and tell her that he was contemplating a visit, accompanied by Ian, but that he had some reservations about the way their last visit had gone and that he didn't want to come if it would be as tense an experience as it had been last time.

Alan's first response was, "Oh, I don't think that will work. She'll just insist that there is no problem and that we should come ahead, and that will be the end of the conversation."

"In that case," I said, "you will have to persist, and tell her if a visit is to be made at all this discussion is crucial to it."

"Hmm," he said a little nervously.

I further suggested that he tell his mother how he felt when she called and didn't ask about Ian though she knew that her son had lived with him, as a mate, for five years.

Alan gave me a long look. He said, "I've never talked to my mother that way."

"Good," I said, "this will be the beginning of a whole new era in your relationship with her. And, while you're at it, you can tell her that you expect to sleep with your partner if you visit her house just as she expects to sleep with her husband when she visits someone else's home. You can tell her how you would like things to be if you and Ian are going to visit her."

Alan looked slightly stricken. "I know you're right. That certainly sounds better than just hoping for the best or not going at all. I will try it."

The next week Alan and Ian came in looking quite relaxed.

Alan said, "Well, we are going to visit my parents, and we both feel good about it. I called my mother, and I said all those things you suggested. She listened. She really listened. She said she hadn't realized that she was avoiding asking about Ian, but she could see that she was. She said that she would change that in the future because it mattered to her how I felt. She said she wanted very much for us to come and that she and my father would do everything they could to make us both comfortable. Frankly, I was amazed."

"New era?" I asked.

"Looks like it," he said.

"How does it feel?"

"Terrific."

And, indeed, Alan and Ian had a visit with Alan's parents that was not just a "test" of their behavior but an enjoyable time shared by all of them.

How easily some of us fall back into the suppliant child's role with our parents. How important it is to remind ourselves, and them, that we now have the power to design our transactions with them according to our adult needs as well as their parental wishes.

FAMILY AS HOUSE GUESTS

I am at times astonished as my clients regale me with tales of a seemingly endless flow of visiting relatives in and out of their homes. Some are tales of good times had by all, some are re-countings of critical events in the ongoing drama of family and lover becoming closer, many are laments over feeling deprived of sufficient private time with a partner to resolve whatever conflicts might be generated by the presence of others in one's home.

People who come from large families usually tend to be quite comfortable with a houseful of people. People who were only children or who grew up in a very small family often have trouble having a lot of people in the house over extended periods. This is one of those differences that partners must learn to accommo-date. What is critical in these situations is effective negotiation. Too often partners will keep their preferences and their gripes about family visits to themselves, not wanting to spoil their lover's fun with the family. What happens when the family stays too long, visits too often, or makes demands that are particularly time con-suming and/or intrusive, is that the partner, by being "kind and considerate" and not complaining, begins to act out her/his re-sentment in ways that convey the message of anger but not the message of what the anger is about. Therefore, without the accu-rate information, the other partner may not be clued in enough about what is going wrong to be able to do something about it.

The family becomes a source of tension and conflict when the issue is really between the partners. They need to work out guidelines for family visits that are okay with both of them.

Of course, if the visiting family is unaware of or chooses to ignore the truth about the couple's relationship, visits can be especially taxing. If family visits are a source of contention between you and your partner, try to clarify what each of you wants and negotiate for any change that you think will improve the situation.

AND THEN THERE'S THE GUILT

A young lesbian cries in my office because she will never give her mother the grandchildren she counted on.

A young gay man avoids his father because he cannot bear to tell him that his only son is the end of the line genetically.

Self-indictment regarding the issue of childlessness can be powerful and pervasive. Lesbian and gay men, too, often internalize the disappointment their parents feel about not being made grandparents by them. They might feel deeply disloyal, as though they violated a code that is as ingrained in them as it is in their parents. They have gone against tradition, and since tradition is so easily confused with normalcy, they are sometimes made to feel abnormal and discredited as human beings because they did not deliver on a promise that was never really theirs to make.

Some parents bedevil their gay or lesbian children by repeatedly bringing up their distress over the you'll-never-give-me-grandchildren issue. They elicit guilt for this "transgression" that sometimes becomes guilt about being gay at all. Trying to live your life according to someone else's unrealistic expectations of you is like trying to climb a mountain with an unbearable weight on your back. Such burdensome obligations cannot help affecting how worthwhile a person eventually comes to feel. If you are carrying this kind of guilt, it is time you did something about it. First, you must assess the effect on your life of your parents' feelings about your not producing children. If the effect is profound, if you feel guilty and feel like less of a person because of it, then you must begin the process of restructuring the way you think of yourself in relation to your parents.

There are parts of gay life that have tended to perpetuate a view of us as eternally young. Often we think of ourselves in that way as though we do not really deserve the prerogatives of adulthood because we have not followed the *traditional* path to maturity. Those inner voices from a past when we were truly children, unable to design our own lives, persist. We find ourselves guided by parental directives even though they might be inappropriate to who we are in a contemporary sense. Once, when we were learning the difference between right and wrong, those directives were relevant. Now they are archaic. We must learn to address those voices from the past, to talk back, to exorcise the critical parent within, to replace that voice with our own, telling ourselves what we need as the people we are now, rather than as the children we were then. We must refuse the guilt because we have done nothing wrong. And, if there is a parent currently trying to reinforce the guilt, we must confront that effort with our adult's voice, as Susan does in the following conversation with her mother.

MOTHER: Susan, I know you don't want me to bring this up, but I have to talk about it. Every time I think about it, I feel terrible. I look at my daughter, and I can't believe I am not going to have any grandchildren from you. I just can't believe it.

SUSAN: Mother, please not again.

MOTHER: Honey, you know I love you, and I want the best for you. That's all. I just want the best for you.

SUSAN: Mother, deciding if we want to have children will be up to my partner and myself, but let's just keep this straight, so to speak—my partner will be a woman. That's not going to change. I am a lesbian.

MOTHER: I know. I know. You keep telling me, but it is hard for me to accept. When you were a little girl, I used to dream about you growing up and marrying a man and having a lovely family of your own.

SUSAN: And you were the doting grandmother?

MOTHER: Of course, what's wrong with that?

SUSAN: Nothing, but that's about *you,* not about me. It's *your* dream of what *you* wanted for *yourself.*

MOTHER: Oh, no, Susan. It's what I wanted for *you.*

SUSAN: No, Mother, it's the loss of *your* dream that you are sad about.

MOTHER: You just refuse to face it, don't you? You refuse to take any responsibility for the pain you are causing me.

SUSAN: All right, Mother. I think it's time we had this out, right now. I am tired of hearing about your sadness about my life. I am tired of your trying to make me feel guilty because you are not going to have a son-in-law. I am no longer willing to be accused of purposely arranging my life in a way that would hurt and disappoint you. I don't want to fight feeling guilty anymore. That means I don't want to hear about this again, ever.

MOTHER: You just don't understand.

SUSAN: I understand all too well. You don't want me to be a lesbian. You had a fantasy about who I would be when I grew up, and you can't stand that I am someone other than that. Well, I am a worthwhile person, and I thank you for that. I have a life that I like, and I will have a partner whom I love. If you want to be part of our lives, you are more than welcome, but only if you stop talking about how sad and disappointed you are about the way I've turned out.

   When I think about seeing you I dread you bringing all this up again. It makes me feel as if I don't want to see you at all. But I do want to see you—I love you.

   So, if we are going to be friends, you are going to have to stop, and I really mean *stop,* this pressuring. If you can't stop I think it's best we not see each other.

MOTHER: That's a pretty serious threat.

SUSAN: It's more than a threat. It is a declaration of the limits of my tolerance for having my wishes ignored by you. It's a statement of how I want our relationship to be. I want you to re-

late to me in terms of who I am, not who you wish I were. If you want to have a loving relationship with me, as I do with you, it is going to have to be more on my terms from now on.
MOTHER: All right, Susan. If that's the way you want it.
SUSAN: That's the way it *has* to be.

Tough talk, but with certain kinds of parents it is the only way to establish a relationship that can offer support in place of criticism, mutual respect and affection in place of guilt producing complaints and condemnation. It's about growing up and separating once and for all from parental domination.

In the final analysis, relations with family always have been and always will be complicated, sexual identity issues aside. Effectively redefining our roles within the family-of-origin once we are adults is a challenge that everyone must meet. While indeed we do have to pay attention to the ramifications our special status may have for the family, we must also not lose sight of the special opportunity we present them to stretch beyond their limitations to embrace us and be enriched by that enlargement of their capacity to learn and grow.

I would particularly like to encourage the reading of any of the helpful books now available on relations between gay men and lesbians and their families. Some of them are:

Bernstein, Robert A. *Straight Families, Gay Children: Keeping Families Together.* New York: Thunder's Mouth Press, 1995.
Berzon, Betty. *Positively Gay: New Approaches to Gay and Lesbian Life.* Berkeley, Calif.: Celestial Arts, 2001. Chapter on "Telling Your Family You're Gay."
Boenke, Mary ed. *Trans Forming Families: Real Stories About Transgendered Loved Ones.* Imperial Beach, Calif.: Walter Trook Publishing, 1999.
Borhek, Mary V. *Coming Out to Parents: A Two-Way Survival Guide for Lesbians and Gay Men and Their Parents.* New York: Pilgrim Press, 1994.
DeGeneres, Betty. *Just a Mom.* Los Angeles: Advocate Books, 2001.

Fairchild, Betty, and Nancy Hayward. *Now That You Know: A Parents' Guide to Understanding Their Gay and Lesbian Children.* San Diego, Calif.: Harcourt Brace Jovanovich, 1998.

Griffin, Carolyn Welch, Marian J. Wirth, and Arthur G. Wirth. *Beyond Acceptance: Parents of Lesbians and Gays Talk About Their Experiences.* New York: St. Martin Press, 1997.

Herdt, Gilbert, and Bruce Koff. *Something to Tell You: The Road Families Travel When a Child Is Gay.* New York: Columbia University Press, 1999.

Jennings, Kevin. *Always My Child: A Parent's Guide to Understanding Your Gay, Lesbian, Bisexual, Transgendered or Questioning Son or Daughter.* New York: Simon and Schuster, 2003.

Rafkin, Louise, ed. *Different Daughters: A Book by Mothers of Lesbians.* Pittsburgh: Cleis Press, 2001.

Resource

PFLAG—Federation of Parents, Families, and Friends of Lesbians and Gays, Inc.
1726 M Street, Suite 400
Washington, DC 20036
(202) 467-8180
(202) 467-8194 (fax)
www.pflag.org

They will provide regional numbers for PFLAG phone contacts in your area.

13

HAVING CHILDREN, TAKING VOWS, TELLING THE WORLD

HAVING CHILDREN

There she stood, the Honorable Mary Morgan, judge of the San Francisco Municipal Court, about to give the keynote address to a distinguished gathering of lawyers. But, wait, what's this? She seems to be quite pregnant. Isn't she a lesbian? Why is she pregnant? Lesbians don't get pregnant, do they?

They do now.

The announcement read:

> Mary and Roberta
> proudly announce
> the birth of their son
>
> BENJAMIN ALEXANDER MORGAN ACHTENBERG
>
> July 26, 1985
> He's terrific!

Mary Morgan was the first open lesbian to be appointed to the bench in the State of California. She is a pretty, petite, and exceedingly pleasant person. She is also formidably smart, tough, and straightforward.

When Mary and her partner, Roberta Achtenberg, made up

their minds to have a child, they decided that Mary would carry the baby. So, Her Honor became a very pregnant lesbian judge.

I like to muse about Mary toward the end of her pregnancy, solemnly presiding over her courtroom, ignoring the quizzical stares of attorneys appearing before her.

And then came Benjamin, mothers and child doing fine, thank you. All three a delight to encounter. Benjamin Alexander Morgan Achtenberg is as wanted, planned for, loved, and cherished a child as one could hope to be.

HETEROSEXUALS' "RIGHT" TO HAVE CHILDREN

People have children for all kinds of reasons, some less than laudable: because they believe they are supposed to; because they can't help it; because they want to please someone else, like a parent or a spouse; because they want something of their own; because they think it will save their marriage, or their source of support, or their soul.

Many of these were children who were unwanted, unattended to, unappreciated, or even punished for the complications they brought to the lives of those who conceived them. Yet the *right* of the parents of these children to have them is rarely questioned. Nobody screens them, evaluates their competence as caretakers. They don't have to pass the muster of social service agencies or the courts.

LESBIAN AND GAY PARENTING OPTIONS

It is easier than it used to be, and much more common now, for a gay man or a lesbian outside of a heterosexual marriage to become a parent. It usually involves a lot of planning and preparation, so much so that you can be pretty sure of one thing— when a lesbian or gay man has gone through the soul searching, the decision making, the legal, medical, and emotional preparation usually involved in having a child under these circumstances, that child is going to be one who is planned for, loved, cherished, and very much wanted.

I believe it is an act of courage for lesbians and gay men to have children, to stand up to the social and legal system that discourages at best, and prohibits at worst, the fulfillment of their need to become parents.

So many of us in the past sublimated the natural need to parent by working in occupations that give us the opportunity to nurture others. It is no accident that so many millions of gay men and lesbians are teachers, nurses, doctors, social workers, and psychologists, or in some other helping profession. We fulfill our altruistic needs by ministering to other adults and to other people's children.

Much has changed in the last few years. We now have a virtual (in the old sense) baby boom in the gay and lesbian community. When the thousands of same-sex couples showed up in San Francisco in early 2004 to stand in line at City Hall to be married, many were accompanied by their children. They were intact families sharing the joy of having their kinship socially and legally acknowledged. That scene has been repeated in city after city, a far cry from the days when gay and lesbian couples having children was considered a challenge to the system that stigmatized gays as parents, and an act of courage. Those days are gone, except of course for the individual hold-outs in our society who will always confuse exclusion and fear of change with adherence to faith.

Much attention has now been given to strategies and methods for same-sex couples having children. A search of "gay and lesbian parenting" on the Internet will yield more information than one may even want or need. Here are some references and resources that can be particularly useful:

Books

Achtenberg, Roberta. *Preserving and Protecting the Families of Lesbians and Gay Men.* 2nd ed. San Francisco: National Center for Lesbian Rights, 1990.

Clunis, D. M., and G. D. Green. *The Lesbian Parenting Book: A Guide to Creating Families and Raising Children.* Seattle: Seal Press, 1995.

Martin, April. *The Lesbian and Gay Parenting Handbook: Creating and Raising Our Families.* New York: HarperCollins, 1993.

Pies, Cheri. *Considering Parenthood.* 2nd ed. Denver, Colo.: Spinsters Ink, 1988.

Magazines Focusing on Gay and Lesbian Famliies

In the Family; (510) 579-8043
And Baby; (718) 422-7613; info@andbabymag.com
Gay Parent; (718) 997-0392; info@gayparentingmag.com

Organizations to Help

COLAGE: Children of Lesbians and Gays Everywhere
2300 Market Street
Box 165
San Francisco, CA 94114
(415) 861-KIDS
KIDSOFGAYS@aol.com

Family Pride Coalition
P.O. Box 65327
Washington, DC 20035
(202) 331-5015
www.familypride.org

Because the legal situation with regard to gay and lesbian parenting changes, and because laws differ from state to state, it is a good idea to consult an attorney in your own community, one who is knowledgeable about such matters and sympathetic to your objective. The following are good resources for legal information and referrals:

Curry, Hayden, Denis Clifford, and Frederick Hertz. *A Legal*

Guide for Lesbian and Gay Couples. Berkeley: Nolo Press, 2004. See the chapter "I'm Mom, She's Mommy (or I'm Daddy, He's Papa)" on having and raising children.

Berzon, Betty. *Positively Gay.* 3rd ed. Berkeley: Celestial Arts, 2001. See the chapter "We Are Family: Gay and Lesbian Parents and Their Rights." Includes a listing of state-by-state laws and references to actual cases.

Having children is *not* the sacred right of heterosexual men and women. You have just as much right to be a parent as your non-gay counterpart. Yes, it may be more complicated, depending on which route you take. Yes, there are some special challenges that children of gay and lesbian parents face. There are special challenges that children born into any misunderstood minority face. These challenges are not insurmountable. Sometimes they even inspire excellence of character in the people experiencing them.

In any case, if you do want to become a parent, read, discuss, learn, consult, think it through, and if you decide to go ahead, more power to you!

TAKING VOWS AND TELLING THE
THE WORLD ABOUT IT

It is no accident that the heterosexual world makes such momentous occasions out of the ceremonies through which two people enter marriage. Weddings not only solemnize the union, but also put others on notice that an important change of status has occurred for the two people involved.

We gay and lesbian people have tended in the past to slip too quietly into our relationships. We sealed the deal privately between ourselves, moved in, mentioned it to a few people, and hoped for the best.

If our liaisons are to be the lasting unions that we want them to be, why don't we enter them with the announcements, rituals, and celebrations they deserve? Why don't we have the people important in our lives sharing the occasion in some way? After all, isn't entering into a partnership for life about as celebratory an event as you'll ever be involved in?

TAKING VOWS

Vows can be taken at any time in a relationship. They can be taken publicly or privately. People who are religious usually prefer a minister or rabbi (gay or gay-supportive) to perform their ceremony. Others may choose a judge or someone else who has importance in their lives. Some may prefer simply to face each other in the presence of family and friends and say their vows unassisted by a third party.

For may people, music is very important as part of the ceremony, as is the exchanging of rings or other tokens. For some, symbolic gestures such as the sharing of wine or the lighting of candles additionally solemnizes the occasion. Prayers would be included by those who are religious.

While there is a growing movement within mainstream organized religion to create opportunities for gay and lesbian couples to receive the ceremonial blessings of the denomination of their choice, by far most of such ceremonies are performed by the Metropolitan Community Church, the gay- and lesbian-oriented religious organization started by Rev. Troy Perry in the 1960s.

At the end of this chapter, I have included a partial list of gay and lesbian religious organizations. You may want to contact one of these organizations for information on the current status of ceremonial blessings in your religion.

For the benefit of those who may decide to give themselves the gift of a ceremony of commitment, or recommitment, I offer a sample of such a ceremony. The following is excerpted from *The Handbook for Commitment Ceremonies,* developed at the Unitarian Universalist Church of Canton, New York. In this example, a third party is conducting the ceremony.

ADDRESS TO THE GUESTS

Friends, we are gathered here at this hour to witness and to celebrate the coming together of two separate lives. We have come to join these two, to be with them and rejoice with them in the making of this important commitment. The essence of this commitment is the taking of another person in his or her entirety as lover, companion, and friend. It is, therefore, a decision which is not to be entered into lightly, but rather undertaken with great consideration and respect for both the other person and one's self.

Love is one of the highest experiences that we human beings can have, and it can add depth of meaning to our lives. The sensual part of love is one of life's greatest joys and, when this is combined with real friendship, both are infinitely enhanced.

The day-to-day companionship—the pleasure in doing things together, or in doing separate things but delighting in exchanging experiences—is a continuous and central part of what people who love each other can share.

This ceremony symbolizes the intimate sharing of two lives, yet this sharing must not diminish but enhance the individuality of each partner. A union that lasts is one which is continually developing and one in which each person is individually developing, while growing in understanding of the other. Deep knowledge of another is not something that can be achieved in a short time, and real understanding of the other's feelings can develop fully only with years of intimacy. This wonderful knowledge of another person grows out of really caring for that person so much that one wants to understand as completely as possible what the other is feeling. Thus, it is possible to share not only joys and successes but also the burden of sorrows and failures. To be known in this way is a priceless thing because such understanding and acceptance make it easier to live with our problems and failings and worries.

On this day of your union, you stand somewhat apart from all other humans beings. You stand within the charmed circle of your love, and this is as it should be. But love is not meant to be the possession of two people alone. Rather, it should serve as a source of common energy, as a form in which you find the strength to live your lives with courage. From this day onward you must come closer together than ever before, you must love one another in sickness and in health, for better and for worse, but at the same time your love should give you the strength to stand apart, to seek out your unique destinies, to make your special contribution to the world which is always part of us and more than us.

VOWS (USING A RING)

The circle is the symbol of the sun and the earth and the universe. It is the symbol of wholeness and of perfection and of peace. The ring is a symbol of unity into which your two lives are now joined in an unbroken circle, in which wherever you go, you will return unto one another.

_____, repeat after me: I, _____, take you _____, as my beloved, to protect, love, respect, and cherish for our lifetime together. Wear this ring as a symbol of our union and as a sign to all the world of our love for and devotion to one another. I proclaim my love for you. I proclaim my trust in you. I am happy to be a part of you. Remember, these words from my heart will always be true, now and forever, with all that I feel, here is my love for you. Each time I see your ring, I will remember all that I have pledged to you this day.

This is one example of vows. For much more advice on all aspects of putting together such occasions, see this treasury of ideas, resources, and planing details: Tess Ayers and Paul Brown. *The Essential Guide to Gay & Lesbian Weddings*. Los Angeles: Alyson Publications, 1999.

ANNOUNCEMENTS

We have tended to keep much too quiet about our relationships. If you are a gay or lesbian person working in a world that is predominantly heterosexual, it is unlikely that you will dance into your workplace on a Monday morning gleefully announcing that you and your same-sex lover have just decided to move in together. "They," on the other hand, are likely to broadcast widely the news that they have decided to share their life with another person. They put notices in the newspaper, mail out announcements, tell perfect strangers. They share their happiness, and, in return, they are reinforced in the rightness of what they are doing by the warm glow they produce in others by merely making the announcement.

For us, it is not so simple.

"Well, guess what? I'm getting married this weekend."

"That's wonderful."

"Yes, it is wonderful. We are both very happy."

"What's her name?"

"Uh . . . Douglas."

(Pause) "Douglas? That's an unusual name for a woman."

"It certainly would be, but, you see, Douglas is a man."

(Pause) "Oh, how interesting. I didn't know. I'm so sorry. I mean, I'm so sorry I didn't know. I hope you and . . . Douglas will be very happy."

No warm glow there. A little red in the face, perhaps. Not exactly reinforcing, either. But that's how it has been. Now, since same-sex marriage became a headline story in 2004, we have the cooperation of the nation's media in calling attention to our commitment events.

Actually, it was Sunday, September 1, 2002, when the *New York Times* published its first same-sex weddings/celebrations announcement: "Daniel Gross and Steven Goldstein affirmed their partnership today in a civil union ceremony at the Shore Acres Inn and Restaurant in North Hero, Vermont. Assistant Judge Barney Bloom of State Superior Court in Monteplier presided. Last evening, Rabbi David M. Steinberg led an exchange of Jewish vows at the Musee des Beaux Arts of Montreal. . . ."

The sky didn't fall.

Now there are literally dozens of mainstream newspapers in the United States that routinely announce same-sex unions occurring in their cities. Still, the personal announcement sent out by the couple is the best way to inform one's world that two gay or lesbian lives have been officially joined together. We need to know this is happening. These are our family stories. They give us a sense of continuity with one another. They are the bond with our community.

THE COUPLES MOVEMENT

The age of the couple has certainly come to the gay and lesbian community. Since the early 1980s there has been a growing grassroots movement involving same-sex couples organizing to expand their social opportunities beyond what the bars have had to offer. Two organizations in particular operate on a national level:

The Couples National Network, with affiliated chapters around the country, is an organization for committed gay and lesbian couples. Their programs include a variety of social events, support groups, and educational activities. See their website at www.couples-national.org, About Us, for information and links to many other relevant gay and lesbian organizations. If there is not an affiliated chapter in your area, you might think about starting one.

Partners Task Force for Gay & Lesbian Couples is a national

service that provides information and support for same-sex couples. Their website contains more than 250 essays, surveys, legal articles, relationship tips, and resources on legal marriage, ceremonies, domestic partner benefits, and parenting and immigration. See their website at www.buddybuddy.com.

Many couples groups begin as an activity of a gay church program or a local gay and lesbian community center. Some have begun spontaneously, unaffiliated with any outside organization, existing only to serve their own member couples.

I strongly encourage participation in couples' organized activity. It can be tremendously supportive for a couple's relationship to have contact with others who are dealing with similar issues in their daily lives. That is especially true if you live outside a large metropolitan center where there are no organized activities for gay people. Even participating with other couples in cyberspace can be informative and validating. We are fortunate to live at a time when the enormous constituency of gay and lesbian families has come out of the closet. We are all enhanced by that.

GAY AND LESBIAN RELIGIOUS ORGANIZATIONS

Affirmation/Mormons
1127 Barnard Drive
Las Vegas, NV 89102-1801
or
Box 46022
Los Angeles, CA 90046-0022
(323) 255-7251
reap@wizard.com; www.affirmation.org

Reconciling Congregation Program (United Methodists)
3801 N. Keeler Avenue
Chicago, IL 60641
(773) 736-5526
www.rcp.org

American Baptists Concerned
P.O. Box 16128
Oakland, CA 94610

Dignity, Inc. (Roman Catholic Church)
1500 Massachusetts Avenue, N.W., Suite 11
Washington, DC 20005
(202) 861-0017

Evangelicals Concerned
Dr. Ralph Blair
311 East 72nd Street, Suite 1-G
New York, NY 10021
(212) 517-3171
ecinc.org

American Friends Service Committee Lesbian & Gay Program (Quaker)
2249 E. Burnside Street
Portland, OR 97214

Honesty (Southern Baptist Convention)
P.O. Box 190869
Dallas, TX 75219
(214) 352-8406
honesty@geocities.com

Integrity, Inc. (Episcopal Church)
Box 5255
New York, NY 10185-5255
(201) 352-2485 (New Jersey)

New Ways Ministry (Roman Catholic Educational Ministry)
4012 29th Street
Mt. Rainier, MD 20712
(301) 277-5674

Seventh Day Adventist Kinship International
Box 7320
Laguna Niguel, CA 92607
(949) 248-1299 or (303) 321-5331
East: (617) 436-5950; West: (213) 876-2076
drbenkc@dimensional.com

Unitarian Universalist Association (National Office)
Office for Bisexual, Gay, Lesbian & Transgender Concerns
25 Beacon Street
Boston, MA 02108
(617) 742-2100, ext. 470
obgltc@uua.org

United Church of Christ (National Office)
Office for Gay, Lesbian, Bisexual & Transgender Concerns
Wilder Church Ministries
700 Prospect Avenue
Cleveland, OH 44115-1100
(216) 736-317
ucc.org

Universal Fellowship of Metropolitan Community Churches
(National Office)
Office of Ecumenical Witness & Ministry
8704 Santa Monica Boulevard, PH2
Los Angeles, CA 90069-4548
(213) 464-5100

World Congress of Gay, Lesbian & Bisexual Jewish Organizations
Box 23379
Washington, DC 20026-3379
(202) 874-4487
leewalzer@mindspring.com

14

THE INEVITABILITY OF CHANGE IN YOUR PARTNERSHIP

You can help me grow, or you can obstruct my growth. If you have a *fixed* idea of who I am and what my traits are, and what my possibilities of change are, then anything that comes out of me beyond your concept, you will disconfirm. In fact, you may be terrified of any surprises, any changes in my behavior, because these changes may threaten your concept of me; my changes may, if disclosed to you, shatter your concept of me and challenge you to grow. You may be afraid, too. In your fear, you may do everything in your power to get me to unchange and to reappear to you as the person you once knew.

   But if you suspend any preconceptions you may have of me and my being, and invite me simply to be and to disclose this being to you, you create an ambience, an area of "low pressure" where I can let my being happen and be disclosed, to you and to me simultaneously—to me from the inside, and to you who receive the outside layer of my being.

Sidney M. Jourard, *Disclosing Man to Himself**

* Sidney Jourard, *Disclosing Man to Himself* (Princeton, N.J.: D. Van Nostrand Co., 1968).

The year was 1976. I was a busy activist in the gay and lesbian community. I lectured, consulted, and conducted educational workshops on a variety of gay-related issues in cities around the country. I sat on the boards of gay organizations, locally and nationally. I helped to found some of the major gay and lesbian organizations.

My lover was young and new to the activist scene. In the early years of our relationship she usually accompanied me in my activities, staying in the background, quietly there, always ready to be helpful. I was clearly the "star" of our relationship, and she never challenged that.

Sometimes I questioned what I was doing with someone seventeen years my junior, unworldly, unsophisticated, an ingenue among the players, but she was good-hearted, unaffected, attractive, and very devoted to me. I would teach her about life. I would be her mentor. I would share my knowledge and experience. She would be the student, and she was a very good one. Those conditions defined the contours of our relationship. It created a kind of order for what we were doing together. Older-younger. Teacher-student. It seemed to work pretty well.

One day I got a phone call from a man who had just begun publishing a local gay community newspaper. He asked me if I would write a column for his publication. I told him I would love to but that I couldn't because I was too busy.

That night I told Terry about the phone call. She looked pensive. Then she said, "I think I'd like to write that column."

"You?"

"Me."

"Well . . ."

"Why not?" she said. "I like to write, and I know what's going on in the community. I think I'd enjoy that."

"Fine, call him up."

That's what I said. What I thought was: This will never work out. She's not up to doing it.

Wrong. She did it, and she did it well. It was a pleasant, chatty, informative column. People liked it and told her they looked forward to reading it.

One night she told me she was thinking of doing a book re-view for her next column. She said that a new book had come into the newspaper and the editor had asked her to review it.

"What's the book?" I asked.

"It's called *The Sorcerer of Bolinas Reef*. It's by a man named Charles Reich."

Good lord, I thought. Charles Reich is a major intellectual writer. His *Greening of America* was a seminal critique of Ameri-can life. She won't be able to handle this. She'll make a fool of herself.

That was what I thought. What I said was, "I don't think you ought to do that."

"Why not?" she asked.

"Well, he's a rather formidable writer. I don't think you'd enjoy that book."

"What you mean is, you don't think I'll understand it. Right?"

"No, no," I protested.

"I think I'll do it anyway."

End of conversation.

She read the book. She reviewed the book. A few weeks later she received a letter from Charles Reich. He said her review had been wonderful, that she was the only person, so far, who had re-ally understood what he was trying to say.

Reading his letter I felt a kind of outrage. What was wrong with this man? How could she be the only person who really un-derstood what he was trying to say? He was a distinguished intel-lectual. She wasn't smart enough or sophisticated enough . . . or was she?

But there it was in black and white. If the author of the book thought she understood it, she must have understood it.

How could I have been so wrong? I didn't like it, but I was forced to begin to look at her in a different way. She may have been naive and unsophisticated when I met her, but that had been three years before. I began to realize that she had changed, and I had not kept up with that change.

It was a rude awakening.

I could no longer think of her as the unworldly ingenue. I could no longer treat her that way. I had to revise my perception of who she was and of who I was in relation to her. Fortunately I had the good sense to do that, or, I believe, we would not have a relationship today.

As she changed, the contours of our relationship changed. She returned to school, got a graduate degree, and began practicing as an independent professional. She emerged from my shadow to cast shadows of her own. Today, thirty-one years later, she is a highly successful human being. She has become a prominent activist in her own right. She has initiated bold ventures, many of them bolder than I would ever have attempted. She is an exceptionally competent, smart, sophisticated person.

And, I almost missed it.

I have come to see that in my own situation I was protecting my rationale for being with someone so much younger by maintaining a view of my lover as someone lacking in the very qualities I saw myself as having in abundance. That gave me permission to lead and guide her.

I was reticent to let go of that view of her because that meant I had to redefine what I was doing with her. I had to face the challenge of a partnership of equality rather than the mentor-student relationship I had defined for us before. I didn't want her to change because I didn't want to let go of the control that the mentor-student arrangement allowed me to exercise over the relationship.

Actually, the more control I was able to exert over her, the safer I felt. As long as I at least saw myself in charge of the relationship, the more surely I could manage the distance between us and the degree of intimacy that might develop. The more of a peer she became, the more democratic the relationship became and the less control I was able to have over what went on between us. I had to face my own fears about increasing intimacy in order to be able to let go of the controlling role I had so systematically structured for myself in our partnership.

It was not easy to accomplish that change. In a sense I had to drag myself, kicking and screaming, out of the controlling role. I did not want things to change. It is clear to me now, however, how crucial keeping up with the changes in her was to our continuing to be together. Which is not to say that I don't to this day sometimes long for the old arrangement, but, alas, it is gone forever. She is not the same person I involved myself with originally. To treat her as if she were would be the height of folly. It would be nothing more than an expression of *my* deepest doubts and fears about being in an open and intimate partnership with someone I can't control. And, I certainly wouldn't want to have all that hanging out, would I?

How often I have seen people in relationships not understanding that their partner was changing, their failure to keep up with that change putting the relationship in serious jeopardy. They cling to a fixed notion of who this other person is and what the relationship is all about. They resist acknowledging change in the other person because that might well mean they would have to make some changes themselves, changes that may discomfort them, or worse.

I was not sure I could succeed in a truly intimate relationship with someone who was my equal. I had previously arranged my life so that I never had to find out. Faced with the choice of continuing that way of life or meeting the challenge, I chose the latter. But it was difficult, and I really appreciate that difficulty when I see it in the people I work with.

THE PYGMALION SYNDROME

Just as I was invested in controlling my partner by being her mentor, I see the same phenomenon occurring in many gay or lesbian relationships in which there is a significant discrepancy in age and/or experience in the world.

It is the Pygmalion Syndrome. In Greek mythology, Pygmalion, the King of Cyprus, sculpts a statue of a beautiful woman with whom he then falls in love. He prays to Aphrodite, the Goddess of Love, who obligingly brings the statue to life so that Pygmalion can marry her.

In George Bernard Shaw's later and more familiar version, his Pygmalion is Professor Henry Higgins, and the creature he "brings to life" is Eliza Doolittle. He does not transform her to marry her. He simply wishes to satisfy his own egotistical need to prove that he can, within a defined period of time, create a beautiful and gracious "lady" out of a mere guttersnipe of a girl. He becomes attached to her, though she proves not as controllable as Pygmalion's statue-come-to-life, making Professor Higgins's story truer to life than that of the mythological Pygmalion. Eliza continued to change, eventually moving beyond Professor Higgins's ability to control her.

The Pygmalion Syndrome, in gay and lesbian relationships, occurs most often when one partner is significantly older than the other.

This kind of relationship can be satisfying and productive for both partners. The younger benefits from the older's experience and wisdom. The older has the pleasure of imparting that wisdom. The problem is that in the usual student-teacher arrangement, the student moves on from the teacher. The order of the relationship is that eventually the student graduates and is no longer a student. Now, where does that leave the "student" in the relationship with an older lover/teacher whose role usually continues to be as rewarding, and as purposeful, as it was the day the two met?

The younger partner, who has grown beyond the need to have her/his life shaped, may begin to chafe at the power imbalance between them. When this partner begins to reject the older partner's teaching, there may ensue feelings of deprivation, anger, and betrayal on the part of the older partner, who may also begin to feel used and unappreciated. In the best of cases, the teacher recognizes and accepts that a change has occurred in his/her partner that calls for redefinition of the relationship. The two partners talk about what is happening and work out ways to effect changes that reflect the reality of what is happening.

In the worst of cases, the older partner begins to criticize the younger partner in an attempt to demonstrate that his/her guidance and counsel are still needed. The younger resents this criticism and fights back or withdraws. The older feels abused. The relationship may well deteriorate from there.

The situation may be (and often is) complicated by the older partner's conviction that love will be forthcoming only if it is "earned." One such person, the older partner in a relationship, said to me recently, "I feel secure when I know he needs me. If he didn't need me, I'm not sure he would stay with me."

On the other hand, the younger partner may feel smothered, tired of fighting off the lover's "helping hand," frustrated that this person does not seem to understand that he/she *is* loved and is needed in other, more relationship-oriented ways, rather than as a mentor and substitute parent.

Much at this point depends on how well the two communicate about what is happening between them. If they can unravel their entangled roles and talk about what they really need from each other, what is happening between them can become a positive turning point rather than a source of new tensions in the relationship.

CHANGES IN PERCEPTION

In addition to the changes in one's partner that actually do occur, there is the matter of one's changing perceptions of a partner. First, we are attracted to the outer package: great face, great body, great hair, great eyes. When we fall in love those are the aspects of the person that we sit around obsessing about, not how well the person deals with conflict, how able the person is to understand what someone else is feeling, how good the person is at articulating his/her feelings and needs, how willing to talk about relationship issues the person is, how similar in values and interests the person is, how emotionally stable, and how committed to work on building a lasting relationship the person is. Do we sit around dreaming of those character traits and relationship skills that make the difference between a partner with whom one can have an easy and fulfilling relationship and one with whom a relationship will be a constant struggle? No, we sit around dreaming of that smile, those eyes, the contour of that face, the way that body moves.

We buy a package, and then we spend the rest of the relationship unwrapping it. Sometimes we like what we unwrap, and sometimes we don't. Sometimes we are shocked and surprised at what we find. "Who is this person!? This is not the person I fell in love with! What's this? I didn't bargain for this!"

Then comes the indictment: "You've *changed*. You weren't like this in the beginning." Of course not. Chances are you didn't really know the person "in the beginning." You were still relating to the outer package and just beginning to unwrap. As the unwrapping goes on, you are coming to know the real person inside the package. That takes time. Finding new facets of your lover's personality and orientation to life is not about your lover changing as much as it is about your perceptions changing as you acquire more accurate information about who this person is.

ROUTINES—BULWARKS AGAINST CHANGE

All couples develop routines. Routines make life simpler. Routines impart that certain comfort that comes from being able to predict what is likely to happen next in your everyday life. You come to depend on your partner to behave in a particular way, at a particular time, under particular circumstances. It feels safe. Being with a person who is consistently unpredictable so that you never know what is going to happen next, sooner or later, feels dangerous. Predictability is a necessary condition for a stable relationship. It produces a sense of feeling in control of one's life. That's the up side.

The down side is that some couples develop unspoken contracts and routines and then become so locked into them that there is no tolerance for changing. But, change is inevitable in all relationships. If a couple is so straitjacketed into its routines that it is necessary to *deny* that it might be desirable to vary the routine and do something different, then it's time for a serious look at what is going on below the surface of the relationship.

For instance, you always have sex on Sunday morning, not during the week, because you are both too tired and too distracted with work. You don't have sex on Saturday night because you get in too late, or the guests leave too late, or one of you has had too much to drink. That leaves Sunday morning. You may be bored with the Sunday morning mode. But, you don't say anything because, well, it's easier not to, you don't want to start a fight, this must be what your partner really wants because he/she hasn't objected to it and seems quite satisfied with things as they are. But, damn it, you really would like something new and different. Oh, well, grin and bear it. There are more important things in life than sex. But you really wish . . .

Or, you always go to the same gay beach on Sunday afternoons and see the same people and talk about the same things, and you feel as if you're caught in a time warp because the two of you have been doing this same thing for so long. Neither of you ever suggests doing anything else on a summer Sunday, and you both assume that there is nothing else to do that either one of you would enjoy. But, you're really tired of the beach scene. You believe you've outgrown it. You're bored with it, but you're afraid to try to change it because you don't want to rock the boat, and you assume that your partner wouldn't do this every Sunday unless he/she really wants to be doing this and nothing else. But you really wish . . .

Or, you and your partner have an unspoken contract to deal with one another's moods in a particular way, as Jeff and Don do.

Periodically, Don gets into one of his black moods. He seems very angry but is unclear what he is angry about. He mopes around, is uncommunicative, and generally inaccessible. As soon as Don slips into one of these moods, it is a signal for Jeff to give him a wide berth. He doesn't press Don for information about what's wrong. He doesn't tell Don how he is being affected by his behavior. He himself lapses into silence and waits.

Don is then free to sink as deeply as he wants into his black mood, and to emerge from it when he is ready, hours later, days later, sometimes weeks later. Jeff waits. Eventually Don comes around. It's a dependable routine. They have discussed the situation and convinced each other, and themselves, that this is the best way to handle Don's moods. It has gone on this way for several years. Then something begins to change. Jeff has endured these black moods of Don's for too long. He is no longer satisfied to wait in silence for Don to get over whatever is troubling him. The next time Don seems to be slipping into one of his moods, Jeff does not follow the usual routine. He does not withdraw from Don. Quite the opposite, he moves toward him and asks what is going on.

"What's wrong? What are you angry about? Is it me? Is it someone else? What can I do to help you? Talk to me about it."

Don is furious. His mood goes to deep black. Why is Jeff behaving like this? Don't they have an agreement about how they handle this situation? What is Jeff trying to pull off here? Why is he doing this?

Don's anger frightens Jeff. He wishes he'd stuck to the routine. At least then he could predict what was going to happen. Don remains angry at Jeff. Weeks go by. Jeff alternates between feeling guilty and being silent, and trying to get Don to open up to him.

They are at an impasse when they come to therapy. Both Jeff and Don are puzzled about what is happening to them. It soon becomes apparent that their unspoken contract regarding Don's moods has a purpose. It has helped them manage the emotional distance between them.

Both Jeff and Don come from families in which there had been a seriously alcoholic parent. Both are discomforted at the prospect of opening up to someone close. Both have learned how to control the amount of closeness they develop with another person, thereby avoiding even the possibility of a repeat of the chaotic and unpredictable experiences of childhood.

Without ever discussing it, they had fallen into a routine that always assured that increasing intimacy would be inhibited. When closeness seemed imminent, Don would become resentful over something going on in their life and slip into one of his black moods. The routine was then that Jeff would withdraw to allow Don to work through his mood on his own. It was the collaborative mechanism they had developed to be able to maintain an emotionally comfortable distance with one another.

It worked just fine for a while. But then Jeff was able to build up the trust and caring necessary to break through his own resistance to closeness with Don. Their routine way of dealing with Don's off-putting moods began to feel wrong to Jeff. The next time Don was in one of his moods, Jeff broke the rules. This required that Don do something different also. The routine that had served as a bulwark to change for so long was now challenged.

As they talked through their feelings both Jeff and Don were able to see what they had been doing. They were able to let go of their need for the routine that had worked for so long to help them manage the degree of intimacy between them. They talked about their fears of loss of control, of not being adequate as a partner, of being hurt by the other.

Soon they were able to approach Don's moodiness in a very different way. They addressed it together, identifying what might have triggered the mood, talking about whatever issues were involved, learning more about one another, growing closer.

Your unspoken contract, and the routine through which it is implemented, may have a different focus from Jeff and Don's. Yours might be a contract never to fight or never to reverse roles in any way or never to express strong feelings or never to look analytically at the relationship. Whatever the theme, the purpose is to thwart change. And, when change occurs, as it inevitably does, these contracts and routines become obstacles to the growth of the partnership that should be identified and called into question.

15

IN PRAISE OF OUR PARTNERS

I looked across the table at my lover and thought, "What a beauty she is." I wanted to tell her at that very moment, though she was at the other end of a table. I said to myself, looking around at our guests, "I'll sound sappy in the middle of all this very adult table talk, suddenly telling my lover that she is beautiful. What will people think of me?" I looked at them. I looked at her. I realized that my priorities were turned around. If she had that thought about me and told me publicly, in the middle of a dinner party, I'd like it quite a lot. I'd feel special and valued and appreciated. Why should she be different? How silly to withhold the gift of love because what I say *might* not fit into someone else's notion of what should be happening.

As soon as there was a lull in the conversation, I said, apropos of nothing in particular, "Terry, you look quite beautiful tonight." A silence fell over the table. As though they were spectators at a tennis match, all heads turned toward me, then toward Terry. She smiled rather shyly at first, and then broke into a grin, obviously pleased. I felt warmed. The spectators turned once again toward me, expectant. I smiled at them. They smiled back. The conversation resumed.

In the past I have thought to myself, "How great she looks tonight!"

I didn't say it out loud.

I took it for granted she knew what I was thinking, by now. She didn't, of course.

How negligent we can be in withholding praise from those we love. We don't mean to withhold. We know better. We know how good it feels when we are told that we look nice or we did a good job of something or we are just so adorable. If it feels good to *us*, it must feel good to *them*. So why don't we give our partners this gift of praise more often? Do we forget that they need it? Are we too preoccupied with what is happening to *us*? Or is it sheer laziness because we've been together so long and we've come to take one another for granted? Perhaps on a given occasion, do we just not understand how important it might be to our partner to hear from us in an affirming, stroking, or reassuring way?

I remember an experience that made me feel a little silly at the time but reminded me dramatically of how *important* it can be to receive praise under certain circumstances. I was in the hospital following surgery. The nursing care was quite thorough and included frequent checking of my various bodily functions. I was told I was doing well and congratulated on my progress, repeatedly, by one nurse after another. I felt quite encouraged by all this positive reinforcement.

One morning a particularly handsome young surgical resident came in to see me. He examined me, then started to leave. He paused in the doorway to say, "Your incision looks terrific! I can't believe how well you are doing!" Then he closed the door behind him.

It took a few seconds for me to realize that I was sitting there in bed, all alone in this room, with a smile from ear to ear. I was so pleased with my terrific-looking incision. No, I was pleased with how well I was doing. No, I was just pleased to be praised so lavishly. Then I began to feel a little foolish. Here I was, a middle-aged woman, sitting all alone in this room beaming because some anonymous ("Hello, I'm Doctor Mumble-Mumble") young resident had praised me for what was probably a fairly routine recovery from a fairly routine operation.

But it felt so good, anyway.

I thought about the previous few days. Many people had told me how well I was doing.

"Oh, you ate some of your lunch. That's very good!"

"You were able to do *that* in the bathroom. Excellent!"

"You walked to the *end* of the hall today. That's marvelous!"

I couldn't remember being praised in that way since I was a child. I thought about that. As adults we are *expected* to live our lives in a competent and responsible way. When we do, no one particularly lauds us for it. No pats on the back. No hosannas. No singing of praises.

How different this experience was. It felt good even though I realized that I was being praised for things I had little control over and that these people, no doubt, had been trained to talk to postsurgical patients in just this way.

Who cared? It worked.

I thought how nice it would be to be talked to this way every day, by someone, anyone. The most logical person is one's lover. Is it unreasonable to expect one's lover to know what one needs to hear and to say it? I didn't think so.

The acid test came all too soon. I came home from the hospital. My lover was her usual devoted, caring self. On the first day at home I ate all of my lunch, walked several times around the bedroom, and did *that* in the bathroom. I proudly informed her of my accomplishments.

She said, "Good."

I was very disappointed. In the hospital they had a lot more to say than "Good." I wanted to hear, "What wonderful progress you're making!" "Marvelous!" "Excellent!"

She clearly was not aware of how important it was to me to hear that I had done a good job. She clearly also was not a nurse talking to a postsurgical patient, and I, clearly, was no longer going to be infantilized.

My adult saw all of this and was amused. My child, on the other hand, was crestfallen.

I thought about the child in all of us who never grows up. That child is sometimes more assertively needy than at other times. Then the child needs to be affirmed (You're doing okay), to be stroked (You are loved), to be reassured (You will continue to be loved because you are lovable).

The opportunity for such affirmation, stroking, and reassurance is present in every intimate partnership. It is one of the main reasons we seek out and open ourselves up to such relationships. How important it is to turn opportunity into reality for your partner, on a regular basis. How important it is to voice your admiration when you feel it, to praise where praise is due, to express love affirmatively and often.

Some people find it hard to say, "I love you." They think about how nice their partner looks, what a good job he/she did on something, how kind, gracious, generous the person is, but those feelings and thoughts are not given expression. It is as though they were trapped in the individual's mind, with no voice available to release them.

Perhaps this person came from a family in which no one spoke of love, no one extended compliments, no one offered praise. This person has no frame-of-reference for such transactions.

These silent partners are the victims of their upbringing, and their partners are victims also, once removed.

Another source for the inhibition of affirmative communication is male gender-role conditioning. Men in our society are taught to turn away from feelings, to avoid vulnerability, to compete with other men. A man who is in competition with his partner (another man) might not want to give away an advantage to him. He might be afraid it would open him up too much to let his partner know just how admiring he is or how much he cares. In heterosexual partnerships, women tend to have a softening effect on men. Love talk with a woman is culturally approved. "Everyone knows that women like to be complimented," as the social myth goes, so men have permission to speak admiringly of the woman's appearance, performance, et cetera. Similar admiration expressed to another male is somewhat suspect, and many males are uncomfortable with such compliments. The exception is in the workplace where there is a context for praising performance and/or presentation, and for criticizing it. Outside the workplace, however, most males do not spend much time telling each other how nice they look or how much they love one another. They are conditioned not to do this. It is considered unmanly.

What if these men are in intimate partnerships with other men? While a loving relationship is an *appropriate context* for the expression of affection, for praise and compliments, for words of admiration, the male conditioning, all too often, still persists. One or both partners hold back, turning away from feelings, avoiding possible vulnerability to another male. But, in an intimate relationship, the story is very different. This person depends on his partner for affection and affirmation. If two men are unable to break out of their conditioning, their relationship will not be the source of warmth and emotional nourishment that it might be. For that reason, it is important for gay men to liberate one another from the constraints of society's definition of how they should run their lives. It is so important to be free to love and to speak often of that love in the many forms available to one.

It is an arid relationship that does not regularly include the verbal expression of affection. If you are in a relationship with someone who seems to fit this description, you can become his/her guide in opening up a new area of interpersonal competence. You can be the gentle teacher, modeling affirmative communication.

You can teach the expression of love by expressing your own. You can facilitate the giving of praise by giving it yourself. You can enable your partner to recognize and respond to your need for affirmation by responding to his or her need. And you can address the matter directly, expressing your feelings about the lack of such communication, listening to what your partner has to say about how his/her inhibitions in this area may have developed. You can become collaborators in the shaping of this new contour in your relationship.

At the end of every workshop I do with gay or lesbian couples, I ask the participants to write something "in praise of their partner." I give them a choice of structures:

1. Write an ad for your partner telling the world what she/he has to offer as a partner/lover/companion. Emphasize what you particularly value, appreciate, cherish, respect, and enjoy. Try to say some things that you have never said before.

2. Write a love poem to your partner, extolling the pleasures and delights of your relationship.

The following is one of my favorites. It was written by someone who had just been through an excruciating examination of his relationship with his partner. I think it is a tribute to our ability to retain the perspective of our life even as we are challenging its order. He wrote of his partner (Richard):

He holds his lover when he's sad . . .
And celebrates with him when he's glad.
He's one of the most compassionate people you'll ever meet, rarely judging anyone for anything.
He's honest and direct to such a degree that it seems he doesn't even understand the word "indirect."
He's quick to forgive
And he loves to play . . . theatre, movies, museums, travel, and *60 Minutes* with homemade popcorn and great cuddling.
Yes, there's even more . . .
He cooks with great care and love (a shrimp, avocado and chicken pasta that you'd leave home for).
He can fix the plumbing, light switches, rewire the stereo, and build cabinets. This talent alone might qualify him for lover of the year.
And he's an artist with a great sense of aesthetics . . . so the house is always changing in new and exciting ways.
And . . .
If you're interested in dating him and becoming his lover . . .
Please don't call

Because Neil is doing everything possible to keep
    him
    Excited,
    Enchanted,
    Intrigued,
    And in love
    For at least the next 50 years.

Have you told your partner recently what you especially value, appreciate, cherish, respect and enjoy about him or her?
    Have you spoken of your devotion?
    Have you spoken of your love?
    If you haven't, isn't this as good a time as any to do so?

AND FINALLY . . .

In the quotation at the beginning of this book, Kate Millett spoke of the energy of our passion that enables us to maintain our love against all the pressure. How powerful our passion must be to endure as it does. What strength there must be for us in its force. If only we can hold on to that passion as we hold onto each other, we might find permanence in these moments out of time that our love has been, too often. We need the roses of those moments to fill our lives, to stay with us, as we need to stay with each other.
    We can have the roses, if we try.

To contact Dr. Berzon, do not write to Plume or Penguin Group.
Please write directly to:

Dr. Betty Berzon
650 North Robertson Blvd.
West Hollywood, CA 90069